Clerk of Works and Site Inspector Handbook

2006 Edition

Clerk of Works and Site Inspector Handbook

2006 Edition

Institute of Clerks of Works

RIBA ⋕ **Publishing**

© Institute of Clerks of Works, 2006
Published by RIBA Publishing Ltd, 15 Bonhill Street, London EC2P 2EA

ISBN-10 1 85946 192 1
ISBN-13 978 1 85946 192 1

Stock code 57698

British Library Cataloguing in Publications Data
A catalogue record for this book is available from the British Library.

Publisher: Steven Cross
Commissioning Editor: John Elkington
Project Editor: Alasdair Deas
Editor: Andrea Platts
Designed by Ben Millbank
Typeset by Academic + Technical, Bristol
Printed and bound by Hobbs the Printer, Hampshire

While every effort has been made to check the accuracy of the information given in this book, readers should always make their own checks. Neither the Authors nor the Publisher accept any responsibility for misstatements made in it or misunderstandings arising from it.

RIBA Publishing is part of RIBA Enterprises Ltd www.ribaenterprises.com

Contents

Foreword

A venerable title

As Peter Lennon points out in his introduction, the title Clerk of Works is a venerable one, going back over 700 years. We cannot claim such antiquity for the title Architect, although our professional body, the Royal Institute of British Architects, has existed somewhat longer than the Institute of Clerks of Works!

In our 170 years of existence we have worked in partnership with all our fellow construction professionals and have long recognised the essential contribution made by the Clerk of Works to the building process.

On a more personal note, I have worked with some superb Clerks of Works who have made very significant contributions both to the projects we were working on and to my own understanding of the construction process.

We welcome and are very pleased to endorse this edition of the *Clerk of Works and Site Inspector Handbook* and look forward to continuing our working relationship with our ICW colleagues.

Jack Pringle RIBA
President of the Royal Institute of British Architects

Acknowledgements

The Institute of Clerks of Works wishes to place on record its thanks and appreciation to the following individuals who have played such a vital role in the development of this handbook – the first of its ilk since 1994:

The Steering Group:

Messrs Peter Lennon FICW, Jerry Shoolbred FICW, John Elkington RIBA.

The Support Team:

Don McGeorge MIAM, Gail Reed, Rachel Morris.

The Team:

Although several members of the team had specific input to certain areas of the handbook, it is appropriate that their input is acknowledged for their team effort and altruistic intentions rather than anything else:

Messrs Rod O'Driscoll (Gulland and Gulland Solicitors), David Cogswell, Don Hussey FICW, Ian Fisher MICW, Graham Cowie (Holbrook Insurance Brokers), Alan White Hon FICW, Bill Moors FICW of William Moors Associates, Bill Higgins FICW of Tarvin Building Consultancy, Gideon Booth FICW of Clerk of Works Services and Building Management, Bob Tucker MICW of R. J. Tucker Freelance Services, Tony Smith FICW, Frank Smith FICW, David Morton MICW, Tom Woodhouse FICW of Tom Woodhouse Associates Limited, Dennis Fryer FICW.

Note:

The term 'Clerk of Works' in this handbook applies to Site Inspector, Building Quality Officer, and other job titles where site quality control is used, but for clarity this document refers only to Clerk of Works.

Introduction

'Ability, Integrity and Vigilance'

One of the most common misconceptions, certainly among the uninitiated, is the belief that, somewhere along the line, a Clerk of Works is an office-bound paper pusher, whose background and experience is of a purely secretarial or administrative nature. Many cannot see beyond the word 'Clerk' and draw their assumptions from that very limited perspective, not even formulating a link to the construction industry. Pitiful really, since it is a title that has been around since the Middle Ages, and has been worn with great pride by many thousands of exponents of the craft since that time.

Let's put this right! Although it is difficult to confirm an exact date, for obvious reasons, the title is traceable as far back as the 13th century when the Church – the richest single entity in the country at the time – was undertaking a vast amount of construction work. It is believed that materials were being pilfered or otherwise sidetracked to such a degree that it was essential that some form of control over quantities and their ultimate usage was required, and the Clerk of Works was born. Initially drawn from the ranks of the Clerics in holy orders – believed to be the most literate and honest of all – with responsibility for the Church works, they were deemed to possess the attributes so essential for the role – 'Ability, Integrity and Vigilance'. 'Cleric of the Church Works' soon became shortened to Clerk of Works and has remained so to this day. One of the earliest known Clerks of Works, although not the first, was the poet Geoffrey Chaucer, who was appointed as 'Clerk of the King's Works' from 1389 to 1391, superintending undertakings in Woolwich and Smithfield in London.

Over the centuries, the role and duties of the Clerk of Works had developed as a part of the great historical and social changes, and exponents were selected from suitable building craftsmen, with proven technical experience, knowledge and personality gained over many years 'on the tools'. The Reform Bill of 1832 and the many Acts that followed it covering education, public health, roads, railways, town improvements and industrial development spawned many technical, professional and scientific associations and institutes.

On 10 March 1882, a group of 17 Clerks of Works met and agreed that they would form a professional body entitled 'The Clerks of Works Association'. At their first general meeting, held just 17 days later on 27 March 1882, and with 31 present, they formed their first governing body, electing Mr Thomas Potter as their first President, issuing their first rulebook and extending the formal title of the association to 'The Clerks of Works Association of Great Britain'. In 1903 the Association gained Incorporated Status and was again retitled 'The Incorporated Clerks of Works Association' which remained in place until 1947 when, for the final time, it changed its name to its current 'The Institute of Clerks of Works of Great Britain Incorporated', more easily known as 'ICW'.

Introduction

It is important to realise that although building practices and procedures have come and gone, and come again in some cases, over the many years since ICW in its original state was formed, the very principles for which Clerks of Works were first established remain as true and valid today as they have ever been. Tragically, in many cases the traditional title has given way to a more modern interpretation of the role – Site Inspector, Quality Auditor – but the principle remains the same. Whether it be in the field of civil engineering, building, landscaping, tunnelling, electrical and mechanical engineering, new build, refurbishment, at home or abroad, the 'Inspectors' ply their craft in ensuring value for money for the client, through rigorous inspection of the materials in use, and the craftsmanship deployed in their usage. Their skills are honed not only from books and study, but also from years of practical, hands-on experience. They know, or will have seen, almost every trick in the book and will know equally well how to counter it, there being no better gamekeepers than, of course, former poachers! They have to remain up to date in terms of legislation and the many building regulations, including those that relate as much to the individual – health and safety, race relations, disability discrimination – as to the act of construction itself. Through rigorous and detailed reporting and record keeping, and thorough inspection of specifications and drawings, their work will, without question, add value to any project – even though it may not be obvious at the time. The question that should always be asked is a very simple one:

'Without the intervention of the Clerk of Works – how much would rectification and/or remedial action have cost?'

After all, their motto is 'Ability, Integrity and Vigilance'!

Peter Lennon FICW
Chairman of the Working Group

Appablearts — 1

Appointing a Clerk of Works

1.1 APPOINTING A CLERK OF WORKS

A Clerk of Works can provide professional services in five main ways.

1 *As a full-time or part-time 'permanent' employee in what the law terms 'a master–servant relationship'*. Such a person might be resident on one project or required to carry out duties as a visiting Clerk of Works on several projects. There will be a contract of employment, and taxation under PAYE. The employer will normally be vicariously liable for the actions of the Clerk of Works in the course of employment. Under current employment legislation, 'part time' means working fewer than 16 hours per week, but if the employee is a long-serving part time worker of over 5 years, this is reduced to 8 hours.

2 *As an employee on a fixed term basis taken on to perform specific tasks under a fixed term contract of employment*. Such a person would be under the control of the employer in a master–servant relationship. There will be a contract of employment and taxation under Schedule E (PAYE).

3 *As a director of a company*, still technically an employee of the company. The contract for the Clerk of Works services will be between the client and the company.

4 *As a sole practitioner, i.e. an independent person in business on their own account offering professional services*. Such a person will perform specific services in return for a fee. There will be a contract of engagement, and taxation under PAYE. Public liability (PL) insurance and professional indemnity (PI) insurance will normally be required.

5 *As a partner in a firm*. Partners will be jointly liable with their other partners for their acts and omissions. The partners in the firm will enter into a contract of engagement to perform specific services in return for a fee and be subject to appropriate taxation. Public liability insurance and professional indemnity insurance will normally be required.

1.2 SELECTION AND INTERVIEW

1.2.1 Factors affecting selection

Various factors are likely to influence the selection of Clerks of Works with the appropriate skills and experience and definition of a proper level of remuneration and conditions of appointment. Consideration should be given to the following:

- the nature of the building project (e.g. new build, refurbishment, engineering, landscaping, etc.)
- the nature of the services required (e.g. traditional construction with recognised basic trades and skills, predominantly specialist with a high content of advanced structural work, with a high content of specialist subcontractor work, etc.)
- the approximate scale of the project and the expected length of the appointment

- the status and level of responsibility envisaged (e.g. as sole Site Inspector, or as part of a team of Clerks of Works) and degree of accountability
- the type of procurement path for the project
- the type of document used for appointing the Clerk of Works.

1.2.2 Pre-interview submission

For the appointment of a sole practitioner or a firm of Clerks of Works, a submission before interview might be called for, and therefore might be a requirement for a free quotation in competition with others. Sometimes interviews are held first and the preferred applicant is invited to negotiate terms with the appointing body subsequently. A submission might include the following information:

- name, location and form of practice and how long established
- names and qualifications of key staff and range of skills available
- details of a minimum of four recently completed appointments (e.g. project names, descriptions, procurement method, cost, programme, with names of clients and lead consultants)
- details of current appointments and present workload
- details of experience in matters relevant to the proposed appointment (e.g. quality management/assurance, quality control, site testing methods, etc.)
- details of financial standing (including name of bankers) and evidence of satisfactory professional indemnity insurance, where appropriate.

1.2.3 ICW membership

For all appointments, employers are recommended to take account of membership of the ICW as offering an endorsement of competence and an indication of an appointee's interest in continuing professional development. For larger contracts, or those which entail a higher level of responsibility, it might be reasonable to require corporate membership. This would ensure a degree of experience gained at an appropriate level (for example, a minimum of eight years, three years of which having been spent on major projects).

Interviews for salaried staff to be employed by an authority or organisation will follow the pattern and procedures used by the particular organisation.

1.3 APPOINTMENT

1.3.1 Appointment documentation

Appropriate terms and conditions of appointment for freelance Clerks of Works are published by the ICW. There is a Memorandum of Agreement between client and Clerk of Works which includes directions for fees on a lump sum, percentage or time charged basis and a separate supporting schedule of services and fees, available from ICW subject to invoice. The memorandum incorporates by reference the conditions appropriate to the appointment, and these are published separately in the Clerks of Works Appointment Document. This has six sections:

1 services pre-building contract
2 services relevant at commencement of contract
3 services generally carried out during contract
4 other services
5 conditions of appointment (e.g. standard of care and skill, suspension and termination, settlement of disputes, etc.)
6 recommended fees and expenses.

There are separate helpful guidance notes on this document, but clients may still welcome professional advice on which of the sections should apply in particular circumstances.

1.3.2 Letter of appointment

The appointment of a Clerk of Works should always be confirmed in a properly formulated letter of appointment that sets out the terms of the agreement between the employer and employee and should include:

- a description of the project, including site layout, etc.
- the conditions on which the appointment is based
- the scope and duration of the appointment
- details of remuneration, method of calculating fees, expenses, etc.
- the identity of client representatives and of other appointed consultants
- arrangements for professional indemnity insurance.

Under current employment legislation, employers are required to issue a written statement of the main terms and conditions of employment within 13 weeks of the start of employment to all full time employees or to full time employees who have worked for the same employer for more than 5 years.

Role and relationships

2.1 THE ROLE OF THE CLERK OF WORKS

The RIBA's Standard Form of Agreement (SFA/99) for the Appointment of an Architect clause 3.10 states:

> 'Where it is agreed that Site Inspectors are to be appointed, the Client shall appoint and pay them under separate agreements and shall confirm in writing to the Architect the services to be performed, their disciplines and the expected duration of their employment'.

It is essential that the role and duties of the Clerk of Works are clearly described in the appointment agreement. The nature and extent of that role will depend in part on the type of procurement path and the construction operations envisaged and will be subject to the provisions of the building contract regarding the Clerk of Works' duties and powers.

2.2 THE FUNCTION OF THE CLERK OF WORKS

In general terms, the functions and attributes required of a Clerk of Works are as follows.

- Anticipation: the ability to identify problems in advance to prevent them materialising or, where they do materialise, to help overcome them quickly. Intelligent anticipation is founded on experience and a thorough knowledge of the contract documents. A competent Clerk of Works functions as an early warning system.
- Interpretation: checking that the contractor fully understands instructions given in words and on drawings and acting to remove ambiguity.
- Recording: making as complete a record as is appropriate, bearing in mind the heavy reliance that may be placed on the accuracy and objectivity of that record by the architect and the others.
- Inspection: detecting workmanship which does not comply or materials which do not conform to the contract standards. This will usually mean inspecting in detail, and checking measurements regularly.
- Reporting: keeping the architect fully informed on a regular prearranged basis. This also means alerting the architect immediately when situations arise which require decisions or actions.

In a traditional building contract, the functions described above will involve the Clerk of Works in the monitoring activities described in sections 2.3–2.5 below. It should be noted that the term 'architect' should be taken to include any other consultant named as administering the contract.

2.3 MONITORING QUALITY CONTROL ON AND OFF SITE

It is a contractual obligation for the contractor to produce work and use materials in accordance with the standards of the building contract. Checking that this obligation is being met is seldom subject to formal procedures. It should be made clear at the outset whether the Clerk of Works is to act as a quality checker or controller, and agreement should be reached about the methods to be adopted. Where there is to be a programme of predictive inspection, the Clerk of Works will need an inspection plan, a quality plan and a test plan.

Where the contractor is required by the employer to apply quality management methods under BS EN ISO 9001:2000, the Clerk of Works should check that the agreed method statement and quality plan for the project are compatible and are being observed, that the quality audits are carried out as programmed and that non-conforming elements are dealt with properly.

2.4 MONITORING THE ADEQUACY AND FLOW OF PROJECT INFORMATION

Incomplete and allegedly late drawings are a serious problem on many projects. The Clerk of Works can make an important contribution by anticipating when certain information will be needed and notifying the architect without delay. Contractors might be required to produce a schedule of information showing what they still need and when it will be needed. They will normally present this at the initial project or pre-start meeting, where it might be accepted or amended by the architect.

The Clerk of Works should check drawings and other information at or prior to issue and draw the architect's attention to inconsistencies in and between documents. Clerks of Works are sometimes required to interpret drawings for the contractor and may be able to supply minor items of missing information, although they should be careful not to exceed their authority or incur unauthorised expenditure or liability.

The Clerk of Works has an important role in assisting with the compilation of record and maintenance information, and, where the contract requires it, in contributing information for 'as-built' drawings. On larger and more sophisticated projects, this might call for a Clerk of Works well versed in information technology and able, at the appropriate level, to access information held on a computer on site or in the architect's office.

2.5 MONITORING THE EFFECTIVENESS OF SITE MANAGEMENT

Efficient site organisation by a contractor is evidenced by a firm management policy, an effective operational structure and clear lines of authority and accountability. Some contractors, particularly those selected by negotiation, are appointed because of their good track record in site management, but on traditional building contracts there is often considerable variation in management performance. In this respect, the Clerk of Works can have an important monitoring function.

Where a contractor's site operations are subject to quality management procedures, the Clerk of Works has a clearly defined framework for monitoring them, but, where they are more difficult, vigilant Clerks of Works will guard against becoming implicated beyond their authority. First-hand knowledge and excellent records are essential; it might become necessary later to show that regular progress was possible but was inhibited by the contractor's inadequate management.

Monitoring the contractor's obligation to comply with statutory requirements is likely to bring Clerks of Works into direct contact with Building Control Officers (BCOs) and other representatives of statutory bodies who visit the site. They will inform the architect immediately of matters raised and agreements reached and will subsequently monitor the contractor's compliance. Health and safety regulations are having an increasing impact on the construction industry. The Clerk of Works should be fully conversant with the Health and Safety Plan required under the Construction (Design and Management) Regulations (CDM Regulations) and should monitor the contractor's compliance and draw any deviations to his or her attention.

2.6 WORKING RELATIONSHIPS

2.6.1 With the employer under the building contract

Many Joint Contracts Tribunal (JCT) building contracts refer to the Clerk of Works as acting solely as an inspector on behalf of the employer under the direction of the architect/contract administrator, who is acting as an agent of the employer. In the traditional situation, where the Clerk of Works has been appointed on a salary basis and is effectively an employee of the employer, the latter is generally vicariously liable for the Clerk of Works' actions.

The employer's interests can be protected in many ways before the works start by doing a conditions survey or dilapidations survey. For example, the Clerk of Works should immediately make a careful record, including photographs, of the condition of pavements, fences and points of site access. Any allegations by adjoining owners or instances witnessed of damage due to the contractor's operations should be reported immediately.

The primary responsibilities of Clerks of Works will arise from their contracts with those who employ them. Clerks of Works are almost invariably employed and paid by the building owner and are intended to assist the architect in the discharge of the architect's duties of supervision and control of the work. However, while this will usually reflect their sole contractual responsibilities and liabilities, Clerks of

Works may possibly be liable to third parties for loss resulting from negligence under the laws of tort.

2.6.2 With a project manager

Many projects are now administered by a project manager (PM). The RIBA has identified the project manager as being a client's representative providing independent management of a project, from identification of business need to completion. In some procurement arrangements the project manager is the supra-consultant placed above the design team, consultants and contractor, to whom they are all directly accountable. The term is not recognised in JCT contracts, which refer to the architect/contract administrator, but there is nothing to prevent the project manager from carrying out this role. However, government construction contracts (e.g. GC/Wks/1 edition 3) refer to the PM as a named person appointed for the purpose of managing and superintending the works. In this context, the PM is permitted to delegate any powers and duties, and a Clerk of Works might be appointed to exercise many of these duties.

Where a PM has been appointed, it is essential to establish in what capacity he or she will operate. The relationship between the PM and the Clerk of Works and the procedures that are to be adopted should be clarified. The Clerk of Works might still work under the direction of the architect or any other consultant named as administering the contract, but there might be some differences in working methods: for example, the intervals at which consultants' reports are to be received (usually monthly), any preferred structure for meetings, specific information to be included in progress reports, particular checklists to be used at practical completion, commissioning and handover.

2.6.3 With the architect

The JCT Standard Building Contract (SBC) refers to the Clerk of Works acting on behalf of the employer under the direction of the architect. This is the conventional situation where the Clerk of Works has a watching and recording brief and is the eyes and ears of the architect. A period working with the architect before going to site can prove invaluable in establishing the basis for a successful working relationship.

The effectiveness of the Clerk of Works will depend to a large extent on a good, clear and complete briefing at the outset, on the adequate and timely flow of project information, and on the architect's experience as a contract administrator.

As an inspector on site, the Clerk of Works will inform the architect immediately it is believed that the work deviates from the contract requirements. Although working under the control of the architect, Clerks of Works are ultimately accountable to their employer, the building owner. Some building contracts empower the Clerk of Works to issue directions (Clerk of Works Direction Form) to the contractor subject to their confirmation as instructions by the architect/contract administrator; some others might confer greater power, including the issuing of instructions to the contractor. In these circumstances, Clerks of Works would be acting as agents, and would thereby attract more onerous liabilities than those attaching to their traditional role. Much will depend on the authority given at the outset, and on the wording of the particular contract and cover under the architect's PI insurance.

In any event, the Clerk of Works should record and report progress, conditions, events, deviations and any matters that may lead to possible future problems. The architect will rely heavily on the Clerk of Works' anticipation of events, frank reports and helpful suggestions. The relationship between architect and Clerk of Works is founded on mutual trust and respect; its effectiveness depends on the Clerk of Works having no doubt about the architect's expectations, being given the appropriate delegated authority and possessing the will to use it.

On some contracts a resident site architect is appointed. In this event, the role of the Clerk of Works in relation to the site architect will need to be clearly defined. It should be established whether reports are to be made to the latter or to a named person at the architect's permanent offices.

2.6.4 With consultants

(a) Quantity surveyor

The quantity surveyor named in the JCT SBC is responsible for measurement, valuation and adjustment of valuations. The Clerk of Works can assist by:

- making a detailed record of items of work before they are covered up
- making a record of all deliveries to site
- keeping a record of work carried out on a day work basis, and checking that such work has been carried out.

Day work sheets should be signed 'for record purposes only', since it is the architect together with the quantity surveyor who will decide whether or not the work is to be paid as day work.

(b) Engineering consultants

Although structural and building services consultants do not usually have any executive power under the JCT SBC, they have an important inspection role. Any instructions which consultants might wish to pass to the main contractor or relevant subcontractor must be channelled through the architect, and it is important for the Project Clerk of Works to be kept fully informed of any instructions issued.

The structural consultant will be concerned that the design performance criteria are met in the construction methods, materials and workmanship, both in off-site fabrication and on-site assembly. The Clerk of Works may be involved in checking tolerances, joints, reinforcement positions, concrete pouring operations and finishes. In each instance, clear instructions from the consultant will be needed. Regular checks of materials (e.g. aggregate) and tests (e.g. piles, slump, concrete cube, reinforcement, mortar) may need to be planned and observed, and the results recorded. The Clerk of Works will maintain correct working relationships with both the consultant and the architect, bearing in mind that the latter has the executive responsibility.

The services consultants will normally be responsible for the inspection, integration and co-ordination of services systems, and for their subsequent installation, testing, commissioning and planned maintenance. Services installations are often complex and the documentation may be difficult for the non-specialist to understand. The Clerk of Works may have to rely heavily on effective communication with the relevant consultant. As work proceeds, it is critical for builders' work and the routeing of pipes and cables to be correctly executed. A programme of progressive inspection on a component, sub-assembly and section basis might be needed and checks implemented. The Project Clerk of Works should make sure that, before services installations work is covered up, the architect is advised and given the opportunity to inspect the completed work.

The Clerk of Works may be required to witness testing, balancing and commissioning, as provided for in the subcontract documents. These operations need to be effectively integrated into an overall programme to avoid delays to completion. Where these considerations are within the remit of specialist consultants (and sometimes Services (Mechanical and Electrical [M&E]) Clerks of Works), integration becomes even more exacting. The services Clerk of Works should also maintain a co-operative working relationship with any specialist on site, and inform the services engineer whenever an instruction from a consultant to a subcontractor seems necessary.

In assisting consultants, the services Clerk of Works may:

- co-ordinate requirements and information
- if requested, make practical suggestions and provide information
- arrange for tests required under the contract to be carried out and observed, and record and report the results.

2.6.5 With the contractor

The Clerk of Works should, as necessary, remind the contractor or 'person-in-charge' (PIC) of the standard of quality required under the contract, dealing promptly and firmly with any departure from good practice or disregard of architect's instructions. However, good co-operation between the Clerk of Works and the contractor's agent can contribute significantly to the success of the contract, particularly in checking that the site is kept in an orderly fashion, unfixed materials are properly stored and completed work is adequately protected. The Clerk of Works should also work closely with the contractor to see that tests, inspections and preparations for formal handover are all effectively supervised.

The Clerk of Works will be particularly vigilant on site in the following respects:

- in inspections, as programmed or as otherwise recognised
- in carrying out tests, as programmed or as otherwise required
- in agreeing measurements prior to work being covered up
- in providing directions or instructions and monitoring work in progress.

2.6.6 With other Clerks of Works

When more than one Clerk of Works has been appointed it is important that one is nominated and recognised as the Project Clerk of Works. This is the person who will receive instructions from the architect, submit reports and attend the site progress meetings for the Clerk of Works items. Only the Project Clerk of Works should be empowered to issue directions under the JCT SBC. A good working relationship with other Clerks of Works is essential, and with any other site supervisory and management staff. It will be important to maintain a consistent interpretation of the situation on site and a co-ordinated approach towards monitoring, inspection, testing, recording and reporting.

Duties of the Clerk of Works/Site Inspector

3

This section provides a general description of the duties of a Clerk of Works. However, it should be noted that these duties will vary depending on the type of procurement and form of contract for each particular project.

3.1 THE CLERK OF WORKS' DUTIES

There are many advantages in appointing a Clerk of Works before work commences on site. This arrangement may prove more difficult in the private sector, but the Clerk of Works can often comment from experience on construction matters and make a significant contribution to production information. A period of two weeks spent in the architect's office before going on site will allow a Clerk of Works to get to know the personnel, procedures and documentation associated with the project.

3.1.1 Pre-project preparations

During this period of familiarisation, the Clerk of Works might be expected to:

- study the architect's office procedures
- study the contract drawings and schedules, and information produced by consultants and specialists
- study the programme for issue of further information
- study bills of quantities and/or specifications
- study the Health and Safety Plan for the project
- study relevant British Standards and Approved Codes of Practice, etc.
- establish lines of communication with the project architect, quantity surveyor, other consultants, other Clerks of Works and the contractor's site supervisory staff
- clarify with the project architect the standards to be met under the contract
- as requested, advise on materials, construction details, samples, etc.
- assemble the record documents supplied for use on site and clarify how they are expected to be used
- as relevant, make contact with the local authority or other approved inspectors
- make arrangements for obtaining weather information
- visit the workshops for proposed nominated suppliers and subcontractors as appropriate.

3.1.2 Documentation

The Clerk of Works might expect to be supplied with the following documents:

- form of building contract, incorporating any supplements or amendments
- contract bills of quantities (unpriced) and/or specification
- 'Numbered Documents' or other information relating to subcontracts
- the employer's health and safety policy requirements and the approved Health and Safety Plan
- the site diary

- report forms
- quality management plan, contractor's method statement, quality control checklist, verification forms, etc.
- relevant record forms
- record chart for rainfall, etc.
- copies of standing orders or instructions applicable to the project.

Site accommodation provided for the Clerk of Works should be checked to see that its position and siting, furniture and equipment are in accordance with what has been specified.

3.1.3 Briefing

Clerks of Works should be briefed about their responsibilities and extent of authority in connection with:

- hours of working and notification of additional hours
- daily labour returns and method of submitting them
- method of recording time lost in site working
- signing of authorised day work vouchers
- samples of materials
- testing of samples
- storage of materials
- notification of work to be covered up after inspection
- general procedures for inspection and recording
- visitors to site and permission to take photographs
- the Party Wall Act 1966 and note if applicable.

Site supervisory staff might be briefed at a special meeting called by the architect or as part of the initial project or 'pre-start' meeting. Ideally, the full project team will be present so that all personnel can be introduced and identified, and responsibilities and lines of communication defined and established.

3.1.4 Initial project or pre-start meeting

The agenda for the meeting will include an item designated 'Clerks of Works Matters', covering inspection, facilities and quantity checks. The architect, who will chair the meeting, will clarify the anticipated pattern of visits to site and will ask for the Clerk of Works' co-operation and assistance in carrying out these inspection duties. The contractor will be reminded of the obligation to provide the Clerk of Works with adequate facilities and access, together with information about site staff, equipment and site operations, and matters relating to site safety. The architect will explain procedures for checking quality control, namely:

- certificates, vouchers, etc., as required
- samples of materials to be submitted

- samples of workmanship to be submitted prior to work commencing
- test procedures set out in the bills of quantities
- adequate measures for protection and storage
- visits to the workshops of suppliers and manufacturers.

3.1.5 Checklist: typical duties of a Clerk of Works

Typically, it will fall within the remit of the Clerk of Works to:

- examine work in the contractor's, subcontractors' and suppliers' yards as necessary
- check that work proceeds according to the programme
- submit periodic reports
- keep a diary of events, a register of drawings and file of instructions received, with relevant observations
- check drawings for errors, discrepancies and divergences and notify the architect if any arise
- witness tests required by the contract or instructed by the architect
- monitor the application of specified techniques
- inform the architect of non-conforming work
- notify the architect immediately of problems arising and decisions needed
- confirm oral directions to the contractor in writing with a copy to the architect
- check the effects of proposed variations on relevant trades and services
- liaise with specialist Clerks of Works, where appointed
- check co-ordination of work by trades on installation, ducting, routeing, etc.
- check day work record sheets and record any wastage
- attend site meetings
- maintain as-built records and drawings
- record delays and the reasons for them
- take site photographs regularly and systematically, ensuring that they are date-endorsed and countersigned
- liaise with the local Building Control Officers (BCOs).

3.1.6 Actions beyond the scope of the Clerk of Works

Unless authorised by the architect or agent, the Clerk of Works will *not*:

- modify the design
- incur extra costs
- instruct the contractor about methods of working
- agree commitments with suppliers and subcontractors
- vary procedures specified in the contract
- issue instructions to the contractor unless authorised by the architect or employer's agent.

The Clerk of Works will not carry out instructions relating to the building contract from anyone but the person empowered under the contract to issue instructions.

3.1.7 Duties on site – quality matters

Quality control, as commonly practised on building sites, requires procedures to establish that work carried out and goods supplied conform to the standards specified in the building contract. Detailed records should provide identification, give the nature and dates of inspections, tests and approvals, and note the nature and extent of any non-conforming work found, together with details of corrective action. While this is the responsibility of the contractor, the Clerk of Works should keep independent records which will be available to the architect.

To the extent required by the contract, the contractor may be required to institute a quality management system. This will entail preparing a project quality plan showing how the contractor intends to meet the requirements; the plan may need to be approved by the architect. The project quality plan will normally give details of project organisation, reports on the performance of subcontractors, the work instructions or method statements to be followed, inspection and test plans listing the verification checks, and the planned dates for the project audits. The Clerk of Works should be informed of the content of the project quality plan, including any amendments and updating, and should check that the contractor implements the associated checks and procedures. However, compliance is wholly a matter for the contractor and the Clerk of Works should not be involved in signing documents. It may be necessary to keep independent notes and to report to the architect.

Effective reporting for a Clerk of Works

4

4.1 EFFECTIVE REPORTING

4.1.1 A professional approach

In the Introduction to this handbook, the motto of the Institute of Clerks of Works was cited as summing up the way in which Clerks of Works are expected to approach and carry out their duties – with ability, integrity and vigilance. This sense of professionalism should be reflected in all site notes, directions and reports which, as well as contributing to the efficient running of a project, are an important part of its recorded history. In the event of litigation, which may take place many months or even years after the project has been completed, they can provide crucial evidence. They should all be methodically compiled in an appropriate format and be legible, clearly and concisely expressed, true and accurate.

However urgent and disruptive an event may be, all the facts about it must be recorded fully as soon as circumstances permit. Clerks of Works need to absorb a constant stream of detailed information in the course of each day and the best approach is to make brief notes as the day progresses so that nothing is forgotten. This approach provides much better insurance than trying to remember everything at the end of the working day.

4.1.2 Writing proficiency

The Clerk of Works' written reports should be seen as an extension of the architect's own project records, and it is essential for Clerks of Works to be able to express themselves clearly and effectively, especially in the written medium.

Writing proficiency is seldom cited as a desirable skill for people whose job is regarded as inherently practical, but it is a crucial competence for most professionals associated with the construction industry, and especially for anyone who is required to inspect and report. Few architects have time to spare for lengthy telephone calls from site on non-urgent matters; a clear, concise and timely written report is more reliable as well as more convenient.

For Clerks of Works, the three principal vehicles for written information are site directions, the site diary and periodic reports. Each of these has a different function and format, and each requires a different approach. Directions are intended to warn of the need for action; the site diary is for compiling a record of day-to-day events on site; periodic reports give an assessment of progress on site and an intelligent forecast of requirements and developments. All must be carefully written and attention must be given to grammar, punctuation and spelling; ignoring these can often lead to misunderstandings, errors and confusion.

4.1.3 Test each written item

The Clerk of Works should scrutinise each item to ensure the following.

- Is it true?
- Is it accurate?
- Does it make sense?
- Will the reader understand what has happened?
- Will the reader understand what has to be done, and how urgently?

4.1.4 Issuing site directions

A clear procedure for the issue and confirmation of site directions in accordance with the contract conditions must be established with the architect at the outset, and the contractor must fully understand this procedure. Under the JCT SBC, directions issued by the Clerk of Works are of no effect unless confirmed by the architect within two working days. In real life, some flexibility is often acknowledged, but this should never be assumed and it is always wise to 'go by the book'.

A published form should be used for site directions so that they are easily recognised and can be distinguished from the architect's instructions, which reflect the powers and duties given to the architect under the contract. Under the JCT SBC, the Clerk of Works may only give directions in relation to matters over which the architect is empowered to issue instructions, so it is important to clearly identify these matters.

Site directions must be clear and unambiguous. Each should be headed with the name of the contract works and any project number, the date of issue and serial number. Drawings should be referred to accurately, with their correct numbers, titles and revisions. Actions, materials and techniques should be described precisely, with times and locations as appropriate. In any form of direction or instruction, sentences should be short and language simple. The top copy of the direction should be sent to the contractor or the contractor's agent, and a copy sent to the architect. With the latter's agreement, a copy should also be sent to the quantity surveyor. The file copy should be kept in a separate file in the site office.

4.1.5 Checks before issuing a direction

The Clerk of Works must check with the architect before issuing any direction that:

- entails additional work
- has new financial implications
- alters any of the contract particulars
- approves working methods that have not been agreed.

4.1.6 Notes and reports

The frequency of reporting required must be established at the outset with the architect. For a Clerk of Works on site full time, a weekly report is usual; if employed on an occasional or part-time basis, the pattern of periodic reports will need to be agreed. For any periodic report, the site diary will be the first point of reference.

4.1.7 The site diary

The site diary is for recording day-to-day events and accidents on site. The amount of detail to be included is a matter of judgment, but Clerks of Works would do well to remember that the diary could be referred to as part of the evidence cited in future arbitration or litigation proceedings. Its cover and binding should therefore be sufficiently sturdy to ensure its survival as a record document. The ownership of the diary and its destination at the conclusion of the project should be clarified with the architect.

Matters that should be entered as a matter of course include:

- verbal instructions or information from the architect
- information given by key consultants
- day works and the reasons for taking them as day works
- the weather, especially extremes of temperature, high winds, rain and snow
- important construction events, such as concrete pouring and striking of formwork
- the start of important subcontract works; any problems of co-ordination or quality
- deliveries of goods and materials to site
- movement of plant and equipment
- description of any tests witnessed, with names of personnel involved
- instances of bad workmanship, and when and if drawn to the attention of the contractor
- any work or materials rejected, with reference to the relevant instructions, and how and when rectified
- delays and reasons for them, either during an operation or between operations
- drawings or information needed or requested
- labour problems, overtime bans, strikes, difficulties with labour-only gangs
- instances of inadequate site management or co-ordination
- any events, discussions, omissions, etc., likely to have knock-on effects or which relate to the contractor's performance
- details of any visitors to site.

4.1.8 Using the site diary to good effect

The following points outline good practice in the use of the site diary.

- The site diary should be opened the day the site is handed over to the contractor.
- Items and events should be noted as soon as possible, and in any event before the end of the day.
- It is good practice to keep observations and records in the same sequence each day, as far as practicable.
- It must be remembered that the site diary is a job record document, not a personal working notebook.
- A new site diary should be compiled for each job.

Clerks of Works should use a separate notebook for compiling a list of their own action items. This will include queries raised by the contractor and the answers given (by the architect or consultants), and the Clerk of Works' own queries to be raised with the architect. This helps to maintain the flow of information and ensures that nothing is forgotten. If the architect does not provide trade or work stage checklists, Clerks of Works might consider preparing their own.

4.1.9 Periodic reports

On many jobs, the Clerk of Works is required to provide the architect with periodic reports to record and assess progress on site. Such reports are often prepared on a weekly basis. Each should include enough information to stand on its own, so that the architect does not need to refer back to previous reports.

Reports should be brief, clear, easy to read and have a consistent structure and format. On some projects, printed forms for periodic reports for the Clerk of Works to complete and sign are provided. These typically include items to be marked or ticked, with space to add notes and remarks. However, on many jobs, particularly small ones, Clerks of Works may have to devise their own format for reporting, and this will vary according to the nature of the work. It should be kept as simple as possible, and the structure for a periodic report might be as follows:

1 Internal works: notes and progress
2 External works: notes and progress
3 Weather records
4 Labour records
5 Information received
6 Instructions required.

Labour returns received from the contractor may be attached to the report, together with relevant reports and records.

The distribution list for the report should be agreed with the architect.

4.1.10 Organisation of reports

To be effective, reports must be properly structured, as detailed below.

- Each report should be headed with the job title and number, report serial number and date.
- The content should be structured appropriately under clear and consistent headings.
- Each section should begin on a new page, unless sections are very short.
- It is best to use a simple numbering system.
- Relevant returns, reports, etc., should be attached.
- The report must be signed and dated.

4.2 MODERN TECHNOLOGY ON SITE

Today, computer and digital technologies have reached construction sites, and these tools have their uses – provided the batteries are charged! Digital cameras and some mobile phones now have the capability to send an image across the ether. Either as a record of non-compliance, or when used to describe a detail to the architect, where one picture could in fact say a thousand words, these tools have proved their use. Hand-held 'palm-tops' can also record details without having to refer to the trusty notepad, but all details and images, regardless of the method of generation, need to be properly catalogued and 'backed up' effectively to provide an adequate future record. As with entries in the site diary, a timely approach to the necessary paperwork is strongly recommended.

Health and safety

5.1 HEALTH AND SAFETY

Health and safety is an integral part of any business and the construction industry is no different from any other in this respect. Clerks of Works have responsibility for liaising with the main contractor and architect in respect of health and safety. During visiting sites, it is imperative that the Clerk of Works ensures that health and safety legislation is being adhered to and, where non-compliance becomes apparent, informs the architect and main contractor immediately.

Since the introduction of the Health and Safety at Work etc. Act 1974 there has been a complete overhaul of the legislative system, which has removed a large number of regulations from the system. Gone are the days of the Factories Act, the Health and Welfare Regulations 1966 plus many others associated with the construction industry. All of this redundant legislation has been replaced by regulations originating in the European Commission (EC).

The following are the most important pieces of legislation:

- Management of Health and Safety at Work Regulations 1999. SI 1999/3242
- Workplace (Health, Safety and Welfare) Regulations 1992. SI 1992/3004
- Provision and Use of Work Equipment Regulations 1998. SI 1998/2306
- Personal Protective Equipment at Work Regulations 1992. SI 1992/2966
- Manual Handling Operations Regulations 1992. SI 1992/2793
- Health and Safety (Display Screen Equipment) Regulations 1992. SI 1992/2792
- Construction (Design and Management) Regulations 1994. SI 1994/3140 (new edition due to be enacted in 2007)
- Construction (Health, Safety and Welfare) Regulations 1996. SI 1996/1592
- Construction (Head Protection) Regulations 1989. SI 1989/2209
- Occupiers' Liability Act 1957
- Occupiers' Liability Act 1984
- Work at Height Regulations 2005. SI 2005/735
- Numerous fire regulations – new Act due to come into force in October 2006
- Party Wall Act 1996.

It is necessary also to adhere to the 'Building Regulations'. The Clerk of Works must be up to date with current Building Regulations and liaise with BCOs regarding any concerns over meeting their requirements.

Clerks of Works must keep themselves up to date with legislation and read articles, etc., on the subject. It should be remembered that ignorance of the law is no defence.

Risk assessments have become the norm for most activities carried out. These are legal requirements. It is part of the Clerk of Works' duties to check that they have been carried out and that procedures have been complied with where necessary.

Two key pieces of legislation that have been specifically drafted for the construction industry, namely the Construction (Design and Management) Regulations 1994 and the Construction (Health, Safety and Welfare) Regulations 1996, are examined below.

5.2 THE CONSTRUCTION (DESIGN AND MANAGEMENT) REGULATIONS 1994

These regulations apply to almost every construction operation and affect health and safety aspects of the design of the building, temporary works required for its construction and systems for maintaining the building and replacement installations.

The client is required to appoint a 'Planning Supervisor' who must supply detailed particulars of the proposed operations to the Health and Safety Executive (HSE) before the commencement of work. The Planning Supervisor is required to prepare a Health and Safety Plan, which details the arrangements for the management and construction of the work, together with the proposals for monitoring progress. The Health and Safety Plan may be adapted by the Principal Contractor to suit each individual programme and methods. The Principal Contractor is wholly responsible for the implementation of the Health and Safety Plan during construction. At completion of the project, the Planning Supervisor must produce a Health and Safety File and this must be securely deposited for future reference.

The Clerk of Works must be informed about the contractor's methods and make routine checks of the contractor's obligations in respect of: first-aid facilities, emergency evacuation procedure, warning signs and the display of the relevant safety signs and notices. The Clerk of Works must be familiar with the method statement and Health and Safety Plan in order that their implementation can be properly monitored. The Clerk of Works may be asked to make a contribution in respect of the Health and Safety File, drawing attention to the materials used and/ or the methods that were adopted. Regular inspections must be carried out.

It is imperative that the Clerk of Works should set in place procedures for:

- regular inspection and spot-checks on health and safety procedures
- reporting to the architect any instances of non-compliance and ensuring that corrective action is taken
- incidents connected with hazardous substances and any delay due to work stoppage because of them.

The CDM Regulations 1994 are due to be replaced in 2007 by the Construction (Design and Management) Regulations 2007 – see Chapter 6.

5.3 THE CONSTRUCTION (HEALTH, SAFETY AND WELFARE) REGULATIONS 1996

These regulations replaced most of the regulations brought into force during the 1960s. Basically, they cover almost every activity that takes place on a construction site, from safe places of work to plant and equipment. Again, the Clerk of Works will have a responsibility to ensure that site practices adhere to the requirements of this legislation. Non-compliance with any section of these regulations should be reported to the architect and the main contractor. One of the duties of the Clerk of Works is to ensure that corrective action is taken and compliance maintained.

These regulations are also due to be replaced in 2007 by the Construction (Design and Management) Regulations 2007 – see Chapter 6.

5.4 FIRE

At present, there is an Act covering fire, namely the Fire Precautions Act 1971, plus more than 60 additional regulations. All of this is due to change, possibly in 2006, when a new Fire Act is due to come into force.

Fire is also dealt with under Section 21 of the Construction (Health, Safety and Welfare) Regulations 1996.

Each year fire destroys many homes and businesses and takes lives, yet most of these fires could have been prevented. It is imperative to ensure that the risk of a fire on site is kept to the lowest level possible. It is also essential that adequate firefighting equipment is provided and that everyone on site knows how to use it. Such equipment must be clearly identified. Emergency escape routes must be clearly defined and kept free from obstruction at all times. The site should have a 'Fire Safety Co-ordinator' with whom the Clerk of Works must liaise at all times to ensure that every element is in place.

Again, Clerks of Works should set up their own inspections and advise both the architect and main contractor of any instances of non-compliance.

5.5 EMERGENCY/DISASTER PROCEDURE

The world is undergoing particularly turbulent times – not only do we face the threat of adverse weather and flooding due to 'climate changes', but we also see an alarming escalation in the threat of terrorist activity. Any of these elements could create an 'emergency' or 'disaster' situation with very little warning.

It is imperative that plans are drafted for use in such emergencies. Such plans must cover every aspect of the possible situation. Ultimately, the first objective is to prevent injury or loss of life, not just of those working on site, but members of the public as well. The other objective is to minimise potential losses to the business. It is imperative that the Clerk of Works participates in the drafting of such plans, and that they are adequately tested. All persons on site must be fully aware of their part of the procedures.

In conclusion, health and safety is a key element in any business; getting it wrong could cost someone their life. Clerks of Works must keep themselves abreast of current developments. When visiting sites it is essential to observe precisely what is happening and determine whether people are adhering to health and safety legislation. It is the duty of the Clerk of Works to ensure that they do, and it is imperative to communicate with everyone involved in the project to make certain that construction sites are healthy and safe places to work.

5.6 HEALTH AND SAFETY SITE CHECKLIST

It is imperative for a Clerk of Works to be aware of health and safety while visiting a construction site, to ensure that health and safety is being treated as an important element of the construction project. The following 'checklist' details some of the elements that should be observed. Obviously, the list is not fully comprehensive as, very often, depending on the project in hand, specialist tools, equipment or processes may be in use. Expert advice on any specific problem can be obtained by telephoning the Health and Safety Executive (HSE) 'Infoline' on 0870 1545500.

5.6.1 Access/egress

Clerks of Works must ensure that a positive answer can be given in response to the following questions.

- Are arrangements in place to deal with visitors and workers new to the site?
- Can everyone reach their place of work safely?
- Are there safe roads, gangways, passageways, ladders and scaffolds?
- Are all walkways level and free from obstructions?
- Is edge protection provided at all edges to prevent falls?
- Are holes securely fenced or protected with clearly marked fixed covers?
- Is the site tidy and are materials stored away safely?
- Is waste collected and disposed of properly?
- Are there chutes for waste to avoid materials being thrown down?
- Are nails in timber removed or hammered down?
- Is safe lighting provided for work in the dark or poor light?
- Are any necessary props or shores in place to make structures safe?
- Are all health and safety notices clearly displayed?
- Are pedestrians separated from site traffic?

5.6.2 Cartridge operated tools

- Are the maker's instructions being followed?
- Has the operator been properly trained?
- Is the operator aware of the dangers and able to deal with misfires?
- Does the operator wear eye protection?
- Does the operator wear ear protectors?
- Is the gun cleaned regularly?
- Are the gun and cartridges kept in a secure place when not in use?

5.6.3 Compressed gases, e.g. liquefied petroleum gas (LPG), acetylene

- Are cylinders stored properly?
- Are all cylinders clearly identified?
- Are cylinders secured in an upright position, with the valve to the top?
- Is the cylinder valve fully closed when the cylinder is not in use?
- Are there 'hot work' procedures?
- Are cylinders in use sited outside huts?

5.6.4 Cranes and lifting appliances

- Is the crane inspected weekly, and thoroughly examined every 14 months by a competent person? Are the results of inspections recorded?
- Is there a test certificate?
- Is the driver trained, competent and over 18?
- Are the controls (levers, handles, switches, etc.) clearly marked?
- Do the driver and banksman find out the load's weight before trying to lift it?
- In the case of a jib crane with a capacity of more than one tonne, does it have an efficient automatic safe load indicator that is inspected weekly?
- In the case of a hydraulic excavator being used as a crane, is the maximum safe load clearly marked and are hydraulic check valves fitted where required by the Certificate of Exemption?
- Is the crane on a firm and level base?
- Is there enough space for safe operation?
- Has the banksman or slinger been trained to give signals and to attach loads correctly and do they know the lifting limitations of the crane?
- If it can vary its operating radius, is the crane clearly marked with safe working loads and corresponding radii?
- Is the crane regularly maintained?
- Is the lifting gear in good condition and has it been thoroughly examined (i.e. are slings and chains currently certified)?

5.6.5 Electricity

- Are all portable electric tools and equipment supplied at 110 V, and have special measures been taken to protect them from mechanical damage and wet conditions?
- Are there any signs of damage to or interference with equipment, wires and cables?
- Are all connections to power points made by the correct plugs?
- Are connections to plugs properly made so that the cable grip holds the cable firmly and prevents the earth wire from being pulled out?
- Are there 'Permit to Work' procedures where necessary to ensure safety?
- Are there any overhead electric lines?

- Where anything might touch overhead lines or cause arcing (cranes, tipper lorries, scaffolding, etc.), has the electricity supply been turned off, or have other precautions been taken?

5.6.6 Emergencies

- Is there an 'Emergency Plan' for use in the case of adverse weather, bomb threats, etc.?
- Is the plan known by all on site, including visitors?
- Are muster points identified?

5.6.7 Excavations

- Have all underground services been located (with scanners and existing plans), and marked and precautions taken to avoid them?
- Has an adequate supply of suitable timber, trench sheets, props or other supporting material been delivered to the site before any excavation work begins?
- Is a safe method in place for putting in and taking out the timbering, i.e. one that does not rely on people working within an unsupported trench?
- If the sides of the excavation are sloped back or battered, is the angle of batter sufficient to prevent collapse?
- Is the excavation inspected daily, and thoroughly examined weekly, after using explosives or after unexpected falls of materials?
- Is there safe access to the excavation, e.g. by a sufficiently long ladder?
- Are there barriers to prevent people falling in?
- Is the excavation affecting the stability of neighbouring buildings?
- Is there a risk of the excavation flooding?
- Are stacked materials, spoil or plant near the edge of the excavation likely to cause a collapse of the side?
- If vehicles tip into the excavation, are properly secured stop blocks used?

5.6.8 Falsework/formwork

- Is there a 'Method Statement' and does it deal with preventing workers from falling?
- Has a 'Falsework Co-ordinator' been appointed?
- Have the design and supports for shuttering and formwork been checked?
- Is it being erected safely from steps or proper platforms?
- Are the bases and ground conditions adequate for the loads?
- Are the props set out on a level bed, plumb and cross-braced?
- Are the correct pins used in the props?
- Are the timbers in good condition?
- Is the falsework inspected by a competent person and checked against the agreed design before permission is given to pour concrete?

5.6.9 Fire

- Does the site have the right number and type of fire extinguishers?
- Are there adequate escape routes?
- Are they kept clear?
- Do all workers know what to do in an emergency?
- Is there a warning system?
- Is it tested?
- Does it work?

5.6.10 Flammable liquids

- Is there a proper storage area?
- Is the amount of flammable liquid on site kept to a minimum for the day's work?
- Is smoking prohibited? Are other ignition sources kept away from flammable liquids?
- Are properly constructed safety containers used?

5.6.11 Health

- Have all hazardous substances, e.g. asbestos, lead, solvents, etc., been identified and the risks assessed?
- Can safer substances be substituted?
- Can exposure be controlled other than by using protective equipment?
- Are safety information sheets available from the supplier?
- Is safety equipment provided and used?
- Are the workers who are not protected kept out of danger areas?
- In confined spaces, has the atmosphere been tested and a fresh-air supply provided if necessary and does it meet statutory requirements?
- Are safety information sheets available from suppliers, e.g. COSHH?

5.6.12 Ladders

- Has a risk assessment been carried out to ensure that the correct access equipment is being used?
- Are ladders the right equipment for the job, or should a scaffold or other access be provided?
- Are the ladders in good condition and properly positioned for access?
- Are they on firm, level ground?
- Are ladders secured near the top, even if they will only be used for a short time?
- If they cannot be secured at the top, are they secured near the bottom, weighted and footed to prevent slipping?
- Do ladders rise at least 1.05 m above their landing place or highest rungs used? If not, are there adequate handholds?

5.6.13 Machinery/plant

- Are there any dangerous parts, e.g. exposed gears, chain drives, projecting shafts?
- Are dangerous parts adequately guarded?
- Are guards secured and in good repair?
- Are plant and machinery regularly maintained?

5.6.14 Manual handling

- Have risk assessments been carried out?
- Can manual handling be avoided where there is a risk of injury?
- If not, have the risks been assessed and reduced?
- Have those engaged in manual handling been properly trained?

5.6.15 Noise

- Has an assessment been carried out of the noise risks?
- Are plant and machinery fitted with silencers/mufflers?
- Do workers wear ear protection if they have to work in very noisy surroundings?
- Are the Noise at Work Regulations 2005 (April 6th) being followed?

5.6.16 Other combustible material

- Is the amount of combustible material on site kept to a minimum?
- Are there proper waste bins?
- Is waste material removed regularly by an authorised operator?

5.6.17 Protective clothing

- Have risk assessments been carried out to determine where protective equipment is required?
- Is the protective equipment suitable for the employee?
- Has training on the use of protective equipment taken place?
- Is suitable equipment provided to protect the head, eyes, hands and feet where appropriate?
- Do workers wear their protective equipment?
- Is protective equipment properly stored?
- Is replacement protective equipment available?

5.6.18 Risk assessments

- Have risk assessments been carried out where required under specific legislation?
- Are risk assessments recorded?
- Are risk assessments implemented?
- Are method statements available?

5.6.19 Risks to the public

- Have all risks to members of the public adjacent to the site been identified, for example material falling from scaffolds, etc., site plant and transport access and egress, and have precautions been implemented (e.g. scaffold fans/nets, banksman, warning notices, etc.)?
- Is there adequate site perimeter fencing to keep out the public, particularly children? Is the site secure during non-working periods?
- Are specific dangers on site made safe during non-working periods, e.g. excavations and openings covered/fenced, materials safely stacked, plant immobilised and ladders removed or boarded?

5.6.20 Roof work

- Are crawling ladders or crawling boards used on roofs that slope more than 10 degrees?
- If not, do the roof battens provide a safe handhold and foothold?
- Are there barriers or other edge protection to stop people or materials falling from sloping or flat roofs?
- Are crawling boards provided and used where people work on fragile materials such as asbestos cement sheets or glass? Are warning notices posted?
- Are suitable guardrails, covers, etc., provided where people pass or work near such fragile materials?
- Are roof lights properly covered or provided with barriers?
- During sheeting operations, are precautions taken to stop people falling from the edge of the sheet?
- Are precautions taken to stop debris falling onto others working under the roof?

5.6.21 Scaffolds

- Was the scaffold erected by competent persons?
- Is there proper access to the scaffold platform?
- Are all uprights properly founded and provided with base plates?
- Where necessary, are there timber sole plates or is there some other way in which slipping or sinking can be prevented?
- Is the scaffold secured to the building in enough places to prevent collapse and are the ties strong enough?
- If any of the ties have been removed since the scaffold was erected have additional ties been provided to replace them?
- Is the scaffold adequately braced to ensure stability?
- Are load-bearing fittings used where required?
- Are the working platforms fully boarded? Are the boards free from obvious defects, such as knots, and are they arranged to avoid tipping and tripping?
- Are the boards fixed down if high winds are forecast?

- Are there adequate guardrails and toe boards at every side from which a person could fall 2 m or more?
- If the scaffold has been designed and constructed for loading with materials, are the materials evenly distributed?
- Are there effective barriers or warning notices to stop people using an incomplete scaffold, e.g. one that is not fully boarded?
- Does a competent person inspect the scaffold at least once a week, and always after bad weather?
- Are the results of inspections recorded, including defects that were put right during the inspections, and are records signed by the person who carried out the inspection?
- Are loading bays properly gated and correctly used?

5.6.22 Transport and mobile plant

- Are all vehicles and plant kept in good repair and serviced?
- Do the steering, handbrakes and footbrakes all work properly?
- Have drivers and operators received proper training?
- Are all vehicles and plant being safely driven?
- Are vehicles securely loaded?
- Are passengers prohibited from riding?
- Are any tipping lorries being used?
- Do workers realise that raised bodies should be propped before reaching underneath?
- Is there a system to control on-site movements to avoid danger, including danger to pedestrians?
- Are there separate routes and crossing points for pedestrians?
- Where vehicles have to reverse, are they controlled by a properly trained banksman following a safe system of operation? Do they have audible alarms?

5.6.23 Welfare

- Have suitable toilets been provided?
- Are all toilets cleaned on a daily basis?
- Are there clean washbasins, hot/warm water, soap and towels?
- Is there a room or area where clothes can be dried?
- Is wet weather gear provided for those who have to work in wet conditions?
- Is there a drying room or canteen where workers can take shelter and have meals with the facility for boiling water?
- Is there a trained First-Aider on site?
- Is there a suitable first-aid box?
- Are the first-aid box contents regularly checked?
- Is the accident book maintained?
- Is there an accident/incident reporting system in use?

Construction (Design and Management) Regulations 2007

6.1 CONSTRUCTION (DESIGN AND MANAGEMENT) REGULATIONS 2007

The Construction (Design and Management) (CDM) Regulations proposed to come into force during 2007 are to replace the Construction (Design and Management) Regulations 1994 and the Construction (Health, Safety and Welfare) Regulations 1996.

Clerks of Works ought to be aware of how the new Construction (Design and Management) Regulations 2007 relate to any building project with which they are involved. In addition, it is important to be aware that the 2007 regulations create a new role, that of 'Co-ordinator', in place of the 'Planning Supervisor', which is in many ways suited to the skills possessed by an experienced Clerk of Works. Co-ordinators need to ensure that all those involved in a building project comply with the CDM Regulations and will therefore require knowledge of the regulations in order to carry out their duties.

6.2 OVERVIEW

The principal aim of the new regulations is to incorporate health and safety matters into the entire building project. The regulations require the client and all trades concerned to be involved in planning, reviewing and updating health and safety issues as a natural part of the building process, rather than as an afterthought.

The regulations identify the duties of the Key Management Team: to facilitate communication and co-operation with each other, providing a structure which allows all involved parties to discuss potential hazards and decide how to deal with those hazards, and provide the appropriate paperwork to the Co-ordinator for the Health and Safety File.

6.3 NOTIFIABLE PROJECTS

The regulations specify that a project is 'notifiable' if the construction phase is likely to involve more than:

- 30 days or
- 500 person hours.

The Health and Safety Executive (HSE) must be notified of these projects, and the particulars to be notified to the HSE as set out in Schedule 1 of the Regulations are:

- date of forwarding
- exact address of the construction site
- name and address of the client
- name and address of the Co-ordinator

- name and address of the Principal Contractor
- date planned for the start of the construction phase
- planned duration of the construction phase
- estimated maximum number of people at work on the construction site
- planned number of contractors on the construction site
- name and address of any contractor already appointed
- name and address of any designer already engaged.

6.4 DUTIES

6.4.1 The client (excluding domestic clients)

(a) Duty in relation to information

The client has a duty to ensure that all members of the management team are promptly provided by the Co-ordinator with all the information in the client's possession, including:

- information for the Health and Safety File
- information about or affecting the site or construction work
- information provided by a designer
- minimum notice which will be allowed to the Principal Contractor and other contractors for planning and preparation of construction work.

(b) Duty in relation to the construction phase

The client must ensure that the Principal Contractor has prepared a 'Construction Phase Plan' allowing work to start without undue risk to health or safety. The plan must be project-specific and must set out the framework for managing health and safety on site and detail any health and safety issues which are likely to arise in the early stages of the project, together with details of any action that will be required to control key risks.

The client, via the Co-ordinator, must ensure that the site is fully equipped, including the provision of welfare facilities.

(c) Duty in relation to the Health and Safety File

The client must ensure that the Co-ordinator has all the information to be included in the Health and Safety File. If the Health and Safety File relates to more than one project, the information for each site or structure should be easily identifiable.

6.4.2 The Co-ordinator

It is the duty of the Co-ordinator to assist and advise the client in fulfilling duties and complying with the regulations, including identifying and extracting information required on the following:

- the Health and Safety File: it is the duty of the Co-ordinator to review, amend and add to the file as the project progresses. At the end of the construction phase, the Health and Safety File is to be passed on to the client
- information regarding the site or construction work
- information from the designer ensuring that notice of the project has been passed on to the HSE
- the minimum notice for the Principal Contractor and other contractors to plan and prepare the construction work.

Other duties that fall within the Co-ordinator's remit are detailed below.

- To obtain necessary details from the designer in order to advise the client on the suitability and compatibility of designs and any modifications. There is no need to approve or check the designs but the Co-ordinator must be satisfied that the designs eliminate and prevent risks.
- To co-ordinate design work, planning and other preparation.
- To liaise with the Principal Contractor concerning any design or change which may affect the construction phase.
- To provide prompt and clear health and safety information to the management team.

6.4.3 Designers

A designer is someone whose trade or business involves preparing designs for construction work, including variations. Areas where a designer may have an influence include:

- drawings
- design details
- specifications
- bills of quantities
- specification of the use of particular articles or substances
- related analysis
- calculations and preparation work.

Designers' duties encompass the prerequisites for all projects, i.e. the designer must check that:

- the client is aware of his or her duties under the regulations
- a Co-ordinator has been appointed for the project, and
- notice of the project has been given to the HSE.

The designer must not commence work until the above checks have been carried out. The designer must be competent and able to address the health and safety issues that are likely to be involved in the design.

Every designer, when preparing or modifying a design to be used in construction work, must avoid risks to any person:

- carrying out the construction work
- cleaning or maintaining the permanent fixtures and fittings of a structure
- using a structure designed as a place of work, or
- anyone likely to be affected by such construction work.

6.4.4 Principal Contractor

The priority for the Principal Contractor is to properly plan and manage the construction phase of the project as far as health and safety is concerned.

The Principal Contractor must ensure that the construction phase is:

- planned and communicated to the management team before the construction work begins
- managed and monitored, taking reasonable steps to ensure that the construction phase plan is implemented
- managed by a full-time manger or supervisor on site, except for small and simple projects.

The Principal Contractor must take the lead and actively encourage co-operation between contractors from the outset to ensure that everyone complies with their legal obligations. Regular and prompt communication is essential to co-operation and risk control.

It is also the duty of the Principal Contractor to take reasonable steps to prevent access by unauthorised persons to the construction site. Each construction site should have its boundaries defined, where practical by suitable fencing.

Finally, the Principal Contractor must display a legible copy of the most up-to-date information notified to the HSE in a place where it can be easily read by people working on the site.

6.4.5 Other contractors

The duties of the other contractors can be summarised as follows. All contractors are obliged to:

- plan and manage the construction work carried out by them or under their control so that, as far as is reasonably practicable, the work is carried out without risks to health and safety and in accordance with the construction phase plan
- provide every worker carrying out the construction under their control with the necessary information and training needed for the project, including ensuring that every worker is aware of the site rules and emergency procedures

- as soon as possible, provide the Principal Contractor with any information which might affect the health or safety of persons on the construction site and which might justify a review of the construction phase plan
- comply with any directions given by the Principal Contractor.

6.5 CONCLUSION

This chapter provides a very brief overview of the duties of each party as set out in the CDM Regulations. The aim is to encourage regular and prompt communication and co-operation within the construction team. It is only through discussing potential hazards from the very early stages that risks to health and safety can either be eliminated or safely monitored. The Co-ordinator plays a pivotal role in aiding communication between the sites and encouraging regular meetings to ensure that everyone has up-to-date information. The Co-ordinator also has a duty to assist and advise the client throughout the project to make sure that any necessary changes are suitable for the progression of the project and meet the client's needs.

Trade elements

7.1 DEMOLITION, ALTERATION AND RENOVATION

1 CONTRACT REQUIREMENTS

7.1.1 Ordnance benchmarks

Unless it is specified, the prior approval of the architect/employer's agent (A/EA) must be obtained when it is necessary to remove bricks, stones or other materials bearing benchmarks. The A/EA should report to Ordnance Survey any proposal to alter an Ordnance Survey benchmark, and the Clerk of Works should advise the A/EA when such action is completed, so that Ordnance Survey may be notified.

7.1.2 Preservation and protection

An early site meeting with the contractor should be arranged to ensure that all items or services to be preserved or protected in accordance with specification are correctly identified, marked and protected. Typically these may include the following.

- Utility services: the Clerk of Works should check that information from the providers is available, and agree any necessary points of disconnection. Service providers' conformity to requirements should be checked. The obtaining of way leaves should be confirmed with the A/EA. It must be confirmed that the local authority has given approval.
- Access: the safety and adequacy of any maintained access for the occupying client must be checked.
- Buildings and features: adequate protection should be in place.
- Trees, grass and plants: the A/EA should agree the method of protection, if not specified. Normally, chestnut fencing maintained in good condition throughout the contract will be required, extending to enclose the full branch spread of the tree. No demolition fires are to be lit within 10 m of the spread of trees to be preserved (if fires are permissible, as the Environment Agency and many local authorities have restrictions – this should be checked with the A/EA).

2 QUALITY CONTROL

7.1.3 Demolition

All demolition work is subject to the Construction (Design and Management) Regulations (the CDM Regulations) and work should be carried out in accordance with the recommendations of BS 6187:2000 *Code of practice for demolition*, and the contractor must appoint a 'competent person' to oversee the works. If the Clerk of Works considers that the contractor is carrying out any dangerous practice which may threaten the safety of personnel, property or the public, the matter must be drawn at once to the attention of the contractor and Health and Safety Co-ordinator (the Co-ordinator as required under the CDM Regulations 2007, or the Planning Supervisor under the CDM Regulations 1994). If satisfactory action is not taken, it should be brought to the notice of the A/EA who may recommend, or action, an approach to the Health and Safety Executive (HSE) inspectorate. Actions should be recorded in the site diary.

7.1.4 Screens

The contractor must comply with any requirements in the specification or in relation to local bye-laws or planning conditions for the provision of screens to protect the public or private property.

7.1.5 Noise

The specification should be checked for any restrictions on weekend working, as construction sites that are close to residential areas can be a cause of distress. It is good public relations for a contractor to letter-drop all local residents to let them know what is going on.

7.1.6 Materials for reuse

The Clerk of Works should check that operations with respect to the recovery of materials to be saved for reuse, the cleaning as specified, and proper storage and custody are being carried out. Materials to be selected for reuse (e.g. bricks) should be approved.

7.1.7 Asbestos

In the event of the discovery of asbestos material it is the responsibility of the contractor to stop work and draw this to the attention of the A/EA and Health and Safety Co-ordinator. The Clerk of Works must advise the contractor, A/EA and the Health and Safety Co-ordinator as soon as the presence of such material is discovered. Similarly, if the Clerk of Works considers that necessary action is not being taken, the contractor should be advised accordingly and the matter reported at once to the A/EA and Health and Safety Co-ordinator. *Only* approved licensed contractors can remove asbestos.

The major risk arises from asbestos dust, particularly from friable material, and damping down with sprayed water is recommended. Incidents must be recorded in the site diary. The HSE provides guidance on procedures and methods of working where a risk of exposure to asbestos has been identified. Work may not be restarted until formal clearance is given and a safe method of working has been detailed in the Health and Safety Plan and implemented.

7.1.8 Contaminated land

Any contamination will normally have been identified by ground surveys, but if evidence of unexpected contamination is uncovered, the A/EA and Health and Safety Co-ordinator must be informed at once. Samples should be taken and sent as instructed.

7.1.9 Temporary works

It is the responsibility of the Clerk of Works to receive and forward to the A/EA for approval contractor's proposals for temporary weather protection and temporary supports to existing buildings or services undergoing alterations.

Contractor's temporary works and falsework

All temporary works and falsework should be designed and checked by the contractor. Calculations and drawings should then be forwarded to the A/EA/ project structural engineer (SE) for comment and appraisal prior to any work starting.

The contractor will formulate a method of work as an instruction for the site staff to follow in conjunction with the falsework drawings. No loading should take place of any falsework until an authorised contractor's engineer has checked and approved its construction.

Regular checks should then be made to ensure that the falsework is not modified or stripped until the permanent structure is ready to be self-supporting.

Some categories of collapses of temporary works or falsework must be reported to HSE under the Reporting of Injuries, Diseases and Dangerous Occurrences Regulations 1995 (RIDDOR).

Any problems must be notified immediately to the A/EA and the Health and Safety Co-ordinator.

7.1.10 Adjoining buildings

It is the Clerk of Works' duty to receive and forward to the A/EA, or approve on the A/EA's behalf as directed, contractor's proposals for the protection of adjoining buildings, including any information subject to the Party Wall Act 1996 (see also 3.1.3).

3 STATUTORY REQUIREMENTS AND TECHNICAL STANDARDS

(Note: under European legislation, the BS prefix will shortly change to EN.)

Publications to which site reference may be necessary include:

BS 5228-2:1997 *Noise and vibration control on construction and open sites. Guide to noise and vibration control legislation for construction and demolition including road construction and maintenance.*
BS 5228-4:1992 *Noise and vibration control on construction and open sites. Code of practice for noise and vibration control applicable to piling.*
BS 6187:2000 *Code of practice for demolition.*
HSG 213 *Introduction to asbestos essentials*, 2001.
HSG 227 *Comprehensive guide to managing asbestos in premises*, 2002.
INDG 188 *Asbestos alert for building maintenance, repair and refurbishment workers*, 2000.
INDG 223 *Short guide to managing asbestos in premises*, 2002.
INDG 289 *Working with asbestos in buildings*, 1999.

7.2 GROUNDWORK

1 CONTRACT REQUIREMENTS

7.2.1 A/EA's actions and approvals

The following is a checklist of items requiring action by the A/EA if specified, for which any delegation to the Clerk of Works in part or whole should be established, and to which the A/EA's attention should be drawn in good time as work progresses if this action or decision is required:

- surplus sub-soil: to be spread where directed or removed from site by a licensed contractor
- imported topsoil: samples to be obtained for approval by the A/EA before delivery
- plants, trees and shrubs to be retained: permission required to cut roots during excavation. Roots over 50 mm should not be cut without the approval of the Landscape Supervising Officer and the local authority Tree Preservation Officer
- turf for reuse: permission to store for more than seven days, and approval of watering
- herbicides: approval of non-residual herbicide before spraying to clear surface vegetation
- weather: contractor to be advised of likely consequences of working in weather conditions specified as unsuitable. Events and conditions should be carefully recorded in the site diary and the A/EA consulted
- supports to excavation: approval of proposals, method statements and agreement of measurement if left in place or to be covered over
- excess excavation: permission to over-excavate, and instruction on backfilling
- foundation bottoms: approval to vary depth to suit ground conditions encountered
- obstructions: instructions and approvals for diversion of waterways, removal and filling of voids for old drains, manholes, foundations and other obstructions

- permanent drains: approval to use for disposal of water from excavations
- antiquities: permission for removal
- explosives clearance: on projects for MOD clients, it must be confirmed that the A/EA has obtained a clearance certificate and any necessary approval from the HSE and local authority inspectorate.

2   QUALITY CONTROL

7.2.2   Setting out

The contractor's setting out must be checked to ensure that it corresponds exactly with the drawings, and the contractor must check and agree the original ground levels before excavation begins. Any disagreement must be reported to the A/EA, since it could have a bearing on quantities and payment.

Arrangements should be made to have temporary benchmarks established by the contractor checked against the nearest Ordnance Survey or other validated benchmark and recorded on the drawings.

7.2.3   Excavation and site clearance

Obstruction: details and dimensions of any large rock or other obstruction sufficient in size and difficulty to delay excavation and require special arrangements for its removal should be recorded for the information of the quantity surveyor.

Bottoms of excavations: the responsibility for carrying out stage inspections for compliance with Building Regulations may be delegated to the Site Inspector. The Clerk of Works should inspect the bottoms of excavations for foundations accordingly. The A/EA will make arrangements when necessary at the briefing meeting for the project civil engineer (CE) to inspect the bottoms of excavations with the Clerk of Works initially. Delegation of the duty should only be accepted when both parties are satisfied that the requirements are understood. Inspections are to be fully recorded in the site diary, and in situations where there is any doubt about the adequacy of a bearing surface the A/EA should be consulted.

Note: when the project is subject to statutory inspection by an approved inspector, the Clerk of Works should attend the inspection and record what transpires. If any problem arises the A/EA should be advised.

When foundation bottoms have been approved, concreting should proceed without delay, any deterioration to the bottom or the sides before concreting begins is to be reported to the A/EA. It is the contractor's responsibility to provide protection against drying out or wetting of the excavation prior to concreting. If the contractor proposes, or the Clerk of Works sees the need for, any resealing or blinding of the bottom, or additional removal of failed side trenching, this should be referred to the A/EA for approval. Any such work carried out is to be recorded for the information of the quantity surveyor.

7.2.4 Materials for filling and method of compaction

Materials to be used for backfilling must be checked to ensure that they meet the specification. The thickness of layers and method of compaction must be confirmed to be as specified.

7.2.5 Piling: sheet, bored, driven, etc.

Piling is a highly specialised operation, and it is important that the Clerk of Works should establish with the A/EA what inspections and other tasks have to be carried out. The Clerk of Works will normally keep a daily progress record, showing on a site plan the location of piles, dates of boring or driving, sets obtained and results of pile testing. The Clerk of Works may also be required to check setting out and tolerances, and to witness sets and tests. The project civil engineer (CE) or structural engineer (SE) will usually require records to be kept of particular conditions, e.g. changes of strata, appearance of water and obstructions encountered.

Advice: normally advice should be obtained from the project CE under the A/EA's arrangements, but if specialist advice is required urgently, the client should be consulted (if employed directly) who will advise on obtaining information on specific problems.

Safety: contract preliminaries and/or the Health and Safety Plan should require the contractor to comply with the safety recommendations in BS 8004 and BS 5573 as appropriate. If the Clerk of Works is required to monitor piling operations, he or she must check compliance. The contractor's attention must be drawn to any unsafe practice and, if it is not corrected, the matter brought to the attention of the A/EA and Health and Safety Co-ordinator who may recommend or action an approach to the HSE Inspector.

Noise: piling is often the noisiest operation on site, and particular limitations may be included in the specification. Special briefing should be provided on any Clerk of Works' duties in this respect, which may range from simply recording periods of piling operation to carrying out noise measurements, and operations must comply with the Noise at Work Regulations 2005. BS 5228 Parts 1 and 2 provide further information. Good public relations can often help to offset the noise nuisance and the Clerk of Works may be called upon to play a part in this.

7.2.6 Diaphragm walls

This is a specialised form of construction for which particular briefing from the A/EA/SE should be obtained in respect of Clerk of Works' duties. These may include delegated inspections for leakage. BS 8102 relating to waterproofing of structures below ground provides detailed information.

Supports to the wall may be provided in temporary or permanent construction, using strutting or ground anchors. Instruction should be obtained from the A/EA or SE on any duties of load testing of supports and de-stressing of anchors.

7.2.7 Underpinning

Particular duties of the A/EA, for which any delegation should be agreed, or for which notification in good time is required, are as detailed below.

Sequence of operations: this and any special procedural requirements are to be agreed with the contractor. Detailed record drawings showing the sequence of operation and curing times should be maintained during this element of the works. Reasons relating to any delays should also be recorded.

Simultaneous underpinning: the A/EA is to approve simultaneous work on adjacent sections at less than a specified limit apart.

Supports: A/EA's approval is required to leave any supports in place when backfilling.

3 STATUTORY REQUIREMENTS AND TECHNICAL STANDARDS

(Note: under European legislation, the BS prefix will shortly change to EN.)

Publications to which site reference may be necessary include:

BS 4428:1989 *Code of practice for general landscape operations (excluding hard surfaces).*
BS 5228-1:1997 *Noise and vibration control on construction and open sites. Code of practice for basic information and procedures for noise and vibration control.*
BS 5228-2:1997 *Noise and vibration control on construction and open sites. Guide to noise and vibration control legislation for construction and demolition including road construction and maintenance.*
BS 8000-1:1989 *Workmanship on building sites. Code of practice for excavation and filling.*
BS 8004:1986 *Code of practice for foundations.*
BS 8102:1990 *Code of practice for protection against water of structures below ground.*

7.3 IN SITU CONCRETE/LARGE PRECAST CONCRETE

1 CONTRACT REQUIREMENTS

7.3.1 A/EA's approval

Approvals required for which the Clerk of Works should establish delegation from the A/EA include the following.

Details, drawings and calculations: these will normally be required only where temporary works are large and complex, and in such cases are likely to be dealt with by the A/EA or project CE. The Clerk of Works may, however, be called upon to assist.

Formed finishes: arrangements for control sampling are to be agreed and examples or photographs of required finishes for inspection purposes obtained from the A/EA or contractor as specified. In the case of superfine and other special finishes, the A/EA's approval is required for details such as panel size and arrangement, use and location of cover spacers and of battens.

Excavation faces: use of these as formwork is not advised unless they are rigid and will stand up to the concrete being placed and the vibration of a vibrating poker and are able to support workmen along the edges. It is essential that some form of sheeting barrier be placed between the cut excavation face and any reinforcement.

Surface retarders: the use of these is to be strictly in accordance with the manufacturer's recommendation and the permission of the design CE.

Striking formwork: the minimum periods to be observed before striking different elements of the formwork should be specified, and may vary with surface temperature of the concrete and its strength. It is the responsibility of the Clerk of Works to check that they are correctly observed. Construction loading, which can be significant, must be taken into account. Re-propping is not permitted without the A/EA's approval, and in any case of doubt the A/EA must be consulted.

2   QUALITY CONTROL

7.3.2   Quality assurance

The quality assurance (QA) system to be implemented must be agreed with the A/EA and instructions obtained. In this workgroup, reference is made to the BSI Registered Firms scheme and CARES (the UK certification body for reinforcing steels).

7.3.3   Quality control

Concrete is a complex product, comprising many materials, which is required not only to comply with specified standards, but also the variable requirements of workmanship. Supervision of concrete work depends on a full understanding of the Code to be followed and the designer's intention. Where the responsibilities are divided between the project CE, the A/EA and the Site Inspector, as is usually the case, it is essential that a clear brief from the A/EA on Clerk of Works' duties is obtained, and that any especially important points to watch are highlighted.

7.3.4 Setting out

The setting out must be checked as directed by the A/EA. This will normally comprise a check on primary setting out of main features such as stairwells and lift wells, random checks on grid, verticality and cambers, section sizes in formwork for beams, and interface with beams and columns.

7.3.5 Formwork

The formwork must be thoroughly clean, undamaged and free from debris. Checks for this are best done when the reinforcement is being inspected, immediately prior to pouring concrete. All inserts, holes, channels, 'blow-holes' for debris removal, embedded parts and services must be confirmed as being in place, and checks made that formwork has not been damaged by loads imposed on spacer blocks. If the contractor proposes to pour the concrete in lifts, it must be established that this is acceptable to the A/EA or project CE.

Cutting away reinforced concrete for service runs is not permitted without the A/EA's prior approval. The Clerk of Works must check therefore, in liaison with the M&E Principal Site Manager (PSM) representative, that provision has been made for service runs by boxing or other method specified.

7.3.6 Concrete mix and materials

The contractor should submit, for the A/EA's approval proposals for meeting the contract specification for concrete, covering sources of materials, suppliers, mixes, chlorides, alkalis and other aspects of concrete quality. Concreting may not be commenced prior to approval of submitted proposed 'design mixes'. All copies should be checked and forwarded to the A/EA. Three copies should be returned to the Clerk of Works on approval, two for the contractor (one for the ready-mix supplier) and one for retention. Where pump mixes are to be used, the specification design will need approval from the SE.

Ready-mix: it is very important that where mix designs are based on a ready-mixed supply, the contractor has provided the ready-mix supplier with a copy of all the relevant specification clauses. There should be a specification clause detailing this requirement and compliance must be checked. The A/EA will arrange for any inspection of the ready-mix plant.

Material orders: early orders by the contractor on suppliers of materials or ready-mixed concrete should be checked for full conformity to the specification. This check may be omitted when the Clerk of Works has full confidence in the correctness of the orders supplied, but should be reimposed with any change in staff responsible.

Certification: all certificates, calculations and other documents relating to supply of materials as required by specification must be obtained and submitted to the A/EA for checking. A record of these submissions is to be kept.

Delivery and storage: the Clerk of Works must check that delivery and storage provisions are as specified, with the aim of ensuring that materials are kept clean, uncontaminated and weather protected, and that they are used in order of delivery.

A/EA's approvals: any delegations must be agreed and the matters requiring the A/EA's attention should be highlighted in good time as work progresses. The following is a checklist of items relating to materials:

- admixtures – admixtures may only be used subject to prior approval of the A/EA. Applications should be submitted to the A/EA quickly to avoid delay to the works
- source of aggregates – to be approved
- colour – where specified, samples of aggregate to be approved
- water – any source other than mains supply to be approved.

7.3.7 Workmanship

Trial mixes: the A/EA may require trial mixes in connection with the approval of mix design proposals. The Clerk of Works should supervise the preparation of trial mixes as directed by the A/EA and keep records. The A/EA's attention should be drawn to any change in constituent materials during the progress of the works which might justify a repeat of the trial mix.

Site concrete production: batch mixing is required for site production of concrete. Satisfactory conditions of mixing plant, which should conform to regulations when such types are used, must be confirmed. During production, the accuracy of the weighing machines should be checked each morning, most conveniently by weighing unopened bags of cement. Batching by weight is required for all solid constituents, except that batching by volume of aggregates is permitted for certain mixes as specified. The regular use of any mixer bigger than necessary for the task should be discouraged since this may lead to error or misuse. Cement should be added by measured number of whole bags, or by weighing on a machine used only for weighing cement. Where pigments or admixtures are to be added, methods of doing so must be confirmed as satisfactory. Cement should be used in date order, from the date of manufacture on the bag.

On sites with large-scale production, the A/EA will lay down a schedule for periodic checking of the calibration of all measuring devices.

Safety: dry cement mixed with water releases an alkali, which can be harmful. Contact between the skin and fresh concrete or mortar should be avoided by wearing suitable clothing. Concrete or mortar adhering to the skin should be washed off with clean cold water as quickly as possible or skin irritation may be caused.

Workability: workability must be appropriate to the casting operation. The Clerk of Works should witness the contractor's slump or compaction factor tests, and carry out his or her own tests if there is any suspicion that the workability is unsatisfactory.

The contractor and A/EA must be informed if the Clerk of Works is not satisfied, and a record made in the site diary.

Placing concrete: conformity with specification must be checked, and the following points requiring site approval noted, which should be agreed as necessary with the A/EA or SE in advance of the work:

- cold weather – approval to place concrete at a temperature below the limit in specification, and of methods to be used to maintain temperature of concrete during and after placing, e.g. thermal matting
- wet weather – approval to start concreting in the open when it is raining heavily, and of the method of protecting finished surfaces from heavy rain.

It should be remembered that concrete should not be dropped into the shuttering from such a height that could cause segregation of the mix, and time periods between pours should be strictly adhered to. Suitable stop-ends and day-joints will need approval from the A/EA and SE prior to pouring.

7.3.8 Curing concrete

Method: the Clerk of Works should discuss with the contractor the proposed methods of curing, and check that all the necessary materials are readily at hand before pouring. The A/EA should be consulted in the case of any doubt arising. Where specified, the A/EA's prior approval for the method proposed should be obtained. Weather conditions should be taken into account and the need to vary curing times considered, as specified.

It is the responsibility of the Clerk of Works to check that:

- curing starts at the proper time
- any curing compound is sprayed on uniformly
- polythene membrane sheeting is sealed at edges and joints, has no tears and is weighted down throughout curing
- hessian or similar material is regularly watered and kept wet until the end of curing
- formwork is kept in place if no other curing is provided instead
- surfaces are protected from solar gain in hot weather
- curing compound is fully degraded before application of any finishes and by the end of construction.

7.3.9 Checking cover to reinforcement

The A/EA and SE must be notified in good time before programmed work of covering, cladding or finishing of concreting ready for checking. The faces to be checked are those specified, and any others as instructed by the A/EA. The A/EA should be advised of any additional areas where a check is considered advisable. Checking should be carried out where so directed by the A/EA, with the assistance of the contractor, and the A/EA notified if the cover is found not to meet the requirements of drawings or specification.

7.3.10 Watertight construction

Workmanship: this construction requires a high standard of workmanship and the Clerk of Works should monitor compliance with the specification very closely, checking with the contractor in advance whether form ties are to be used and the acceptability of the ties. The A/EA should be notified of any necessary check on tie stress. Kickers must be formed at the same time as the slab, not separately, and any pipe penetrations must incorporate puddle flanges to form water barriers.

Inspection: the A/EA must receive due notification when joint inspections with the contractor are to be carried out as specified (i.e. after completion of slab-over and after the main frame of the building is complete) or the Clerk of Works may inspect on the A/EA's behalf as directed and report any signs of leakage.

Grouting: if grouting has to be carried out, the A/EA's approval of the proposed method should be obtained, and the A/EA notified when work is ready for inspection or the Clerk of Works may inspect on the A/EA's behalf as directed. Socket holes, etc., may not be made good until the grouting method is accepted as satisfactory.

7.3.11 Testing of concrete

Reference should be made to BS 8501-1:2002, BS 8501-2:2002 and BS EN 206-1:2000.

Test cubes: the proper casting of test cubes by the contractor must be witnessed and checked, in accordance with the specification. Cube moulds should be calibrated to BS 1881 and QSRMC requirements. The A/EA's approval for the contractor's proposed independent laboratory must be obtained. Some concrete delivery firms will certificate instead of offering a cube-testing service.

Independent tests: any requirements and delegation to the Clerk of Works to take cubes for independent testing should be discussed with the A/EA, e.g. for sensitive elements of the structure or where there has been any problem, and samples despatched to the laboratory as directed by the A/EA.

Workability: random sampling should be carried out at the specified rate per m^3. The Clerk of Works should witness and record measurements of workability in accordance with the method approved.

Records: a record of concrete test cubes taken and a record of the results of cube tests must be kept. A record of the locations from which cubes were taken should be made on appropriate drawings and cross-referred to the relevant form.

7.3.12 Steel reinforcement

Quality assurance: reinforcing steel is normally to be supplied by a firm belonging to the CARES scheme (CARES is the UK certification body for reinforcing steels), and is also to be cut and bent by a CARES licensee. Certificates should be obtained from the contractor for suppliers showing the CARES certificate of approval number and forwarded to the A/EA.

Materials: the Clerk of Works should check that steel bars and fabric bear the CARES marking (see CARES leaflet; www.ukcares.co.uk) and that delivery notes bear the CARES certificate number.

Workmanship: the work of a CARES licensee should not require close inspection, but it remains essential to carry out sample checks on bar diameters and other dimensions, spacing and positioning of reinforcement, especially in critical areas. If there are any doubts about the standard of work, the A/EA should be consulted.

Site work carried out by anyone other than a CARES licensee should be confined to minor adjustments and cutting of random lengths of secondary reinforcement made on site. The A/EA should agree on the delegation to approve cold bending machines and the conditions under which hot bending and re-bending or straightening after fixing may be approved. No site heating or welding of reinforcement should be permitted without the approval of the A/EA. The use of couplers may be acceptable, but the A/EA should be consulted.

Spacers and chairs: any delegation of approval from the A/EA for material and type of spacers and sizes of chairs should be confirmed. Details are normally the responsibility of the contractor, but in special circumstances, such as deep slabs or areas of congested or complex reinforcement, details may be included in drawings or bending schedules. The Clerk of Works should check adequacy and, when wood wool permanent formwork is used, check that supports are sufficient to avoid indentation. The A/EA should be informed in the event of any dissatisfaction. During the pouring of concrete, the Clerk of Works should check that spacers are stable and not displaced and that reinforcement maintains its specified clearance from the shuttering.

Discrepancies: it is the responsibility of the contractor to draw attention to any incompatibility with the drawings. Any discrepancy that cannot be simply resolved should be reported to the A/EA for instruction.

Verification tests: these should not be required for materials supplied under a CARES licence, but if any doubt arises about the quality of material, it should be reported without delay to the A/EA for instructions. The location(s) of suspect material must be recorded. If the A/EA directs that a verification test be carried out, the Clerk of Works should identify the suspect material from which test pieces are to be cut. The results of tests should be forwarded to the A/EA.

7.3.13 Precast and composite concrete decking

Components for such work will be largely the subject of off-site or other specialist inspection and test. The Clerk of Works should obtain briefing from the A/EA on any particular duties, but they will normally include a check on the condition on delivery to site and subsequent checks in the course of construction, e.g. during propping, erection and placing of in situ topping.

7.3.14 Suspending and rejecting concreting work

The contractor should be warned of the advisability of suspending work if there are compelling reasons. The A/EA must be consulted in all such cases.

Rejection of completed work will normally require consultation with the project SE, who will wish to check the site diary records of casting. Typical examples of situations where rejection may be called for are:

- failure of cube tests to meet specified limits – at least four test results per pour are required, and decisions rest with the A/EA, who may order loading tests where cube results have shown failures
- movement of formwork or reinforcement during pour
- unsatisfactory finish, including any 'honeycombing'
- failure of steel validation test
- excessive cracking
- lack of proper curing
- failure to protect against frost.

7.3.15 Building regulations

The Clerk of Works must monitor that the contractor is acting in compliance with Building Regulations and that inspection is carried out prior to covering up of foundations, or oversite concrete with other oversite material. Where the project is subject to statutory inspection by an approved inspector, the Clerk of Works should attend the inspection and record what transpires. The A/EA should be informed of any problem that arises.

3 STATUTORY REQUIREMENTS AND TECHNICAL STANDARDS

(Note: under European legislation, the BS prefix will shortly change to EN.)

Publications to which site reference may be necessary include:

Building Regulations 2000.
BS 8000-2.1:1990 *Workmanship on building sites. Code of practice for concrete work. Mixing and transporting concrete.*
BS 8000-2.2:1990 *Workmanship on building sites. Code of practice for concrete work. Sitework with in situ and precast concrete.*
BS 8110-1:1997 *Structural use of concrete. Code of practice for design and construction.*
BS 8501-1:2002 *Concrete. Complementary British Standard to BS EN 206-1. Method of specifying and guidance for the specifier.*

BS 8501-2:2002 *Concrete. Complementary British Standard to BS EN 206-1.*
  Specification for constituent materials and concrete.
BS EN 206-1:2000 *Concrete. Specification, performance, production and conformity.*

7.4 MASONRY

1 CONTRACT REQUIREMENTS

7.4.1 A/EA's actions and approvals

It is the responsibility of the Clerk of Works to go through the specification and identify all items in material and workmanship sections which require an action or approval by the A/EA (normally but not always specified as A/EA's responsibility). These should be brought to the notice of the A/EA in good time for the A/EA's attention as the works progress and any delegations, in part or whole, established. Typical examples are listed below.

Samples: where approval of samples or sample panels is specified, the Clerk of Works should ensure that these are submitted or that readiness is notified to the A/EA before the contractor confirms an order. An approved sample should be obtained for retention on site to match against deliveries. Random samples should be taken as specified from initial deliveries and approved or referred to the A/EA as delegated. If there are any doubts about compliance the A/EA should be consulted.

Tolerances: normally to BS 6649 for bricks and BS EN 771-3:2003 and BS EN 772-2: 1998 for blocks. Any relaxation of specified tolerances must be agreed with the A/EA.

Tipping of loads: tipping of loads of masonry units should not be allowed unless this has been authorised by the A/EA.

Carved stone: the A/EA will normally approve the selection of stone for carving and will decide whether profiles will be carved before or after the stone has been built in.

Finishes and facework: any special requirements should be identified and the A/EA's instructions and any delegation of approvals obtained.

Overhand work: normally permitted only where the bricklayer cannot gain access to a normal working position.

Admixtures: the specification may permit plasticisers to BS EN 934-3:2003 to be used in mortars, but any proposal to use other admixtures should be referred for the A/EA's decision. The use of calcium chloride by itself or in admixtures is not permitted.

Alternative mixes: any proposal for alternative mortar mix should be referred for the A/EA's decision. The specification may also permit the use of factory-produced pre-mixed and retarded mortars, or batched mortars produced and delivered to site. If site mixes are agreed, the method of gauging for mortars should also be established. In all cases the manufacturer's instructions are to be adhered to precisely.

Frost damage: the contractor is required to take down and rebuild any work damaged by frost. If any doubts arise the A/EA should be consulted.

Broken bonding: if the masonry bond is not specified the A/EA's instructions should be obtained. Where bonding is specified, the A/EA's instructions on the location and arrangement of any broken bond in faced work must be sought. On corners, 'toothing out' should not be allowed unless specifically required. 'Racking back' is best practice on corner work.

Daily progress: any proposal to raise walls at a rate above that specified should be referred to the A/EA for approval or otherwise. It is good practice to bring the walls up together if possible, and either leaf should not be raised more than 1.5 m high before the second leaf is added.

Wall ties, cavity trays and weep-holes, etc.: the A/EA should be consulted for types of wall tie permitted, and whether fixed sloping or level. Reference should be made to the manufacturer's instructions. Cavity insulation should be confirmed as appropriate to the design, and cavity closers are to be mechanically fixed and not left fitted loose.

2   QUALITY CONTROL

7.4.2   Quality assurance

The specification should be checked for any quality assurance (QA) schemes applicable, and the A/EA's instructions obtained on any duties arising. Agrément Certification is used in this workgroup.

Quality control: it is one of the duties of the Clerk of Works to check conformity with the specification and drawings. Where materials are specified to British Standards or Agrément certificates, the appropriate markings must be checked and any additional or particular requirements which may require certification or test noted.

7.4.3   Setting out

All setting out of masonry must be checked in relation to the established centrelines of the building and the given building line. All dimensional checks must be made with a steel tape. Additional checks should be carried out as the work rises. The Clerk of Works should be familiar with the bonds specified, ensure that the setting out of the first course is accurate, and that the work is related to established datum levels. A datum at finished ground floor level is a convenient point. The use of storey rods for setting out storey heights from datum and showing the tops and bottoms of openings, course levels, etc., should be encouraged.

7.4.4 Weather protection

The adequacy of the protection of materials from frost and rain should be confirmed, as should the provision of insulated covering to new masonry walling where specified for low temperatures. Newly erected masonry should be top covered during rain to prevent saturation and future efflorescence and mortar being washed out of joints.

7.4.5 Certification

In addition to conformity to relevant British Standards, bricks and blocks may be required to meet particular specifications of type, colour, strength, durability, water absorption, manufacturing control level, etc. The Clerk of Works should check that the contractor's orders properly cover these requirements, and check the delivery documentation for evidence of compliance. The A/EA's instructions should be obtained on acceptable certification. Some suppliers may meet QA standards, in which case their certificate of compliance will normally be acceptable (e.g. Kite-marked and Agrément-certificated products). In other cases the A/EA may require independent testing.

7.4.6 Testing

Mortar: this is normally required only for structural masonry. Initial testing of mortars to be used is to be carried out by the contractor *at least six weeks* before commencing masonry work. The Clerk of Works should witness preparation of test specimens and record details of mix and ball penetration tests. Comprehensive strength test certificates received should be submitted to the A/EA for approval to start masonry work. The A/EA's instructions should be obtained on further testing to be carried out as the work progresses.

Bricks and blocks: independent testing should be arranged as directed by the A/EA. The following are normally tested:

- comprehensive strength of load-bearing bricks and blocks
- water absorption of facing bricks and those to be used below the damp-proof course
- thermal conductivity of dense aggregate, aerated or lightweight aggregate concrete blocks for load-bearing walls and partitions.

7.4.7 Scaffolding

If it is not specified, the A/EA's decision should be obtained as soon as possible on whether putlog or independent scaffolding is to be used.

7.4.8 Manufacturer's instructions

The Clerk of Works should obtain copies of the manufacturer's instructions and Agrément certificates where applicable and check that they are followed.

7.4.9 Weighing plant

If weighing machines are employed in site mortar mixing plant, the Clerk of Works should carry out or witness regular checks on their accuracy. The maker's instructions should be followed on this. An unopened bag of cement makes a convenient weight for checking.

7.4.10 Conditioning bricks and blocks

Where a conditioning period is specified, the date of supply should be noted and checks carried out that the material is not used before the period expires.

7.4.11 Damp-proof course (DPC)

In addition to the specified workmanship, attention should be paid to the following points:

- rolls of bitumastic DPC should be checked to ensure that they do not crack when unrolled in cold weather
- where the DPC is stepped, the DPC may not be laid less than 150 mm above the finished ground level
- the edge of the DPC must not be bridged by mortar. It should be flush or slightly projecting. If used as a drip, it should extend 5 mm
- if cavity walling has to be cleaned out, it must be established that the method employed will not damage the DPC or any insulant
- the connection and sealing between horizontal wall DPC and damp-proof membrane to a floor must be checked
- vertical DPCs should be left proud of brickwork around doorways, etc., and extend beyond horizontal DPCs for lapping
- the Clerk of Works must be vigilant where the specification provides for forming bridges with DPC material. If the contractor proposes the use of pre-formed cavity trays, these should be Agrément-certificated.

7.4.12 Services

Where services penetrate an exterior wall below ground, in addition to sleeving and sealing against passage of gas it may be necessary to provide protection against ingress of groundwater. The A/EA's instructions should be obtained.

3 STATUTORY REQUIREMENTS AND TECHNICAL STANDARDS

(Note: under European legislation, the BS prefix will shortly change to EN.)

Publications to which site reference may be necessary include:

BS 3921:1985 *Specification for clay bricks*. Appendix F2 deals with the preparation of sample panels. [Partially replaced by BS EN 772-3:1998 *Methods of test for masonry units. Determination of net volume and percentage of voids of clay masonry units by hydrostatic weighing*, and BS EN 772-7:1998 *Methods of test for masonry units. Determination of water absorption of clay masonry damp proof course units by boiling in water.*]

BS 5628-3:2005 *Code of practice for the use of masonry. Materials and components, design and workmanship.*

BS 5642-1:1978 *Sills and copings. Specification for window sills of precast concrete, cast stone, clayware, slate and natural stone.*

BS 5642-2:1983 *Sills and copings. Specification for copings of precast concrete, cast stone, clayware, slate and natural stone.*

BS 6100-5.1:1992 *Glossary of building and civil engineering terms. Masonry. Terms common to masonry.*

BS 6100-5.2:1992 *Glossary of building and civil engineering terms. Masonry. Stone.*

BS 6100-5.3:1984 *Glossary of building and civil engineering terms. Masonry. Bricks and blocks.*

BS 6649:1985 *Specification for clay and calcium silicate modular bricks.*

BS 8000-3:2001 *Code of practice for masonry.*

BS EN 771-3:2003 *Specification for masonry units. Aggregate concrete masonry units (dense and light-weight aggregates).*

BS EN 772-2:1998 *Methods of test for masonry units. Determination of percentage area of voids in masonry units (by paper indentation).*

BS EN 934-3:2003 *Admixtures for concrete, mortar and grout. Admixtures for masonry mortar. Definitions, requirements, conformity, marking and labelling.*

7.5 STRUCTURAL/CARCASSING: METAL/TIMBERWORK

The contents of the Quality Control section are divided into subsections as follows:

2A structural steelwork
2B structural timber.

1 CONTRACT REQUIREMENTS

7.5.1 Quality assurance

The specification should be checked for any quality assurance (QA) schemes applicable and the A/EA's instructions obtained on any duties arising. Reference is made to the use of the Timber Research and Development Association (TRADA) scheme under Trussed Rafters (see 7.5.14) and to the project specification.

Part of the normal duties of the Clerk of Works is to check conformity with the specification and drawings. In the case of structural steelwork and timber framing, guidance on inspection and approval of fabrication in workshops should be sought from the A/EA. The Clerk of Works will be required to inspect condition on delivery to site and monitor the site works. Some site decisions may be delegated while others are reserved to the A/EA or the Project Engineer. In this situation it is important that clear written instructions on the delegation of duties are obtained from the A/EA.

2A QUALITY CONTROL: STRUCTURAL STEELWORK

7.5.2 Fabrication

When inspection of fabrication in workshops, either on or off site, is carried out by others, the Clerk of Works may be required to provide liaison between them and the contractor for notification in good time of readiness of test pieces, forwarding drawings and other documentation as required by specification, and submitting test results for approval. A record of such actions should be made in the site diary.

Where responsibility for inspecting fabrication rests with the Clerk of Works, the delegation of duties should be established with the A/EA. Tolerances for accuracy of alignment, level and verticality are normally as given in BS 5950-2, and for lengths, as specified. The setting out of holes and cuts should be checked.

7.5.3 Handling and transportation

To prevent primitive practices of handling and transportation it is now common practice to require a method statement not only for handling but also for the erection of components. The requirements are to be strictly enforced. Both the main contractor and the steelwork contractor should be informed in writing of any case of non-compliance, with copies to the A/EA and also to the Health and Safety Co-ordinator if there are safety implications.

The Health and Safety Plan and the Health and Safety Co-ordinator should be consulted in the case of any uncertainty over the methods being used.

Damage: the Clerk of Works must be strict in the rejection of components found to be damaged on delivery to site, rejecting without question dented hollow sections and distorted flanges of compression members and insisting on removal of oil and grease.

Repairs: any proposals for site repair of damage should be reported to the project SE via the A/EA. If not rejected, details should be agreed with the A/EA as necessary.

7.5.4 Steel quality

The A/EA will have approved the method of steel manufacture, but the Clerk of Works may be required to inspect deliveries of steel for conformity of surface quality to BS 7668, BS EN 10029, BS EN 10025 or BS EN 10210. Any steel with defects beyond the permissible limits in BS 7668, BS EN 10029, BS EN 10025 or BS EN 10210, or where pitting by surface rust is excessive and visible to the naked eye, should be rejected.

7.5.5 Steel identification

Steel must be correctly identified with quality and other marks as specified, and these marks transferred to any cut sections.

There should be an erection sequence drawing on site showing the location of members, and members should be marked in accordance with it.

7.5.6 Site fabrication

The section on Workmanship at 7.5.10 below provides additional information. The following are typical matters that may require the Clerk of Works' decision.

Plane table for fabrication: if used, it is important to ensure that it is level in both directions to guarantee accuracy of fabrication.

Temporary attachments: welding or bolting is not permitted in tension areas. If there is any doubt about whether an area is in tension, the A/EA or project SE should be consulted.

Cutting: any proposal for cutting other than by sawing, shearing or machine flame should be referred to the A/EA.

Faying surfaces: machining of deformed surfaces is not allowed without the A/EA's approval.

Holing: any members with incorrect holing are to be rejected.

Welding: this is normally confined to the workshop, but may be specified for some site works. Detailed instructions should be obtained from the A/EA. Certification of the welder's competence for the class of work as directed should be obtained *before work commences*.

Burrs: any burrs or sharp arises are to be removed by grinding, as these can reduce the durability of surface protection.

Indented anchor bolts: these are to be used only for locating, not for load.

High strength friction grip bolts: these must be tightened only by use of indicating washers and *not* by torque wrench.

Holding down bolts: joint holes must be aligned prior to the installation of bolts. Bolts should never be driven into position as this can damage threads or deform the bolt. Hot dip galvanised steel is normally acceptable for Grade 8.8 bolts unless stainless steel is specified. Galvanising should be carried out by the bolt manufacturer.

Fit of nuts: the fit should be checked as specified. The aim is to avoid zinc-to-zinc contact between nut and bolt threads to reduce the danger of the nut seizing. Internal threads are protected by close contact with the galvanised threads of the bolt.

Stress relieving: submission of stress relief certification to the A/EA and galvaniser should be confirmed.

Galvanised steel: the Clerk of Works should check for transit damage and seek approval for remedial works. For cutting and welding of galvanised steel, the SE's approval and directions should be obtained and the Health and Safety Plan and the Health and Safety Co-ordinator referred to because of associated health hazards.

7.5.7   Steel erection

Setting out: setting out must be checked.

Safety: the Clerk of Works should check compliance with the Health and Safety Plan, *BCSA code of practice for erection of low rise buildings* and applicable sections of BS 5531 and ensure that the provision of access for inspection is satisfactory: a different standard is applicable to that for erectors. The A/EA's directions should be obtained on allowing additional bolt holes or weldments to the permanent structure.

Stability: the contractor is responsible for ensuring the stability of the structure at all stages of construction and for the proper sequencing of stages of construction, taking into account other structural elements. The Health and Safety Plan should be examined for prescribed safe sequences of erection. The Clerk of Works should bring immediately to the attention of the contractor, A/EA and Health and Safety Co-ordinator any departure from the method statement or any other potentially unsafe situations. Any further instructions can be obtained from the A/EA.

Cutting and drilling: site cutting and drilling is not normally permitted because it is seldom done satisfactorily and weakens surface coatings, but is sometimes unavoidable. Any proposal should be referred to the A/EA for authorisation and the A/EA's method statement laying down conditions for such work obtained.

Note: at no time will the contractor be allowed to form holes with a burning torch.

Distortion: distortion of steelwork in the course of erection may exceed design stresses. Any instance should be reported to the A/EA.

Weather: if instability is suspected due to severe weather conditions, the A/EA and Health and Safety Co-ordinator should be informed and the contractor instructed to check the safety of the work.

Column bases: casting dates for maturity to accept erection loads should be confirmed. The A/EA's directions should be obtained on approval for raising or lowering column bases beyond specified limits, and for subsequent packing or grouting. The concrete must be sloped away from the embedded steel and the steel must not stand in water. The holding down bolt pockets must be cleaned out and ready for grouting up *before* the steel columns are positioned over them.

Tolerances: the Clerk of Works should check that erection tolerances generally comply with BS 5950-2 and confirm any particular tolerances specified. The fitting of gantry beams and crane rails should be checked against those required by the manufacturer of the traveller.

Temporary fixings: no temporary fixings which might damage protective surfaces are to be attached to the structure. The contractor's proposals should be presented to the A/EA for approval in advance.

Hoisting: the Clerk of Works should obtain and forward to the A/EA and Health and Safety Co-ordinator details of any proposed method of lifting and winching using equipment fixed to structural members, identifying the members clearly and, if approved, monitoring any loading restriction. Care should be taken with loads from cranes. The steel erectors must use guide-lines or ropes to control the swinging of loads during hoisting.

Phased connections: the A/EA's agreement and/or any restrictions for any proposed phasing must be obtained.

Holes: any misalignment should be reported to the A/EA. If not rejected, consideration should be given to the necessity for a larger bolt and the A/EA's agreement obtained.

Spanners: imperial spanners may not be used to tighten metric nuts and bolts.

HSFG bolts: the use of high strength friction grip (HSFG) bolts requires a high level of supervision and inspection. The average gap of 0.25 mm to which an HSFG bolt should be tightened relates to galvanised bolts. For other finishes the gap should be specified. BS 4604 provides further information.

The correct washers must be used in assemblies. Over-tightening can damage bolts and they could subsequently fail from brittle fracture in cold weather. When the gap of more than one fastener is zero and the average gap of the connection is as specified, the Clerk of Works should inform the A/EA, who should instruct replacement of the assembly (this may be a more rigorous requirement than the manufacturer's recommendations). Any fasteners which require to be slackened after full tightening should be discarded and not reused.

7.5.8 Inspection, certification and testing

Formal inspections, certification and testing are generally of a specialised nature, and the instructions of the A/EA should be obtained on any particular duties. These may include ensuring that samples, trial assemblies, test specimens, etc., are prepared and submitted in good time for the A/EA's attention and forwarding the results of the tests to the A/EA. A record of all such actions should be kept. The Clerk of Works will normally be required to attend and supervise site tests, such as load testing in accordance with BS 5950-1, unless the Project Engineer does so.

The Clerk of Works must ensure that the structure is complete before it is loaded for testing. This applies particularly to crane rails. Any problem should be reported to the A/EA and Health and Safety Co-ordinator.

Inspection at workshops should always be carried out in the presence of the contractor, and the A/EA will normally require a report.

Particular attention should be paid to the production in good time of all material test certificates. The Clerk of Works should identify these from the specification, check that they are submitted, forward them to the A/EA and keep a record.

Where there is any reason to doubt the quality of steel supplied, the A/EA may instruct the contractor to carry out special tests. Any suspicions should be reported immediately to the A/EA.

7.5.9   Protective coating

The Clerk of Works should check that the contractor orders protective coating materials as specified. Paint containers should be checked immediately after delivery, and accepted only if labelled as described and provided that they are within shelf life.

Where a poor quality of paint is suspected, the contractor will be asked to report this to the supplier and inform the A/EA, with details of supplier and material as on the container label. An unopened container should be set aside for testing.

Other materials: the Clerk of Works should agree delegation by the A/EA for approval of other materials, for example:

• rust removers
• detergent.

Decorative painting of zinc-rich coatings: the contractor must submit details in advance by the time specified for the A/EA's approval.

Cement wash: the A/EA is to instruct if rainwater from rusty steel is likely to damage finishes before embedding in concrete.

Sampling and testing: each batch of paints is to be sampled in accordance with BS 3900: Part A. The A/EA's instructions should be obtained on the number of samples required, and whether unopened containers are to be despatched to the nominated testing authority, or samples only from containers. Each different batch should be identified on delivery. Arrangements should be made for the contractor to set aside containers as appropriate and despatch for testing with subsequent test results forwarded to the A/EA.

The methods to be followed in sampling from containers, paint kettles and finished work are detailed in BS EN ISO 15528:2000. Samples should be taken from paint kettles and finished work if there is reason to check that the correct paint is being applied and if faults occur during or after application.

Paint thickness: the A/EA's instructions should be obtained on the number and locations of measurements to be carried out using an elcometer (electromagnetic meter). The correct calibration of the meter must be confirmed before use. Coats of paint must be compatible with other coats, e.g. if intumescent paints are used then primer coats must be compatible.

Sample panels: the contractor must prepare sample panels of the specified finishes in good time for the A/EA's approval. Approved panels should be kept on site for comparison purposes.

7.5.10 Workmanship

Attention is drawn to the following points of workmanship.

Barrier coatings: aluminium coatings must never be allowed to have direct contact with rain-washed concrete, concrete in wash-down areas, brickwork, plaster or plaster products. A barrier coat of black bitumen is required. Dissimilar metals should also be separated by a barrier coat or sleeve of bitumen plastics. Steelwork embedded in brickwork should be protected with black bitumen. The A/EA should be consulted in any case not covered by specification.

Welding of galvanising: the limits in specification on sizes of contact areas relate to the risk of explosion in enclosed areas if welding is to be carried out. The Clerk of Works should check the Health and Safety Plan for method statements, and inform the A/EA, Health and Safety Co-ordinator and contractor immediately should any problems become evident.

Faying surfaces: if the contractor has a standard method of protecting faying surfaces equal to or better than the method specified, it may be accepted.

Repair of damaged zinc or aluminium coatings: if the method does not satisfactorily clean down to bare steel, grit blasting to SA2.5 (semi bright) may be authorised. Sealant needs to be removed from overlap areas to obtain metallic contact.

Colours: pigments are not to be added on site to tint zinc-rich coatings. Colours are to be prepared by the paint manufacturer.

Stripe coats: where zinc-rich paint is applied to welds and edges of steelwork in stripe coats, the Clerk of Works should check that thorough preparation as specified is carried out, paying particular attention to the thickness of the coat at the edges as well as to overlaps as specified.

Pot life: the Clerk of Works should check that mixed multi-component materials are used within pot life as recommended by the manufacturer.

Protection of fasteners: the A/EA's approval must be obtained for the contractor's proposed method.

2B   QUALITY CONTROL: STRUCTURAL TIMBER

7.5.11   Quality assurance

The Clerk of Works should check the specification for any QA schemes applicable and obtain the A/EA's instructions on any duties arising. Reference is made to use of the TRADA scheme under Trussed Rafters (see 7.5.14).

Quality control: it is part of the Clerk of Works' normal duty to check conformity with specification and drawings, to inspect condition on delivery to site and supervise site work. Some site decisions may be delegated to the Clerk of Works while others are reserved to the A/EA or the Project Engineer. In this situation it is important that clear instructions on the delegation of duties are obtained from the A/EA.

7.5.12   Structural timber

All timber for structural purposes should be specified in the contract documentation to stress grades. The Clerk of Works must check project specification and that delivered timber is marked with its stress grading and used as specified. The A/EA should be informed of any unmarked or suspect materials. Timber should have had a preservative treatment applied – normally tanalised timber will have treatment documentation. TRADA publishes a guide to stress-graded softwood.

7.5.13   Timber frame buildings

It is vitally important to check that all horizontal cavity barriers are installed correctly to prevent the spread of fire through the cavity. The A/EA must be informed of any non-compliance.

7.5.14   Trussed rafters

Timber Research and Development Association (TRADA): trussed rafters are subject to a QA scheme, and may only be supplied by a member of the Trussed Rafter Quality Assurance Scheme operated by TRADA Quality Assurance Services Limited. The supplier should be verified through the A/EA or by direct enquiry to TRADA (see Chapter 15 for contact information). Marking will be either:

- a stamp or label stating that the supplier is a member of the Trussed Rafter Quality Assurance Scheme, or
- a stamp or label with the trademark and the scheme mark.

Unloading, handling and workmanship generally should be specified to comply with recommendations in the Trussed Rafters Association's *TRA technical handbook*, and guidance on erection is contained in BS 5268-6. The limitations to the TRADA QA scheme should be made clear, in that the building designer is held responsible for the overall design and structural integrity of the building, a roof designer may undertake only detailed design of the roof structure, and the trussed rafter designer is responsible only for the design of the trussed rafter.

Deliveries should be checked for any damage and damaged rafters returned to the supplier; rafters should not be repaired on site unless the A/EA has given permission after the manufacturer has specified the repair and issued a method statement for site work.

The following points should be checked, particularly during storage and erection:

- stress grading marks
- storage clear of the ground and weather protected
- verticality ensured during storage, lifting and installation
- rafters to be lifted only at the manufacturer's lifting points, which should be marked on the rafters
- sufficient bracing provided during erection and permanent stability and wind bracing on completion
- satisfactory fixing to the building structure
- no cutting of any member (excluding overhangs)
- no site repairs in the event of damage, except as approved by the manufacturer (see above)
- if gang-nail plates are to be used, they must have 'nailable' type nail holes for the sections to be joined and correct length nails to be used.

Shop drawings: where required, these must be obtained from the contractor at least four weeks before the programmed fabrication date and submitted to the A/EA for approval.

Testing: the A/EA's instructions for testing should be obtained. Normally a prototype rafter is load tested, and the A/EA may require testing of water content of timber.

3   STATUTORY REQUIREMENTS AND TECHNICAL STANDARDS

(Note: under European legislation, the BS prefix will shortly change to EN.)

Publications to which site reference may be necessary include:

Steelwork
BS 3900-Group A *Method of tests for paints. Tests on liquid paints.*

BS 4604-1:1970 *Use of high strength friction grip bolts in structural steelwork. Metric series. General grade.*

BS 4604-2:1970 *Use of high strength friction grip bolts in structural steelwork. Metric series. Higher grade (parallel shank).*

BS 5493:1977 *Code of practice for protective coating of iron and steel structures against corrosion.* [Partially replaced by BS EN ISO 12944 parts 1 to 8 1998 *Paints and varnishes,* and BS EN ISO 14713:1999 *Protection against corrosion of iron and steel in structures. Zinc and aluminium coatings. Guidelines.*]

BS 5531:1988 *Code of practice for safety in erecting structural frames.*

BS 5950-1:2000 *Structural use of steelwork in building. Code of practice for design. Rolled and welded sections.*

BS 5950-2:2001 *Structural use of steelwork in building. Specification for materials, fabrication and erection. Rolled and welded sections.*

BS 7668:2004 *Specification for weldable structural steels. Hot finished structural hollow sections in weather resistant steels.*

BS EN 10029-1991 *Specification for tolerances on dimensions, shape and mass for hot rolled steel plates 3 mm thick or above.*

BS EN 10025-1:2004 *Hot rolled products of non-alloy structural steels. General delivery conditions.*

BS EN 10025-3:2004 *Hot rolled products of non-alloy structural steels. Technical delivery conditions for long products.*

BS EN 10025-4:2004 *Hot-rolled products of structural steels. Technical delivery conditions for the thermomechanical rolled weldable fine grain steels.*

BS 10210-1:1994 *Hot finished structural hollow sections of non-alloy and fine grain structural steels. Technical delivery requirements.*

BS EN ISO 15528:2000 *Paints, varnishes and raw materials for paints and varnishes. Sampling.*

British Constructional Steelwork Association (BCSA), *BCSA code of practice for erection of low rise buildings,* 2004.

Timber

BS 3900-A7.1:2000, ISO 2884-1:1999 *Methods of test for paints. Tests on liquid paints (excluding chemical tests). Determination of the viscosity of paint at a high rate of shear. Cone and plate viscometer.*

BS 3900-A7-2:2003, ISO 2884-2:2003 *Methods of test for paints. Tests on liquid paints (excluding chemical tests). Determination of the viscosity of paint at a high rate of shear. Determination of the viscosity of paint at a high rate of shear. Disc or ball viscometer operated at a specified speed. Section A7-2: Disc or ball viscometer operated at a specific speed.*

BS 5268-3:1998 *Structural use of timber. Code of practice for trussed rafter roofs.*

BS 5268-6.1:1996 *Structural use of timber. Code of practice for timber frame walls. Dwellings not exceeding four storeys.*

BS 5268-6.2:2001 *Structural use of timber. Code of practice for timber frame walls. Buildings other than dwellings not exceeding four storeys.*
BS 5531:1988 *Code of practice for safety in erecting structural frames.*
BS 8000-5 *Code of practice for carpentry, joinery and general fixings.*
British Constructional Steelwork Association (BCSA), *BCSA code of practice for erection of low rise buildings*, 2004.
TRADA *Timber strength grading and strength classes*, 2003.
Trussed Rafter Association (TRA) *TRA technical handbook*.

7.6 CLADDING/COVERING

1 CONTRACT REQUIREMENTS

7.6.1 Duties

It is part of the Clerk of Works' normal duties to check conformity with specifications and drawings. Cladding and coverings are often of a proprietary type, and it is important to check their particular fixing requirements and tolerances. This aspect is considered further below.

7.6.2 Manufacturer's instructions

Many clauses in the specification refer to the need to store, handle and fix in accordance with the manufacturer's instructions. Such references should be identified, copies of these instructions obtained and compliance confirmed, including the use of sealants and other accessories as recommended by the manufacturer. Reference may also be made to compliance with application requirements of a relevant British Standard. If any doubts arise, the A/EA should be consulted.

7.6.3 A/EA's approvals

The A/EA's instructions should be obtained on any approvals required in the specification which may be delegated in part or whole to the Clerk of Works. The following are examples:

- patent glazing: approval to cut or drill parts of the structure for fixing
- metal profiled flat sheet: evidence of compliance with fire rating classification
- glass reinforced plastics: approval to repair damage and if given, approval of method
- precast concrete slabs: approval of purpose-made lifting devices and testing of fixings for lifting. The A/EA may also specify test loading of a sample of panels. Fixing may not normally be carried out until panels reach their 28-day strength, unless the A/EA agrees otherwise

- natural stone slab: supplier's guarantee that stone is from the quarry and bed specified
- natural slating: supplier's certificate of compliance with atmospheric pollution resistance requirements. The Clerk of Works should check whether slates are to be fixed via nailing or clipping
- lead sheet: laying otherwise than in accordance with BS 6915
- aluminium sheet: laying otherwise than in accordance with CP 143-15
- copper sheet: laying otherwise than in accordance with CP 143-12.

2 QUALITY CONTROL: SLATING AND TILING OF ROOFS

7.6.4 Quality assurance

The specification should be checked for any QA schemes applicable and the A/EA's instructions on any duties arising obtained.

7.6.5 Warning notices

Warning notices (e.g. Fragile Roof Covering – Use Crawling Boards) are to be supplied by the contractor. Orders are to be placed in time before completion and must conform to HSE Standards. Notices will be required as part of the contractor's own safe working precautions.

7.6.6 Materials

Delivery documents should be checked for evidence of compliance with particular performance requirements, such as thermal conductivity, fire performance, light diffusion class, etc. The contractor should be asked to provide additional certification as necessary. In case of any doubt, the A/EA should be consulted.

7.6.7 Samples

The specification should be checked for requirements to submit samples and these should be submitted in good time for the A/EA's approval. Approved samples are to be kept on site to check against deliveries.

7.6.8 Fabrication drawings

The specification should be checked for requirements to submit fabrication drawings and these are to be submitted by the date specified for the A/EA's approval. A copy of the approved drawing(s) should be kept and the A/EA notified of any variation or discrepancy occurring in construction.

7.6.9 Approved firms

Where the specification provides for supply and/or fixing by approved firms, the Clerk of Works should check that these firms do in fact carry out the service. It should be noted that precast concrete cladding units are to be obtained from a firm on the BSI register of firms of assessed capability.

7.6.10 Off-site inspection

The Clerk of Works will provide liaison, if required, for off-site inspections.

7.6.11 Safety precautions

The contractor is responsible for preventing unsafe access and egress to areas where roofing work is in hand and for ensuring the use of crawling boards as necessary. The contractor's attention should be drawn to any unsafe/dangerous practice, and the Health and Safety Co-ordinator and A/EA informed and a record made in the site diary.

7.6.12 Workmanship

The specification should be consulted as to the type of underfelt to be used and the manufacturer's instructions as to the required laps. Battens should have preservative treatment applied and must be laid with no more than three straight joints to a single rafter, with no battens less than 1200 mm in length laid. The specification should be checked on slating or tiling, whether they are to be clipped or nailed, and in the case of tiles, how many and which courses should be fixed. Generally, the eaves, ridge line and edges to gables, hips and valleys are fixed, and every fourth or fifth course, depending on the roof pitch. If any doubt arises, the matter should be referred to the A/EA.

3 STATUTORY REQUIREMENTS AND TECHNICAL STANDARDS

(Note: under European legislation, the BS prefix will shortly change to EN.)

Publications to which site reference may be necessary include:

BS 5534:2003 *Code of practice for slating and tiling (including shingles)*.
BS 6100-1.3.2:1987 *Glossary of building and civil engineering terms. General and miscellaneous. Parts of construction works. Roofs and roofing*.
BS 6915:2001 *Design and construction of fully supported lead sheet roof and wall coverings. Code of practice*.
BS 8000-6:1990 *Code of practice for slating and tiling of roofs and cladding*.
CP 143-12:1970 *Code of practice for sheet roof and wall coverings. Code of practice for sheet roof and wall coverings. Copper. Metric units*.
CP 143-15:1973 *Code of practice for sheet roof and wall coverings. Code of practice for sheet roof and wall coverings. Aluminium. Metric units*.

7.7 WATERPROOFING

1 CONTRACT REQUIREMENTS

7.7.1 Duties

It is the normal duty of the Clerk of Works to check conformity with specifications and drawings. Specialist subcontractors are involved and work prepared by one contractor to be finished by another must be carefully checked. It is becoming more common to obtain confirmation in writing from the asphalter before asphalting work starts that the preparation of areas to be covered is acceptable. This avoids any opportunity of claiming that defects in roofing were due to poor preparation. In certain areas a 'Permit to Work' may be required for operatives.

2 QUALITY CONTROL

7.7.2 Quality assurance

The specification should be checked for any QA schemes applicable and the A/EA's instructions obtained on any duties arising. Use is made in this workgroup of BSI Kitemarked products.

7.7.3 Materials

Delivery documents should be checked for evidence of compliance with particular performance requirements, such as thermal conductivity. The contractor should be asked to provide additional certification as necessary. Unmarked materials should be rejected. The A/EA should be consulted if any doubt arises. Kitemarks should be checked where specified. In cases where the contractor offers materials as equivalent to those specified, these should be referred to the A/EA for approval or otherwise.

7.7.4 Roofing

Bonding: where a high bond primer is required for cementitious or masonry surfaces, the Clerk of Works should check that the primer is acceptable to the asphalter.

Mastic asphalt or felt roofing: written agreement by the roofing contractor that the base and falls are satisfactory for work to commence must be obtained.

Cauldrons: the A/EA's instructions on the acceptability of using cauldrons should be obtained.

Thermometer: the contractor should have an appropriate thermometer on site and should use it to observe specified temperature limits when laying asphalt.

7.7.5 Asphalt samples

The specification should be checked for requirements to test samples of asphalt. These must be taken in accordance with BS 5284 section 4 as specified and despatched to an independent laboratory for analysis. Analyses received should be forwarded to the A/EA. The contractor is required to keep a record of locations; the Clerk of Works should check that this is done, but make a separate record in the site diary. It should be noted that BS 5284 requires sampling to be carried out at the time of laying.

7.7.6 Liquid applications

The Clerk of Works should check for any temperature restrictions in the manufacturer's instructions where damp-proof membranes are applied in liquid form and monitor compliance.

7.7.7 Protection against traffic

The contractor is responsible for ensuring that traffic on felted roofs does not exceed the design category. The A/EA should be asked to confirm what this load limit is and compliance should be monitored. It is also important that the contractor keeps all traffic on the finished roofing to a minimum to prevent damage.

3 STATUTORY REQUIREMENTS AND TECHNICAL STANDARDS

(Note: under European legislation, the BS prefix will shortly change to EN.)

Publications to which site reference may be necessary include:

BS 747:2000 *Reinforced bitumen sheets for roofing. Specification.*
BS 1446:1973 *Specification for mastic asphalt (natural rock asphalt fine aggregate) for roads and paths.*
BS 1447:1988 *Specification for mastic asphalt (lime stone fine aggregate) for roads and footways.*
BS 5284:1993 *Methods of sampling and testing mastic asphalt used in building and civil engineering.*
BS 8000-4 *Workmanship on building sites. Code of practice for waterproofing.*
Mastic Asphalt Council (MAC) *Roofing handbook.*

7.8 LININGS/SHEATHING/DRY PARTITIONING

1 CONTRACT REQUIREMENTS

7.8.1 Duties

It is part of the normal duties of the Clerk of Works to check conformity to specifications and drawings. Where panels of similar appearance but of different performance requirements are being installed, it is important to check that the correct types are used.

2 QUALITY CONTROL

7.8.2 Quality assurance

The specifications should be checked for any QA schemes applicable and the A/EA's instructions obtained on any duties arising. Schemes which may be used in this workgroup include Agrément Certification.

7.8.3 Material

The delivery documents should be checked for certification of edge and other treatments and fire performance, as specified. The contractor should be asked to provide additional certification as necessary. The A/EA should be consulted if any doubt arises.

7.8.4 Manufacturer's instructions

Requirements in the specification to fix in accordance with the manufacturer's instructions or recommendations should be identified, copies of these obtained and compliance monitored.

7.8.5 Samples

The specification should be checked for requirements to submit samples and these should be submitted in good time for the A/EA's approval. Approved samples should be kept on site for checking against deliveries.

7.8.6 Workmanship

BS 8000-8 applies. It should be remembered that double-boarded partition walling should have staggered joints, for example.

Plasterboard dry lining: metal angle bead reinforced angles should be used where external angles need maximum protection. Taper-edged boards are to be used where flush finish joints are required.

Veneers: there are no British Standards specifically covering timber veneers or timber veneered products. The A/EA's instructions on matching requirements should be obtained.

7.8.7 Loose insulants

Loose insulants should be used and placed correctly to achieve the specified requirement for sound or thermal insulation.

7.8.8 Demountable partitions

The setting out of partition centre lines by the subcontractor and the marking out of positions of vertical abutment to structure by the main contractor should be checked.

7.8.9 Raised access floors

The specification may require supply and fixing by an Agrément-certificated contractor, be it computer flooring, timber stage flooring or access duct panels. The information required from the manufacturer will normally have been submitted at tender stage.

7.8.10 Tests

Site testing is required for earth bonding continuity, in liaison with the M&E Site Inspector. Results should be forwarded to the A/EA. The Clerk of Works should carry out any other tests of demountability and transferability as required by the A/EA.

3 STATUTORY REQUIREMENTS AND TECHNICAL STANDARDS

(Note: under European legislation, the BS prefix will shortly change to EN.)

Publications to which site reference may be necessary include:

BS 8000-8:1994 *Workmanship on building sites. Code of practice for plasterboard partitions and dry linings.*
British Gypsum, *The white book.*
Lafarge Roofing, *The red book.*

7.9 SURFACE FINISHES

The contents of the Quality Control section are divided into subsections as follows:

2A cement–sand floor screeds and concrete floor toppings
2B plaster and cement rendering
2C wall and floor tiling
2D decorative wall coverings and painting
2E mastic asphalt
2F terrazzo finishes
2G sheet floor finishes – rubber, plastics, cork, linoleum and carpeting.

1 CONTRACT REQUIREMENTS

7.9.1 Duties

It is part of the normal duty of the Clerk of Works to check conformity with specifications and drawings.

7.9.2 Quality assurance

The specifications should be checked for any QA schemes applicable and the A/EA's instructions obtained on any duties arising.

7.9.3 Materials

Delivery documents should be checked for evidence of compliance with particular performance requirements or limitations (e.g. admixtures). The contractor should be asked to provide additional certification as necessary. The A/EA should be consulted if any doubt arises.

Compliance with specification and drawings should be monitored. The A/EA should be informed and the A/EA's approval obtained for any alternative products proposed by the contractor before their use is allowed. Any delegation by the A/EA to approve materials, such as proprietary paints and coatings and materials offered by the contractor as equivalent to those specified, should be approved.

7.9.4 Manufacturer's instructions

The specification should be checked for reference to installation in accordance with the manufacturer's instructions, copies of these obtained and compliance checked.

7.9.5 Specialist firms

Where the contractor is required to select from listed firms for specialist work, the Clerk of Works should check that the work is in fact carried out by an approved firm.

7.9.6 Samples

The specification should be checked for requirements to submit samples or to prepare sample panels, and the Clerk of Works must ensure that these are submitted in good time for the A/EA's approval. Approved samples of materials should be kept on site for comparison.

2A QUALITY CONTROL: CEMENT–SAND FLOOR SCREEDS AND CONCRETE FLOOR TOPPINGS

7.9.7 Quality assurance

The specification should be checked for product QA if applicable. For screeding, cement is to be supplied by a BSI-registered firm.

7.9.8 Materials

Delivery notes should be checked for evidence of compliance with performance requirements or limitations, e.g. admixtures. The contractor may be asked to provide additional documentation if necessary. Any offer of equivalent materials to those specified should be referred to the A/EA for approval.

7.9.9 Items for specific attention

Aerated cement screeds: for proprietary lightweight aerated cement screeds where the structural slab is laid to falls of 1:40, the screeds should be laid to a consistent thickness not exceeding 50 mm. Where the structural slab is level, the screed should be laid to falls with a maximum thickness of 200 mm. Where this means that a fall of 1:40 is not obtainable, a lesser fall is acceptable, except that for asphalt covering it should not be less than 1:80. Any difficulty should be reported to the A/EA.

Water: use of any source other than mains supply is to be approved. A sample analysis should be obtained in case of any doubt.

Concrete bases: preparation of hardened smooth concrete by mechanical scabbling may damage bases of less than 100 mm thickness. In such cases preparation should be by shot or grit blasting. If the contractor proposes water pressure hoses, the A/EA should be consulted.

Monolithic screeds: these are specified to be laid within three hours of laying base concrete, but in hot weather a lesser period may be agreed with the contractor. In the absence of agreement the A/EA should be consulted.

Curing: the A/EA is to approve any alternative method of curing proposed by the contractor.

Impact test – dense floor screeds: the A/EA should determine locations for test and any delegation of approval if the BS centres and specific testing parameters are to be varied. The Clerk of Works should witness tests and record readings on record drawings and in the site diary. For acceptance, other defects are to be taken into account such as curling, excessive cracking material and breakdown of hollowness. Additional tests may be ordered as necessary. The A/EA's instruction or agreement for remedial action should be obtained where required.

Screed tolerances: project specification should be checked for finished tolerances; normally, 3 mm in 3 m.

2B QUALITY CONTROL: PLASTER AND CEMENT RENDERING

7.9.10 Quality assurance

The specification should be checked to see if Product Quality Assured items have been requested. All items covered by this scheme will be accompanied by a certificate.

7.9.11 Quality control

Conformity with the specification and drawings should be checked. No additives are to be included in mortar mixes without prior approval from the A/EA.

7.9.12 Special points to watch

Suction: any excessive suction must be addressed either by means of damping down with clean water or by sealing the surface with a bonding agent prior to the first coat of render being applied.

Shrinkage: some forms of lightweight block when saturated shrink to a great extent on drying and cause render to debond. It is the Clerk of Works' responsibility to ensure that this form of blockwork does not get excessively wet during storage or construction.

Cement: supplies must come from a BSI-registered firm.

Water: use of a source other than mains supply is to be approved. In cases of doubt a sample should be sent for analysis.

Sample areas: preparation of sample areas of external render finishes must be undertaken in good time for the A/EA's approval before works proceeds.

Surface salts: where surface salts repeatedly appear on masonry or concrete backgrounds despite dry brushing as specified, the A/EA's instruction should be obtained.

Mechanical application: the A/EA's approval is required if the contractor proposes to use machine-applied plaster. If approved by the A/EA, the plaster must be applied by means acceptable to the plaster manufacturer and by experienced operatives.

Internal working areas: the Clerk of Works must ensure that there is enough natural or artificial light for tradespeople to carry out their work correctly. Any areas with inadequate lighting should be reported to the A/EA.

Surface finish: an accuracy of finished surface within 3 mm is required under a 1.8 m straight-edge for smooth untextured plaster unless otherwise specified: reference should be made to the project specification. The A/EA's instruction must be obtained for any plaster finish other than trowelled smooth.

Formed joints: the A/EA's approval is required for any cutting of formed joints instead of using scrim reinforcement at junctions of gypsum baseboard and solid background.

Scraped finish: where the surface is to be scraped to an approved finish the A/EA's instructions must be obtained. Scraping removes about 3 mm of coating.

2C QUALITY CONTROL: WALL AND FLOOR TILING

7.9.13 Quality control

The Clerk of Works should check and monitor conformity with the specification and drawings and that products are installed in accordance with the manufacturer's instructions.

7.9.14 Special points to watch

Samples: the A/EA's approval must be obtained prior to the ordering. Approved samples should be kept on site for comparison.

Sample areas: preparation of sample areas in locations as directed by the A/EA must be undertaken in good time for the A/EA's approval before work begins.

Tolerances: if, on new concrete, specified tiling tolerances cannot be met, then the A/EA's approval must be sought for rendering the concrete background.

Impact protection: certain wall tile areas, such as corners, pillars and those near to door openings, may be subjected to impact. These locations can be protected by securing metal angles over the tiling or building in special recessed corner angles. Any gaps or crevices caused by securing these metal angles should be completely filled, especially if in a hygienic area.

Falls: adequate falls should be incorporated in floor areas likely to come into contact with acidic residues, such as lactic acid in dairies and detergent spillages. Gradients between 1:80 and 1:40 are recommended. The direction of falls should be planned with the traffic flow in mind and so that the traffic will move across rather than up and down the slope. The position of drainage channels and gulleys should be given special attention.

Substrates: unusual substrates (in existing buildings) may be encountered and specialist advice may be required from the A/EA and specialist adhesive manufacturers.

General design considerations are discussed in section 3 of BS 5385: Parts 1 and 3.

7.9.15 Movement joints

Movement joints should be provided in accordance with BS 5385-1 section 3.5 for walls and in accordance with BS 5385-3 sections 19 and 23.6 for floors. Their type and location should have been decided at the design stage. Each movement joint should be at least 6 mm wide and of a depth at least equal to the thickness of tile and bedding. Movement joints should be impervious and the sealant well bonded to the sides of the joints.

It is important that any movement joints already incorporated in the structure should not be tiled over but be carried through to the face of the tiling.

In large areas of wall tiling, movement joints should be provided at internal vertical corners and at 3–4.5 m centres horizontally and vertically.

Movement joints should be provided around the perimeter of the floor and where floor tiles abut fixed machinery and structural fixtures such as columns, bases, etc. Intermediate movement joints should be incorporated in large floor areas, as described in BS 5385-3 sections 19 and 23.6.

Brass or stainless steel reinforced movement joints using bonded neoprene should be used for intermediate joints, especially where there is the likelihood of wheeled traffic.

All other movement joints should be filled completely with appropriate sealant.

7.9.16 Materials

Cement: cement should comply with the requirements of BS EN 197-1:2000, BS 4027 or BS EN 413-1:2004.

Sand: sand for rendering should comply with Type A of table 1 of BS 1199. Sands for cement/sand screeds and mortar beds should comply with grading in BS EN 12620:2002.

Water: use of source water other than mains supply is to be approved. In case of any doubt a sample should be sent for analysis. Water should be fresh and clean.

Tiles: project specification should be checked, but wall tiles are to comply with BS EN 14411:2003. Floor tiles are to comply with BS EN 14411:2003 and should be selected to suit service conditions.

Adhesives and grout: the most frequent failures occur because of the use of the wrong combination of adhesive and grout for the service conditions. The Clerk of Works should check particularly for adequate water resistance of both: e.g. adhesives to comply with the performance requirements of BS EN 12004:2001 possessing Class AA water resistance.

2D QUALITY CONTROL: DECORATIVE WALL COVERINGS AND PAINTING

7.9.17 Safety

The Health and Safety Plan should be examined for procedures and method statements relating to paint storage, handling and application. Any failure to observe safe methods should be brought to the contractor's attention and the Health and Safety Co-ordinator should be informed. Compliance with mandatory safety clauses relating to the Lead at Work Regulations and the need to ensure adequate ventilation for all painting processes or provide air demand respirators should be monitored.

Danger areas

For areas where explosives or highly flammable materials are stored or handled, the specification should cover any restriction on materials, but it should be noted that aluminium paints are not to be applied to rusty surfaces in such situations. In case of doubt the A/EA should be consulted.

7.9.18 Sample areas

Sample areas of each type of coating should be prepared in good time for approval by the A/EA (or the Clerk of Works if delegated) before the work proceeds. An area of about 1 m^2 is sufficient, preferably in a corner of a wall where varying light and shade will give greater definition of colour than a central panel. Sample areas for joinery are best applied to a panel of plywood of similar finish and appearance to the article to be coated rather than to the article itself, to avoid the labour of cleaning it off.

7.9.19 Special points to watch

Background preparation: all paintwork will fail, regardless of quality of product, if the background is unsuitable, badly prepared or is contaminated with oil, grease or even excessive amounts of moisture. Correct background preparation should be monitored. Oil or grease spots may be touched over with a 'stiptic' paint, such as aluminium paint, before undercoat and topcoat are applied. This should seal them in.

Labelling: paint containers should be checked immediately after delivery and accepted only if labelled as described in specification. The requirement that all coats of each paint system are to be obtained from the same supplier should be noted.

Paint quality: where poor quality paint is suspected, the contractor should be asked to report this to the supplier and the A/EA should be informed with details of supplier and material as shown on the container label. An unopened container should be set aside for testing.

Flame-retardant paint: the Clerk of Works must ensure that certification as specified is obtained and forwarded to the A/EA. Primer coats must be checked for compatibility. (See also 7.5.9 above.)

Sampling and testing: the A/EA's direction must be obtained on sampling and testing.

Sample areas: sample areas must be prepared for each type of coating in good time for approval by the A/EA (or the Clerk of Works if delegated) before the work proceeds. An area of about 1 m^2 is sufficient, preferably in a corner of a wall where varying light and shade will give greater definition of colour than a central panel. Sample areas for joinery are best applied to a panel of plywood of similar finish and appearance to the article itself to avoid the labour of cleaning it off.

Paint thickness: a wet paint thickness gauge (if available) should be used to check applied thicknesses.

Batch matching: the batch numbers of wallpaper to be used on adjoining walls within a room should be checked. If differing shades do occur, this should be brought immediately to the attention of the contractor, the A/EA informed of any instances and a record made in the site diary.

Disposal of paint containers: many paints (especially lead and solvent based) should be treated as 'special waste' and disposed of by segregated skips.

7.9.20 Workmanship

The following are matters which may require the A/EA's approval or decision, for which any delegations should be agreed.

Concrete surfaces: the A/EA's instructions should be obtained for removal of releasing agents if these cannot be removed by washing down.

Defective zinc coating: the A/EA's instructions should be obtained before painting. The preferred action is that the defective coating be made good by the subcontractor or supplier concerned. An inferior remedy is to wire brush the defective areas back to bare steel and prime immediately with primer as instructed by the A/EA.

Grease and dirt: the specification provides for washing off with detergent and warm water, but this should be done sparingly and only as necessary. Wet preparation should generally be avoided, particularly on plaster.

Unsound timber: the contractor is to inform the A/EA on discovery of unsound timber and await the A/EA's instructions.

Thinning: thinning of paints and varnishes is only permitted if recommended by the manufacturer or by agreement of the A/EA. If allowed, in the case of oil paint a limit of 5 per cent by volume of thinners is specified, but in the case of emulsion paint, the specified limit of 10 per cent by volume of water may be exceeded with the A/EA's approval.

Sealing: the A/EA's instructions are to be given where sealing as specified proves inadequate or may be harmful to subsequent paint coats.

2E   QUALITY CONTROL: MASTIC ASPHALT

7.9.21 Samples for analysis

If specified, samples should be taken in accordance with BS 5284 section 4 and sent for independent analysis. All analyses received should be forwarded to the A/EA. The contractor is required to keep a record with locations and to check that this is done, but the Clerk of Works should make a separate record in the site diary. It should be noted that BS 5284 requires sampling to be carried out at the time of laying.

7.9.22 Sample area

The A/EA's approval should be obtained before work proceeds, unless delegation to the Clerk of Works has been agreed.

7.9.23 Cauldrons

The A/EA's instructions on acceptability of using cauldrons must be obtained.

2F QUALITY CONTROL: TERRAZZO FINISHES

7.9.24 Special points to watch

BS 8000-11 gives detailed information.

Cement: must be supplied by a BSI-registered firm.

Water: use of a source other than mains supply is to be approved. A sample should be sent for analysis in case of any doubt.

Samples: samples are to be obtained from the specialist subcontractor for the A/EA's approval. Approved samples should be kept on site for comparison.

Sample areas: preparation of sample areas in locations as directed by the A/EA must be carried out in good time for the A/EA's approval before work begins.

Grinding: the A/EA's instructions on the use of any alternative method to wet process must be obtained.

2G QUALITY CONTROL: SHEET FLOOR FINISHES – RUBBER, PLASTICS, CORK, LINOLEUM AND CARPETING

7.9.25 Conditions prior to laying

Orders must be placed in adequate time for fixing.

The A/EA is to be satisfied that the building is weathertight, all wet trades have been completed, the building has dried out, paintwork is finished and dry and all fixtures abutting the floor covering have been fixed.

The contractor is to confirm that *the flooring contractor's written agreement has been obtained* that the base is suitable to receive the specified covering.

Tests for moisture content of screeds or substrate are to be taken prior to laying. The Clerk of Works should confirm acceptable relative humidity of storage and laying area and obtain the assistance of the M&E Site Inspector to carry out tests as required.

7.9.26 Points to watch

Storage: many sheet finishes should be stored for a period of time prior to laying in the same conditions as the area to be covered. The supplier's and manufacturer's instructions should be consulted.

Sample areas: where specified, the A/EA should be informed when the sample area is ready for inspection.

Repairs: only minor repairs may be carried out by the contractor. Any case of serious damage should be referred to the A/EA for instructions.

Seams: seams are to be avoided on traffic routes. If unavoidable, they should run parallel to the route.

3 STATUTORY REQUIREMENTS AND TECHNICAL STANDARDS

(Note: under European legislation, the BS prefix will shortly change to EN.)

Publications to which site reference may be necessary include:

Screeds and concrete finishes
BS 6100-1.3.3:1987 *Glossary of building and civil engineering terms. General and miscellaneous. Parts of construction works. Floors and ceilings.*
BS 8000-9:2003 *Workmanship on building sites. Cementitious levelling screeds and wearing screeds. Code of practice.*
BS 8204-1:2003 *Screeds, bases and in situ floorings. Concrete bases and cement sand levelling screeds to receive floorings. Code of practice.*

Rendering and plastering
BS 5262:1991 *Code of practice for external rendered finishes.*
BS 5492:1991 *Code of practice for internal plastering.*
BS 8000-10:1995 *Workmanship on building sites. Code of practice for plastering and rendering.*

Ceramic floor and wall tiling
BS 5385-1:1995 *Wall and floor tiling. Code of practice for the design and installation of internal ceramic and natural stone wall tiling and mosaics in normal conditions.*
BS 5385-2:1991 *Wall and floor tiling. Code of practice for the design and installation of external ceramic wall tiling and mosaics (including terracotta and faience tiles).*

BS 5385-3:1989 *Wall and floor tiling. Code of practice for the design and installation of ceramic floor tiles and mosaics.*

BS 5385-4:1992 *Wall and floor tiling. Code of practice for tiling and mosaics in specific conditions.*

BS 5385-5:1994 *Wall and floor tiling. Code of practice for the design and installation of terrazzo tile and slab, natural stone and composition block floorings.*

BS 8000-9:2003 *Workmanship on building sites. Cementitious levelling screeds and wearing screeds. Code of practice.*

BS 8000-10:1995 *Workmanship on building sites. Code of practice for plastering and rendering.*

BS 8000-11.1:1989 *Workmanship on building sites. Code of practice for wall and floor tiling. Ceramic tiles, terrazzo tiles and mosaics.*

BS 8000-11.2 *Workmanship on building sites. Code of practice for wall and floor tiling. Natural stone tiles.*

BS EN 12004:2001 *Adhesives for tiles. Definitions and specifications.* [Withdrawn and superseded by BS EN 14411:2003 *Ceramic tiles. Definitions, classification, characteristics and marking.*]

Painting and decorating

BS 2015:1992 *Glossary of paint terms and related terms.*

BS 3046:1981 Specification for adhesives for hanging flexible wall coverings.

BS 5493:1977 *Code of practice for the protective coating of iron and steel structures against corrosion.* [Partially replaced by BS EN ISO 12944 Parts 1 to 8 1998 *Paints and varnishes* and *BS EN ISO 14713:1999 Protection against corrosion of iron and steel in structures. Zinc and aluminium coatings. Guidelines.*]

BS 6150:1991 *Code of practice for the painting of buildings.*

BS 8000-12:1989 *Workmanship on building sites. Code of practice for decorative wall coverings and painting.*

Mastic asphalt

BS 5284:1993 *Methods of sampling and testing mastic asphalt used in building and civil engineering.*

Floor coverings

BS 5325:2001 *Installation of textile floor coverings. Code of practice.*

BS 5385-3:1989 *Wall and floor tiling. Code of practice for the design and installation of ceramic floor tiles and mosaics.*

BS 5385-5:1994 *Wall and floor tiling. Code of practice for the design and installation of terrazzo tile and slab, natural stone and composition block flooring.*

BS 8203:2001 *Code of practice for the installation of resilient floor coverings.*

Materials

BS 1199 and 1200:1976 *Specifications for building sands from natural sources.* [Superseded but remains current.]

BS 4027:1996 *Specification for sulfate-resisting Portland cement.*
BS EN 197-1:2000 *Cement. Composition, specifications and conformity criteria for common cements.*
BS EN 413-1:2004 *Masonry cement. Composition, specifications and conformity criteria.*
BS EN 12004:2001 *Adhesives for tiles. Definitions and specifications.*
BS EN 12620:2002 *Aggregates for concrete.*
BS EN 13139:2002 *Aggregates for mortar.*
BS EN 14411:2003 *Ceramic tiles. Definitions, classification, characteristics and marking.*

7.10 FURNITURE, EQUIPMENT AND INTERNAL PLANTING

1 CONTRACT REQUIREMENTS

7.10.1 Duties

It is a normal duty of the Clerk of Works to check conformity with specifications and drawings. In the case of items obtained through the buying agency or client direct supplier, their inspectors may carry out checks. For internal planting, the A/EA may arrange specialist inspections.

2 QUALITY CONTROL

7.10.2 Quality assurance

The specification should be checked for any QA schemes applicable and the A/EA's instructions obtained on any duties arising. For supply of sanitary appliances and fittings, use is made of BSI Kitemark schemes.

7.10.3 Delivery of items for inclusion in the works

Together with the contractor, the Clerk of Works should inspect delivery of items for compliance with the specification. Any damage or missing items, which the contractor is required to record on the carrier's consignment note, should be agreed. The contractor must order replacements as necessary. A record should be kept in the site diary.

Specified requirements for maintenance of temperature and humidity conditions in storage and after installation should be noted. The Clerk of Works should check these (with the assistance of the M&E Site Inspector) and report any problems arising to the A/EA.

7.10.4 Sanitary appliances – A/EA's approvals

The following matters may require contractual approval.

Location of taps and valves: approved practice is to set the hot tap to the left to aid disabled and partially sighted people, and valves should be located in an accessible position.

Chemical closets: to be fixed in accordance with the manufacturer's instructions and as directed by the A/EA. The A/EA's instructions should be obtained.

Testing: performance testing of sanitary appliances is normally carried out when testing the drainage installation. Guidance on testing is given in BS 8000-13.

Compliance with water regulations: it is usually necessary to inspect for compliance with water regulations, particularly for correct provision of air-gaps and warning pipes. BS 8000-15 provides detailed guidance.

7.10.5 Internal planting

Where there is significant provision of internal planting, it is probable that the A/EA will arrange for specialist inspection of the work, particularly off site. The following are points that may require the attention of the Clerk of Works.

Certification: deliveries of plants and materials should be checked for labelling and certification to specified requirements. Verification that such deliveries are correctly certified will normally be a specialist task, but where delegated to the Clerk of Works the A/EA should be consulted in case of any doubt.

Sampling and testing: sampling of compost mixes for approval or test as directed by the A/EA should be arranged and the results of the tests arranged by the contractor forwarded.

Replacements by the client: the conditions in the specification relating to relocation of plants, temperature, lack of water or unauthorised watering, change in lighting and effect of toxic chemicals which could place responsibility for replacement on the client/user should be noted. Any such problem arising should be reported to the A/EA and a record kept in the site diary.

Use of peat-based products: the use of peat is increasingly being criticised because of the environmental impact of extraction. Where specification excludes peat products, delivery should be checked for compliance.

Pesticides: similar concerns are raised over the use of certain pesticides, nitrate fertilisers, etc. The A/EA should advise on any environmental requirements. Unused chemicals and their containers are likely to constitute 'special waste' for disposal.

Maintenance: the A/EA should be able to supply a copy of the maintenance programme and instructions on any delegated duty. It is common for the landscape contractor to maintain the planting for a defined period. Liaison arrangements with the client/user for contractor's access after handover should be confirmed.

Notice to A/EA: where specified, the Clerk of Works should ensure that sufficient notice is given to the A/EA of commencement of specified operations.

Cleanliness: The site is to be left clean on completion to the A/EA's satisfaction.

3   STATUTORY REQUIREMENTS AND TECHNICAL STANDARDS

(Note: under European legislation, the BS prefix will shortly change to EN.)

Publications to which site reference may be necessary include:

BS 8000-13:1989 *Workmanship on building sites. Code of practice for above ground drainage and sanitary appliances.*
BS 8000-15:1990 *Workmanship on building sites. Code of practice for hot and cold water services (domestic scale).*

7.11   BUILDING FABRIC SUNDRIES

NBS reference: P20 Unframed isolated trims/skirtings/sundry items.

The contents of the Quality Control section are divided into subsections as follows:

2A   skirtings/architraves/trims/sundries
2B   ironmongery.

1   CONTRACT REQUIREMENTS

7.11.1   Duties

Part of the normal duty of the Clerk of Works is to check conformity with specifications and drawings and, in the case of ironmongery, any schedules produced. It is important that cross-checks with a door schedule, if produced, are carried out as external door manufacturers may have their own locking provisions or isolated trims to be included. The A/EA may utilise the services of a specialist to produce an ironmongery schedule.

2A   QUALITY CONTROL: SKIRTINGS/ARCHITRAVES/TRIMS/SUNDRIES

7.11.2   Quality assurance

The specification should be checked for any QA schemes applicable and the A/EA's instructions obtained on any duties arising. For skirtings and architraves, reference is made to the TRADA scheme under Trussed Rafters (see 7.5.14).

7.11.3   Skirtings and architraves

The specification should be checked for requirements to provide samples before-hand, and when delivered to site off-loaded materials should be checked for any splits, shakes, excessive knots or ribbed planed timber. Any disputes for rejection should be immediately referred to the A/EA.

Softwood material due to be painted should be treated for knotting, stopped and primed prior to cutting into the required lengths for fixing. Softwood or hardwood due to be varnished should be carefully checked for imperfections prior to the finish being applied. Where hardwood skirtings and architraves are fixed via pelleting, the Clerk of Works should check that the pellets are as close a match as possible to the surrounding timber and, when glued in, run with the grain of the surrounding material as post-varnishing will highlight cross-graining.

Moisture content at the time of fixing should be between 8 and 12 per cent.

7.11.4   Trims

For timber trims, quadrants and glazing beads, the specification should be checked for sample requirements beforehand. Delivery and finishes inspection should be treated as skirtings and architraves. (See 7.11.3.)

Softwood trims are normally fixed with galvanised or sheridised nails and stopped prior to decoration. The Clerk of Works should be mindful of excessive splits and refer any disputes to the A/EA.

Metal trims around door or window frames, where not part of that particular trade package, should be non-ferrous and straight and true. Where powder-coated to match existing, the Clerk of Works should be vigilant to check for a true colour match and report any non-compliance to the A/EA.

7.11.5   Sundry items

Often included in sundry items, but too numerous to have their own relevant section, are:

- plywood shelves
- medium density fibreboard window boards or boxings
- visible timber packers to posts, linings or frames.

2B   QUALITY CONTROL: IRONMONGERY

7.11.6   Quality assurance

The specification and schedule should be checked for any QA schemes applicable and the A/EA's instructions obtained before proceeding further.

7.11.7 Manufacturer's instructions

Requirements in the specification to fix in accordance with manufacturer's instructions or recommendations should be identified, copies of these obtained and compliance checked. It is often better for the Site Inspector to obtain a copy of the manufacturer's brochure, for readily identifiable reference.

7.11.8 Samples

The specification should be checked for requirements to submit samples, for example where powder-coated, and these must be submitted in good time for the A/EA's approval. Approved samples should be kept on site to check against deliveries.

7.11.9 Special points to watch

Lubrication: as ironmongery generally has several moving parts, it must be lubricated before installation, and, in any case, the manufacturer's instructions must be checked. A sealed case should never be broken for lubrication purposes as this might invalidate any guarantees.

Door signage: the A/EA's agreement should be sought for heights and positions of door signage. Consistency throughout gives a neater and more professional appearance.

Handle fixing: before the tradespeople fix handles to internal timber doors, the Clerk of Works must make sure that the screws used are long enough to do the job. Far too often shorter screws pull out with misuse, in many instances taking a piece of flax-board core with them. For heavily used doors, through-bolts might be a better option. In cases of doubt the A/EA should be consulted.

Completion: at completion, the Clerk of Works should check that the ironmongery has been adjusted and lubricated if necessary and ensure that any protective films are removed.

3 STATUTORY REQUIREMENTS AND TECHNICAL STANDARDS

(Note: under European legislation, the BS prefix will shortly change to EN.)

Publications to which site reference may be necessary include:

Skirtings, architraves, trims and sundry items
BS 1186-3:1990 *Timber for and workmanship in joinery. Specification for wood trim and its fixing.*
BS 4072:1999 *Copper/chromium/arsenic preparations for wood preservation.* [Current but obsolescent.]
BS 5499-1:2002 *Graphical symbols and signs. Safety signs, including fire safety signs. Specification for geometric shapes, colours and layout.*

BS 5499-2:1986 *Fire safety signs, notices and graphic symbols. Specification for self-luminous fire safety signs.*
BS 5499-4:2000 *Safety signs, including fire safety signs. Code of practice for escape route signing.*
BS 5499-6:2002 *Graphical symbols and signs. Safety signs, including fire safety signs. Creation and design of graphical symbols for use in safety signs. Requirements.*
BS 5499-11:2002 *Graphical symbols and signs. Safety signs, including fire safety signs. Water safety signs.*
BS 8000-5:1990 *Workmanship on building sites. Code of practice for carpentry, joinery and general fixings.*
BS EN 314-2:1993 *Plywood. Bonding quality. Requirements.*
BS EN 635-1:1995 *Plywood. Classification by surface appearance. General.*
BS EN 635-2:1995 *Plywood. Classification by surface appearance. Hardwood.*
BS EN 635-3:1995 *Plywood. Classification by surface appearance. Softwood.*
BS EN 635-5:1999 *Plywood. Classification by surface appearance. Methods for measuring and expressing characteristics and defects.*

Ironmongery

BS 476-22:1987 *Fire tests on building materials and structures. Methods for determination of the fire resistance of non-loadbearing elements of construction.*
BS 8000-5:1990 *Workmanship on building sites. Code of practice for carpentry, joinery and general fixings.*
BS EN 12209:2003 *Building hardware. Locks and latches. Mechanically operated locks, latches and locking plates. Requirements and test methods.*

7.12   PAVING, EXTERNAL PLANTING, FENCING AND SITE FURNITURE

1   CONTRACT REQUIREMENTS

7.12.1   Duties

It is part of the Clerk of Works' normal duties to check conformity with specifications and drawings. Paving, planting and sports surfaces may require landscape or other specialist supervision which the A/EA will arrange, but for small-scale work this duty may fall to the Clerk of Works. The A/EA will provide instructions on these matters and contact points for specialist advice.

7.12.2   A/EA's approvals

Matters which may require prior A/EA's approval under the specification are set out in the respective work sections below.

2 QUALITY CONTROL

7.12.3 Quality assurance

The specification should be checked for any QA schemes applicable and the A/EA's instructions obtained on any duties arising. In this workgroup reference is made to BSI-registered firms and BSI Kitemarks.

7.12.4 Paving

Setting out: the setting out of road lines, kerb lines, radii and level datum points should be checked. Levels and grades should be rechecked as work proceeds.

Materials: delivery documents should be checked for evidence of compliance with specification requirements. The contractor should be asked to provide additional documentation as necessary. The A/EA should be consulted in case of any doubt. In cases where the contractor offers materials as equivalent to those specified, this should be referred to the A/EA for approval or otherwise. The following requirements should be noted:

- frost-resistant materials: the contractor should be asked to provide evidence (in the form of test results) that the materials provided are non-frost susceptible as defined in TRL SR 829. The A/EA should be consulted as necessary
- cement: should be obtained from a BSI-registered firm
- steel: dowel bars, mesh reinforcement and tie bars are to be obtained from a CARES licensee
- thermoplastics paint: to be supplied by a Kitemarked licensee.

7.12.5 A/EA's approvals

The following matters may need contractual approval as specified and any delegations by the A/EA to the Clerk of Works should be established:

- waterproofing compounds: material to seal edges of cement-bound sub-bases and road bases to be approved
- air entraining agents: to be approved (e.g. for use in in situ concrete)
- bond breaking agents: to be approved (e.g. for use in in situ concrete)
- blinding materials: alternatives to sand for curing concrete if proposed require approval
- surface finishes: pedestrian pavings may be finished to the A/EA's requirements
- bitumen: bitumen binders are generally to be penetration grade unless the A/EA authorises the use of cutback
- reflecting studs: the A/EA is to approve the supplier
- adhesion agents (to improve adhesion between cutback bitumen if approved and uncoated chippings): to be approved, in conformity with TRL Road Note 39, 5th edition, 2002.

7.12.6 Testing

Where sampling and testing are to be carried out on paving materials, the A/EA will approve the test laboratory for the purpose. Test results are to be forwarded to the A/EA. On large-scale works, site testing laboratories may be set up, in which case the Clerk of Works' particular duties will be as directed by the A/EA. On small works, the Clerk of Works may be required to carry out sieve analysis checks on grading of aggregates. Where materials are mixed off site, the A/EA will arrange for any off-site inspection.

7.12.7 Workmanship

The following contractual requirements should be noted and documentation or the A/EA's instructions obtained as necessary.

Type 2 sub-base: requirements for checking compaction with correct moisture content should be agreed.

Concrete bases: requirements for checking compaction to required average dry density should be agreed.

Trial concrete mixes: the A/EA's instructions on approval of trial mixes should be obtained.

Air entrainment: the Clerk of Works should approve the pressure type meter to be used, witness tests, check calibration of meter and monitor compliance with specification in accordance with BS EN 12350-7:2002.

Coated macadam: workmanship is to be in accordance with BS 4987 and BS 434-2.

Hot rolled asphalt: workmanship is to be in accordance with BS 594, by machine unless otherwise instructed (the A/EA's requirement should be established).

Mastic asphalt: workmanship is to be in accordance with BS 1447 Appendix A. The Clerk of Works should check that the contractor has a suitable thermometer on site and uses it to conform to specified temperature limits for laying.

Dense tar: workmanship is to be in accordance with BS 5273.

Surface dressing: workmanship is to be in accordance with TRL Road Note 39, 5th edition, 2002. The A/EA's instructions should be obtained on whether to use section 7 or 8.

Slurry sealing: workmanship is to be in accordance with BS 434.

Tack coats: to be laid in accordance with BS 434-2.

Perforated concrete units: a copy of the manufacturer's instructions for laying should be obtained and compliance monitored.

Interlocking blocks: workmanship is to be in accordance with BS 7533. Manufacturer's instructions for any special requirements for the laying and protection of blocks during vibration should be obtained and compliance monitored. If samples are required to be approved by the A/EA, the A/EA must be given notice of readiness for inspection in good time.

Sand: sand for brushing into joints must be completely dry otherwise gaps may not be completely filled. Project specification for oven-dried sand or similar should be checked and compliance monitored.

7.12.8 Special surfacing and pavings for sport

This work will usually be carried out by a specialist contractor and may involve landscape or other specialist supervision. Such visits (contractor and supervisor) should be recorded in the site diary. The A/EA's instructions should be obtained on the Clerk of Works' particular duties.

7.12.9 Seeding and turfing

This work will usually be carried out by a landscape contractor and may involve supervision by a consultant appointed by the client or A/EA. Such visits should be recorded in the site diary. The A/EA's instructions on the Clerk of Works' particular duties should be obtained. Certification of materials delivered to the site should be checked and any discrepancies reported to the A/EA. Prior notice to the A/EA may be required for setting out, application of weedkillers and fertilisers, seeding, turfing, initial cutting and for maintenance visits by the specialist contractor. Such notice should be forwarded to the A/EA without delay.

7.12.10 A/EA's approvals or decisions

The following may require contractual approval or decision by the A/EA and agreement of any delegations to the Clerk of Works:

- samples of seed and turf: for approval
- equivalent manufacturer: for approval, where offered
- worm and weedkillers: approval of manufacturer. To be applied when directed by the A/EA
- weather and site conditions: to be agreed as suitable for work to proceed
- damage: reinstatement to the A/EA's satisfaction of grassed areas
- turf stacking: approval where period exceeds seven days, and on completion
- cutting grass: prior consent is required for the initial cut
- re-seeding: where growth is unacceptable to the A/EA
- protective fencing: to be removed when directed by the A/EA
- rolling: to be directed by the A/EA
- top dressing: to be directed by the A/EA
- Tree Preservation Orders: the Clerk of Works must check with the A/EA that none exist on the site and obtain directions for protection if the A/EA so directs.

7.12.11 Planting

This work will usually be carried out by a specialist contractor and may involve supervision by a consultant appointed by the client or A/EA. Such visits should be recorded in the site diary. The A/EA's instructions on the Clerk of Works' particular duties should be obtained. Certification of materials delivered to the site should be checked and any discrepancies reported to the A/EA. Prior notice to the A/EA by the contractor may be required for setting out, weedkilling, fertilising, delivery, plant and maintenance visits.

7.12.12 A/EA's approvals and decisions

The following may require contractual approval or decision by the A/EA. Any delegations to the Clerk of Works must be agreed:

- certification: the contractor must provide certification of materials and compliance with specification where required by the A/EA
- alternatives: the contractor may propose alternative plants or equivalent manufacturers for the A/EA's approval
- inspection: the A/EA is to inspect and approve plants in the nursery prior to lifting
- compaction: the A/EA is to decide when soil has become compacted and requires to be broken up
- hedge plants: the A/EA is to instruct if leaders are to be cut back
- watering: the A/EA is to decide whether or not to water-in plants to saturation
- sub-soil: the A/EA is to direct disposal of excavated sub-soil
- stakes: tree stakes should be sawn off below first branch, unless the A/EA instructs otherwise
- stumps: to be disposed of as directed
- tree surgery: the A/EA's prior permission may be required for use of retained trees as anchors for winching, use of artificial drying before application of fungicides, use of filler in splits, removal of major branches and severing of roots. Any defects or weaknesses not covered by specification should be reported to the A/EA
- burning: ash is to be disposed of as directed. However, site fires may not be permissible and this should be checked with the A/EA
- fencing: the A/EA is to direct when to remove protective fencing
- chemicals: prior approval of the A/EA may be required for application of chemicals to control weeds. The Health and Safety Plan should be consulted for method statements.

7.12.13 Fencing

Fence erection: may be specified to be carried out by a BSI registered firm or by a specialist subcontractor, if not by the main contractor. Generally, fence erection should be carried out in accordance with the appropriate part of BS 1722.

Preservative: any proposal by the contractor to provide an equivalent to the specified treatment should be referred to the A/EA for approval or otherwise.

3 STATUTORY REQUIREMENTS AND TECHNICAL STANDARDS

(Note: under European legislation, the BS prefix will shortly change to EN.)

Publications to which site reference may be necessary include:

Roads and pavings
BS 434-2:1984 *Bitumen road emulsions (anionic and cationic). Code of practice for use of bitumen road emulsions.*
BS 594-2:2003 *Hot rolled asphalt for roads and other paved areas. Specification for transport, laying and compaction of hot rolled asphalt.*
BS 1447:1988 *Specification for mastic asphalt (limestone fine aggregate) for roads, footways and pavings in building.*
BS 4987-1:2005 *Coated macadam (asphalt concrete) for roads and other paved areas. Specification for constituent materials and for mixtures.*
BS 4987-2:2003 *Coated macadam (asphalt concrete) for roads and other paved areas. Specification for transport, laying and compaction.*
BS 5273:1975 *Specification. Dense tar surfacing for roads and other paved areas.*
BS 7533 *Pavements constructed with clay, natural stone or concrete pavers.*
BS EN 12350-7:2000 *Testing fresh concrete. Air content. Pressure methods.*
Transport Research Laboratory (TRL) SR 829 *Specification for the TRRL frost-heave test*, 1984.
TRL Road Note 39 *Design guide for road surface dressing*, 5th edition, 2002.

Landscape
BS 1722 Parts 1–13: *Fences.*
BS 3882:1994 *Specification for top soil.*
BS 3969:1998 *Recommendations for turf for general purposes.*
BS 3998:1989 *Recommendations for tree work.*
BS 4043:1989 *Recommendations for transplanting root-balled trees.*
BS 4428:1989 *Code of practice for general landscape operations (excluding hard surfaces).*

7.13 DISPOSAL SYSTEMS

1 CONTRACT REQUIREMENTS

The contents of the Quality Control section are divided into subsections as follows:

2A   above ground drainage and sanitary appliances
2B   below ground drainage.

7.13.1 Duties

Conformity with specification, drawings and with Building Regulations should be checked. In addition, the Clerk of Works should ensure that the drainage system and appliances fitted to it are operational. Guidance on inspection is given in BS 8000-16. Guidance on responsibilities of the A/EA arising in the specification which may be delegated to the Clerk of Works is included in the duties listed in the remainder of this section.

2A QUALITY CONTROL: ABOVE GROUND DRAINAGE AND SANITARY APPLIANCES

7.13.2 Quality assurance

The specification should be checked for any product QA schemes applicable and the A/EA should be consulted about duties arising. For drainage work, use is made of BSI Kitemarked products and Agrément Certification.

7.13.3 Special points to watch

Internal pipe work: where not shown on drawings, the line and grade of pipe runs should be agreed, but the maximum branch lengths allowed by Building Regulations should always be borne in mind.

Discharge errors: the Clerk of Works should listen for traps being syphoned when two or more adjoining fittings are being discharged. Back-fall errors are basic but are still a regular item found on snag lists.

Overflow connections: when performance testing sanitary fittings, the Clerk of Works must ensure that the overflow connections are checked for leaks in addition to their full operation.

Water supply: it is not uncommon for hot taps to be fitted to the cold water supply in error and the cold tap to the hot water supply. To ensure that no accidents occur, the correct orientation of taps should be checked. The cold tap should be on the right-hand side of the basin (a convention helpful to blind and partially sighted persons).

Testing internal pipe work: pressure must be released from the end furthest away from the pressure gauge to prove that the whole pipe has been under test.

Fire protection: any plastic drainage pipe over 50 mm in diameter passing from one fire zone into another must have a fire sleeve or 1 m of cast iron drain pipe either side of zone barrier to comply with Part B of the Building Regulations.

Air admittance valves (AAVs): where an internal AAV is fitted to the top of a stub stack, the valve must be mounted above the height of the highest sanitary appliance fitting overflow point. AAVs should not be used at the head of a drain.

2B QUALITY CONTROL: BELOW GROUND DRAINAGE

7.13.4 Setting out

External drainage: the Clerk of Works should check that invert levels are the point of discharge of new drainage against level shown on drawings. The correct setting out and depth relative to building lines, roads, paths and other service runs must be confirmed. It is important that manholes and inspection chambers are correctly sited to avoid acute bends at branch connections. The A/EA's agreement to the use of a laser instrument instead of sight rails must be obtained if proposed. The Clerk of Works should confirm that the contractor sets up the lasers accurately.

7.13.5 Safety

The Health and Safety Plan should be checked for any special provisions with regard to safe working in trenches, etc. Any potentially dangerous situations should immediately be brought to the contractor's attention. The Health and Safety Co-ordinator and A/EA should also be informed as necessary.

7.13.6 Special points to watch

Falls: falls to required levels should never be achieved by supporting pipe work on bricks, stones or any hard objects. The supporting medium should be consistent in support.

Rocker pipes: unless otherwise specified, a short length of pipe (normally under 300 mm) from the manhole (rocker pipe) should be included to allow for differential movement between pipe runs and manholes. The junction of this pipe with the adjoining pipe run should have a movement joint of approximately 20 mm if pipes are being concreted for protection.

Pipe protection: the pipe runs must have protection from loads and traffic vibration appropriate to the depth of cover.

Pressure testing: the Clerk of Works must always ensure that the pressure is released from the end of the pipe work furthest away from the test gauge to make certain that the whole pipe has been under test. All other tests should be as specification and BS 8000-16. The requirement for profile testing must be kept in mind: in case of any doubt the A/EA should be consulted and advice sought, especially with regard to CCTV surveys.

7.13.7 Materials

Manufacturer's instructions: the specification should be checked for reference to these, copies obtained and compliance monitored. This applies particularly to proprietary pipe couplings.

Granular fill: testing must be arranged as specified or as directed by the A/EA.

Coarse sand: the source must be approved.

Backfill: the reuse of trench spoil must be approved where suitable and subject to test.

3 STATUTORY REQUIREMENTS AND TECHNICAL STANDARDS

(Note: under European legislation, the BS prefix will shortly change to EN.)

Publications to which site reference may be necessary include:

BS 437:1978 *Specification for cast iron spigot and socket drain pipes and fittings.*
BS 416-1:1990 *Discharge and ventilating pipes and fittings, sand-cast or spun in cast iron. Specification for spigot and socket systems.*
BS 416-2:1990 *Discharge and ventilating pipes and fittings, sand-cast or spun in cast iron. Specification for socketless systems.*
BS 6465-1:1994 *Sanitary installations. Code of practice for scale of provision, selection and installation of sanitary appliances.*
BS 6465-2:1996 *Sanitary installations. Code of practice for space requirements for sanitary appliances.*
BS 8000-13:1989 *Workmanship on building sites. Code of practice for above ground drainage and sanitary appliances.*
BS 8000-14:1989 *Workmanship on building sites. Code of practice for below ground drainage.*
BS 8000-16:1997 *Workmanship on building sites. Code of practice for sealing joints in buildings using sealants.*
BS EN 877:1999 *Cast iron pipes and fittings, their joints and accessories for the evacuation of water from buildings. Requirements, test methods and quality assurance.*

7.14 PIPED SUPPLY SYSTEMS

1 CONTRACT REQUIREMENTS

The contents of the Quality Control section are divided into subsections as follows:

2A water supply systems
2B gas supplies.

7.14.1 Duties

Conformity with the specification and drawings should be confirmed. The many variable performance requirements specified for products to be installed require particular vigilance to be exercised in checking the documentation and certification of deliveries and conformity with appropriate standards, bye-laws and other statutory requirements. Competent personnel are obligatory for some tasks and the Clerk of Works may be asked to confirm their qualifications.

The specification should be checked for product QA schemes applicable and the A/EA's instruction obtained on any duties arising.

2A QUALITY CONTROL: WATER SUPPLY SYSTEMS

7.14.2 External pipe work

Excavation for pipe work runs should be dealt with under BS 8000-1. The Clerk of Works should check that correct setting out and depth relative to building lines, roads, paths and other service runs has been achieved.

7.14.3 Internal pipe work

Where not shown on drawings, the line and grading of pipe runs and points of connection to risers should be agreed. Air locks must be avoided. Cold and hot water pipe runs should be co-ordinated for appearance in exposed sections, but avoiding heat transfer from hot to cold pipe work. Any cutting through the building structure not specifically provided for in the drawings requires prior approval and instruction on sleeving and fire stopping. In case of doubt the A/EA should be consulted. The spacing of support brackets is to be as the project specification.

7.14.4 Lead

Where capillary fittings are to be utilised, the Clerk of Works should check that lead-free solder is used to make the joints on potable water systems. If integral solder ring fittings are to be used, they must be stamped as lead-free.

7.14.5 Compliance with the Water Supply Regulations

All water installations must be installed, tested and disinfected in accordance with the project specification, local water bye-laws (if applicable) and the Water Supply Regulations.

Copies of test and inspection certificates including initial pipe work pressure test, disinfection initial and residual level results, final sampling after flushing, plus bacteriological tests are required. There may also be a requirement for Legionella assessment.

7.14.6 Disinfection

Method statements should be obtained from the contractor, paying particular attention to the disposal of flushing and disinfecting water. The Clerk of Works should check with the A/EA, Environment Agency or local authority that the contractor's proposals are acceptable.

Flushing and disinfection must be monitored to ensure that procedures are properly carried out and that required chlorine residuals are obtained. Water samples should be taken and despatched as directed by the A/EA and bacteriological reports must be available for handover. If there is any question that water or distribution systems may have been contaminated, the A/EA must be informed accordingly.

Treated water

Water supplies that receive additional treatment over and above initial disinfection must be clearly labelled and identified to avoid confusion with standard mains water: colour coding should conform to BS 1710. After disinfection, the pipe work must be flushed with the same type of water that it is designed to distribute.

7.14.7 Pressure testing

A sudden escape of water at high test pressures can cause considerable damage and may even cause personal injury. Particular attention should be paid to any temporary anchorages, supports and temporary connections, especially where existing premises are at risk from leakage. When testing mains water installations and fire mains the pressure may be particularly excessive, in which case clearing the area and placing danger signs may be in order.

7.14.8 Storage cisterns

Storage cisterns must be checked to ensure that they comply with water bye-laws, especially with regard to support, placing, valves, access for maintenance and supply pipe work.

2B QUALITY CONTROL: GAS SUPPLIES

7.14.9 Generally

All gas pipe work and installations, including final connections, must be carried out by trade-approved personnel, i.e. CORGI, which approves trades for different types of gas work. A CORGI-approved operative is only approved to work on certain types of gas installations. Operatives approved only for domestic installations are not qualified to work on commercial gas installations. All tradespeople should carry a card to say what type of work they are allowed to undertake.

All installations and materials should comply with the relevant sections from a wide range of statutory instruments and British Standards, such as BS 6891. Those applicable should be listed in the contract specification but an outline list is included at the end of this section for reference.

7.14.10 External pipe work

Excavation for pipe work runs should be dealt with under BS 8000-1. The Clerk of Works should check that the correct setting out and depth relative to building lines, roads, paths and other service runs has been achieved. Service routes must be confirmed to be fully co-ordinated with other service routes, with particular attention paid to areas where services cross.

7.14.11 Internal pipe work

Where not shown on drawings, the line and grading of pipe runs must be agreed. Pipe runs should be co-ordinated for appearance in exposed sections. Where distribution pipes are routed through ceiling voids, floor voids or ducts they should be naturally ventilated. In the event that the pipe run crosses a fire barrier within a ceiling void, then each fire-stopped section must be separately ventilated. Pipes should not pass through areas which could be prejudicial to their safety without special fire safety provisions; these may include enclosing the pipe within a sleeve or duct which should be ventilated at each end. Any cutting through the building structure not specifically provided for in the drawings requires prior approval and instruction on sleeving and fire stopping. In case of doubt the A/EA should be consulted.

Regulation 18 of the Gas Safety Regulations 1984 gives detailed information with regard to enclosed pipes, protection against failure due to movement, shortest routes through walls and gas-tight sleeves.

7.14.12 Entry to buildings

Where services enter buildings, particular attention should be paid to sealing the point of entry to prevent seepage from possible leaks on external pipe work entering the building. In the event that a service crosses a cavity wall it should be sleeved to prevent seepage into the cavity. Plastic type gas entry pipe work is permitted inside a building, but should not be exposed to sunlight.

7.14.13 Primary meter

The location of the meter is subject to agreement with the gas utility company. The meter enclosure, be it a purpose-built box or meter room, should be ventilated to outside air.

7.14.14 Secondary meters

Any secondary meter serving a kitchen or other building or building compartment, which, because of its use, may present a particular fire hazard, should preferably be housed in a room or chamber used for no other purpose, ventilated directly to the open air and fire-separated from the building by a construction having a fire resistance required by the Building Regulations.

7.14.15 Isolation

Each appliance should be provided with a valve or cock in an accessible location. In addition, where more than one appliance is situated in a self-contained area the installation pipe serving that area must also be fitted with a readily accessible isolating valve or cock. Non-domestic kitchens and boiler rooms, etc., should be fitted with an isolating valve or cock which should preferably be located at the point of exit from the room. This valve or cock is for emergency and maintenance isolation only and should be suitably labelled.

7.14.16 Flexible tubes

Where flexible tubes are to be used for the connection of kitchen appliances these must comply with the requirements of BS 669-2 and BS 6173. For commercial and industrial works, refer to the Institution of Gas Engineers and Managers (IGEM) utilization procedure IGE/UP/2.

7.14.17 Pressure testing

Testing of gas services should be undertaken in accordance with Institute of Gas Engineers and Managers publications. Where existing services are to be altered or added to, a pressure test to ascertain the condition of the existing service should be undertaken before modifications begin.

7.14.18 Equipotential bonding

Electrical 'equipotential' bonding is a statutory requirement for protective multiple earthing (PME) installations and is also recommended by the Institute of Electrical Engineers (IEE) Wiring Regulations in other circumstances.

7.14.19 Flues

The Clerk of Works should check that flues are complete, continuous and free from obstruction; with reference to relevant Building Regulations.

7.14.20 Ventilation for appliances

The provision of adequate air supply for open-flued appliances and ventilation for gas appliances in accordance with the Building and Gas Safety Regulations should be confirmed.

7.14.21 Maintenance access

It must be possible to gain access to an appliance for operation, maintenance and inspection.

7.14.22 Identification

Pipe work should be colour coded throughout its entire length in accordance with BS 1710.

3 STATUTORY REQUIREMENTS AND TECHNICAL STANDARDS

(Note: under European legislation, the BS prefix will shortly change to EN.)

Publications to which site reference may be necessary include:

General
BS 8000-1:1989 *Workmanship on building sites. Code of practice for excavation and filling.*

Water
BS 6700:1997 *Specification for design, installation, testing and maintenance of services supplying water for domestic use within buildings and their curtilages.* [Partially replaced by BS EN 806-2:2005 *Specifications for installations inside buildings conveying water for human consumption. Design.*]

BS 8000-15:1990 *Workmanship on building sites. Code of practice for hot and cold water services (domestic scale).*

Gas
BS 669-2:1997 *Flexible hoses, end fittings and sockets for gas burning appliances. Specification for corrugated metallic flexible hoses, covers, end fittings and sockets for catering appliances burning 1st, 2nd and 3rd family gases.*

BS 1710:1984 (1991) *Specification for identification of pipelines and services.*

BS 6172:2004 *Installation and maintenance of domestic gas cooking appliances (2nd and 3rd family gases). Specification.*

BS 6173:2001 *Specification for installation of gas-fired catering appliances for use in all types of catering establishments (2nd and 3rd family gases).*

BS 6891:2005 *Installation of low pressure gas pipework of up to 35 mm ($R1\frac{1}{4}$) in domestic premises (2nd family gas). Specification.*

Gas Safety Regulations 1972 SI 1972/1178

Gas Safety (Installation and Use) Regulations 1984. SI 1984/1358

Building Regulations 2000. SI 2000/2531

Institute of Gas Engineers and Managers IGE/UP/2 *Gas installation pipework, boosters and compressors on industrial and commercial premises.*

Water Regulations Advisory Scheme (WRAS) *Water fittings and materials directory.* Available online at www.wras.co.uk/Directory/

7.15 MECHANICAL HEATING, COOLING AND REFRIGERATION SYSTEMS

1 CONTRACT REQUIREMENTS

The contents of the Quality Control section are divided into subsections as follows:

2A   mechanical heating – sources of heat
2B   heat distribution systems
2C   refrigeration systems.

7.15.1 Duties

Conformity with the specification and drawings should be checked. The many variable performance requirements specified for products to be installed require particular vigilance to be employed in checking the documentation and certification of deliveries and conformity with appropriate standards, bye-laws and other statutory requirements. Competent personnel are obligatory for some tasks (electrical, water, gas and oil) and the Clerk of Works may be asked to confirm their qualifications or registration. In some areas of the site there may be a 'Permit to Work' system in operation and any non-compliance with this system should be reported directly to the A/EA.

The specification should be checked for product QA schemes applicable and the A/EA's instruction obtained on any duties arising.

Section 7.16 below deals with ventilation and air conditioning systems.

2A QUALITY CONTROL: MECHANICAL HEATING – SOURCES OF HEAT

7.15.2 General

This section deals with boiler plant and other sources of heat within a mechanical services installation. The setting out details of boiler plant must be checked with the contractor and in particular that adequate space is available around plant for its assembly and maintenance. Plant should be examined on arrival to site, any damage noted and a check made that tappings are adequately protected and capped or plugged. If plant is to be craned into the building, check that it is slung in a manner approved by the manufacturer so as not to impose undue stress or strain. Where particularly large plant is being installed it may be necessary for this to be positioned well in advance of the rest of the installation and may require greater attention to protection during the remainder of the construction period. Particular attention should be given to future maintenance with regard to how the plant can be safely accessed or dismantled for replacement.

The Clerk of Works should check that all sources of heat are sited so as to minimise the risk of heat damage to the building fabric and that means of isolation are easily and safely accessible in an emergency. They should be mounted and secured strictly in accordance with the manufacturer's instructions. Additionally, installation should be by qualified personnel, especially for gas-fired and electrical equipment. Checks should be made that adequate air for combustion is available and that airways are not obstructed by other building works if the plant is operational (dust can block airways and/or damage gas burners, leaving them in an unsafe condition). All safety devices must be confirmed as operational and secure from unauthorised access before the plant is commissioned.

7.15.3 Builders' work

The Clerk of Works should check that preparatory builders' work associated with the installation of plant and equipment has been undertaken in accordance with the approved drawings. Further, the Clerk of Works should also check what allowance has been made for the draining of the systems and what permanent drainage is provided in the boiler room to the foul drain – chemical discharge directly into rivers will contravene legislation enforced by the Environment Agency.

7.15.4 Ventilation

Adequate ventilation must be afforded to the boiler room/location, both for the provision of combustion and relief air and for the dissipation of heat. Reference should be made to Institution of Gas Engineers and Managers' publications, British Standards, CORGI publications, the Chartered Institution of Building Services Engineers (CIBSE) Guide B, etc., for guidance. Where mechanical ventilation is provided this should be interlocked with the boiler controls to shut down equipment.

7.15.5 Boiler mountings

The contract documents and any associated documents should be referred to for the requirements for the installation of boiler mountings. All mountings must be easily reachable and accessible for maintenance. Floor mountings in basements should be on a concrete plinth to prevent burners and electrics being submerged in water.

7.15.6 Tools

Where required by the contract documents, maintenance and operating tools must be provided. Where these are to be hung on a rack or similarly provided in the boiler room, their location must be agreed with the contractor and training for their use may be required.

7.15.7 Solid fuel

Solid fuel boilers are seldom selected at present, as maintenance and attendance costs are now higher than automated gas- or oil-fired boilers. They can be manually or automatically stoked or fed with pulverised fuel. Greater space is required around and in particular in front of the boiler for maintenance, stoking and removal of ash and clinker.

7.15.8 Oil fuel

Oil fuels are supplied in varying classifications designated by their viscosity. The heavier oils will require preheating and pumping from the storage tank to the burner. All fuels are susceptible to thickening at lower temperatures and even the lighter fuels may need to be trace heated where oil lines are susceptible to freezing conditions. Tanks should be positioned within a bund, to allow for containment of oil to prevent any escape into the drainage system, not less than 110 per cent of total tank capacity. Bunding tanks are now used and should be designed for catastrophic failure, and manufactured from rotationally moulded UV-stabilised medium-density polyethylene. Advice from the local environmental offices should be sought.

At the point of entry to the boiler room a fire valve will be installed to cut off the supply of oil in a fire condition. This may be mechanically or electrically activated.

A means of containing an oil spillage and raising an alarm should be provided. This will generally be in the form of a sump with a level switch, which should shut down the plant and cut off the oil supply. This facility must be easily accessible and maintainable.

7.15.9 Gas

Any requirements for secondary metering or for the provision for a test meter at the burner should be noted. This is sometimes required in larger installations. At the point of entry to the boiler room, a gas cock or a fire valve will normally be installed to cut off the supply of gas in a fire situation. This may be mechanically or electrically activated by a fire alarm or emergency stop button, with a reset control fitted within the boiler room incorporated (if possible) on the main control panel.

7.15.10 Combination boilers

Combination boilers are fed direct from the mains water supply and in addition to providing heating also provide domestic hot water with no storage. These should be installed in accordance with the Gas Regulations, with reference to the manufacturer's instructions and having due regard for the requirements of the Water Regulations, in particular regarding cross-contamination of supply.

7.15.11 Condensing or high efficiency boilers

Conventional boiler design seeks to avoid flue gas side corrosion by condensation, and as a consequence boiler efficiency is limited to about 85 per cent. By comparison, a condensing boiler seeks to recover the latent heat in the flue gases by returning the boiler water at a lower temperature; efficiency can then be increased to about 93 per cent. The flue gas condensate will be slightly acidic and the boiler will be designed to accommodate this. The condensate from the boiler flue will, however, need to be piped away to a foul drain in a material suitably resistant to the acidity of the condensate. In addition, because of the low flue temperatures (65 °C), a natural draught will not be present in the flue and mechanical ventilation will be necessary. It should be noted that as the boiler return water temperature is lower than in conventional design, the system mean water temperature will therefore also be lower. This will result in radiators and other emitters having to be larger when compared to conventional design.

7.15.12 Electrically heated boilers

This type of boiler is heated with single, twin or three-phase electrical heating elements installed in the water pressure unit, and is primarily for small domestic premises or where there is no possible storage space or gas supply available. A competent person should be qualified and registered to install this type of pressurised system.

7.15.13 Multi-boiler installations

The control requirements for sequencing or step control should be noted. Motorised isolating valves are provided on the return connection to each boiler and will be interlocked with the burner operation to each boiler. Particular attention should be paid to the piping up of the boilers. A loop header system is becoming the norm as it is proving to be the most flexible. It is not unusual for a reverse return method of piping to be adopted.

7.15.14 Specialist inspections

Boiler plant, in particular steam raising plant, may require inspection by insurance, safety and building control officers. The Clerk of Works should note the requirements of the contract documents, discuss them with the A/EA and liaise with any specialists as necessary. It is likely that plant will have been pressure tested off site, in which case copies of the relevant test certification should be obtained from the contractor and securely retained, but there may be a requirement for site-assembled plant to be on-site tested. The Clerk of Works should liaise between the contractor and any specialists in this latter instance.

Any system operating at temperatures and pressures defined to be medium or high temperature is required to be examined by a 'competent person' before it is put into use. It is recommended that for *any* sealed system the Project Engineer is consulted as early as possible and that the contractor is made fully aware in good time if there are requirements for additional inspections or tests, or if the client/engineer wish to apply any higher standards. The following section provides further information and advice.

2B QUALITY CONTROL: HEAT DISTRIBUTION SYSTEMS

7.15.15 General

This section deals with the distribution systems for transfer of the heating medium throughout an installation. These may be steam and condensate or low, medium or high temperature hot water. This section covers both external and internal installations, and pre-insulated pipe work.

7.15.16 Water/oil systems

Heat distribution systems generally use water as the transfer medium but occasionally oil may be encountered. For oil systems the mechanical engineer should be consulted if insufficient information is contained in the specification for the Clerk of Works' duties to be carried out effectively.

7.15.17 Storage of pipe work and materials

Pipe work should be stored clear of the ground on racking, with ends capped and protected and, ideally, sheltered from rain. Tube ends should be cleaned of scale, paint, oil, etc., and any rusting should be removed and treated with a suitable primer before installation. Threaded and reamed iron pipes should also be reprimed before installing. Pipe work fittings should be sorted, binned and stored under cover.

Valves and cocks, particularly with flanged faces, should be plugged or plated to prevent the ingress of foreign objects and damage to seats and seals. Expansion devices should be similarly protected and retaining or sizing bars left in place until installed (reference should be made to the manufacturer's instructions).

7.15.18 Setting out

External pipe work: excavation for pipe work runs should be dealt with under BS 8000-1. The correct setting out, grading, venting and draining of pipe work and depth relative to building lines, roads, paths and other service runs should be confirmed. Sand covering of pipes and identification tapes are placed in the top 400 mm of the trench to protect the services.

Internal pipe work: where not shown on drawings, the line and grading of pipe runs and points of connection to risers must be agreed. To avoid air locks, vents should be positioned at high points and pipe work should be completely drainable to an accessible safe point. Particular attention should be paid to pipe gradients on steam pipe work where the effective removal of condensate is of importance.

Pipe runs should be co-ordinated for appearance in exposed sections but avoiding heat transfer from hot to cold pipe work. Any cutting through the building structure not specifically provided for in the drawings requires prior approval and instruction on sleeving and fire stopping. In case of doubt the A/EA should be consulted.

7.15.19 Installation

For all systems, the Clerk of Works should check that as work proceeds it is installed to its co-ordinated location, is adequately supported and braced and laid evenly to avoid trapped pockets of air. Supports should allow for thermal expansion, preventing stress to pipe joints.

Air bottles and vents need to be installed where designed and/or where high spots cannot be avoided. Equally, drain cocks should be provided to allow full and effective removal of all liquid from the system by gravity.

Open ends of pipe work left during the progress of work should be closed temporarily with purpose-made metal, plastic or wood plugs, caps or blank metal flanges. Joints should not be made in the thickness of any wall, floor or ceiling and pipe work passing through the building structure should be sleeved in a material similar to the pipe. Sleeves must be fire-stopped where passing through a fire barrier. Galvanised fittings are only to be used on galvanised pipe work.

Particular attention must be paid to the bracketing of pipe work as required by the contract documents and any requirements for the guiding and anchoring of pipe work for the purpose of expansion or bellows should be noted.

The type and manufacture of valves must be as specified and access to valves must be feasible.

7.15.20 Thermal insulation

The requirements of the contract documents for the application of thermal insulation should be noted: many specifiers require that pipe work be painted prior to the application of insulation to eliminate damage to the primer during installation. Pressure testing should be undertaken before the application of insulation, and on pre-insulated pipe work joints should be left exposed for testing.

Unless using pre-lagged pipe, no insulation should be applied until all pressure testing and inspections have been completed but if circumstances dictate that insulation commences earlier, no joints, either welded or screwed, should be covered until testing has been completed.

Insulation material should be checked for conductivity, quality and wall thickness against the specification. Valves and flanges must be insulated if specified and the correct surface finish applied. The Clerk of Works should check that circuit name, colour code for medium and directional arrows are correctly applied.

Adequate identification banding must be applied in accordance with the BS and contract documents.

7.15.21 Flushing and dosing

Method statements should be obtained from the contractor, paying particular attention to the disposal of flushing and dosing water. The Clerk of Works should check with the A/EA, Environment Agency, local authority and the local water authority/company that the contractor's proposals are acceptable.

Flushing and dosing must be properly carried out and required water conditions obtained. A negative or acidic reading of pH 7.1 with a low bacteria count will help to prevent noise and a build up of oxides. Water samples should be taken and despatched as directed by the A/EA. Disposal of flushing and dosing water should be in accordance with any discharge consents.

7.15.22 Chemical cleaning

If chemical cleaning is required, a method statement should be obtained via the main contractor from a specialist chemical cleaning contractor. Cleaning follows on from the flushing out of the systems to remove loose scale and other deposits in the pre-commissioning stage. The pipe work is thoroughly cleaned of oils, greases, mill scale and other corrosion-forming deposits. Reference should be made to CIBSE Commissioning Code W for procedures of flushing, chemical cleaning and passivating.

7.15.23 Inspection

Many water systems need to be inspected and tested in accordance with the Health and Safety at Work etc. Act 1974 and the Pressure Systems and Transportable Gas Containers Regulations 1989. If the system that is being installed does not have an open vent, the specification should be checked for inspection and testing requirements to meet the regulations (e.g. Competent Person Inspection) and the Project Engineer consulted if these are not specified.

The pressurisation tank should be checked to ensure that it has the correct maximum pressure test stamped on the top or side to meet the design specifications, also the size of vent pipe has to increase as the distance runs, and it should be confirmed that the pressure relief valve spring is for 'high' pressure (this should always be one size larger than entering pipe to vent).

Normally, it will be the responsibility of the contractor to engage the services of a competent person to carry out these duties and the Clerk of Works should refrain from carrying out the duties of a competent person without the written authority of the project manager or client. The contractor should be asked to confirm *in writing* the company that is being employed to carry out these duties; and if the Clerk of Works is not familiar with the name and reputation of the company, it is reasonable to request a list of similar works that they have undertaken recently.

If any cause for concern still lingers, the Project Engineer and A/EA should be consulted. The 'competent person' must witness any large-scale pressure testing of the system, unless he or she has visited site and agreed to specific inspection and testing arrangements.

7.15.24 Pressure testing

A sudden escape of water or air at high test pressures can cause considerable damage and may even cause personal injury. Particular attention must be paid to any temporary anchorages, supports and temporary connections, especially where existing premises are at risk from leakage. Adequate precautions must be taken to prevent the deformation or distortion of expansion devices. When testing steam or high pressure hot water mains installations, the pressure may be particularly excessive, in which case clearing the area and placing danger signs may be in order.

Where pre-insulated external mains are to be pressure tested, the test may be for a 24-hour duration and, further, require monitoring of ambient air temperatures by chart recorder. Reference should be made to the contract documents for further clarification. A check should always be made that pressure is present at the furthest point in pipe runs.

7.15.25 Certificates

Copies of *all* inspection and test certificates, including welder's assessment certificates where necessary, must be available for inclusion in the handover documents.

2C QUALITY CONTROL: REFRIGERATION SYSTEMS

7.15.26 Application

This section covers all refrigeration plant, refrigerant and chilled water pipe work.

7.15.27 Safety and environment

Although mainly aimed at refrigeration plant for air conditioning systems, the safety procedures apply equally to split refrigeration installations for food storage or beer cellars.

Most refrigerant gases are hazardous to health and extensive safety procedures must be followed when charging and discharging refrigerant systems. BS EN 387 contains detailed requirements for their safe design, construction and installation. Many refrigerants are also environmentally destructive and precautions must be taken to prevent release.

Hazard warnings are required to be displayed for semi-sealed systems and gas detectors with audible alarms installed where natural ventilation of the room is not available. The Clerk of Works should ensure, in conjunction with the Health and Safety Co-ordinator, that the Health and Safety Plan and the Health and Safety File at handover contain safety procedures.

7.15.28 Storage of pipe fittings and valves

Pipe work fittings should be sorted, binned or bagged and stored under cover. Valves and cocks, particularly those with flanged faces, should be plugged or plated to prevent the ingress of foreign objects and damage to seats and seals. Expansion devices should be similarly protected and retaining or sizing bars left in place until installed (reference should be made to manufacturer's instructions).

7.15.29 Setting out

External pipe work: excavation for pipe work runs should be dealt with under BS 8000-1. The correct setting out, grading, venting and draining of pipe work and depth relative to building lines, roads, paths and other service runs must be confirmed.

Internal pipe work: where not shown on drawings, the line and grading of pipe runs and points of connection to risers should be agreed. Air locks should be avoided and pipe work must be completely drainable. Particular attention should be paid to pipe gradients. Pipe runs should be co-ordinated for appearance in exposed sections and services routed so as to avoid unwanted heat gain. Any specified noise attenuation must be incorporated and installed correctly.

7.15.30 Installation

Open ends of pipe work left during the progress of work should be closed temporarily with purpose-made metal, plastic or wood plugs, caps or blank metal flanges. Joints should not be made in the thickness of any wall, floor or ceiling and pipe work passing through the building structure should be sleeved in a material similar to the pipe. Any cutting through the building structure not specifically provided for in the drawings requires prior approval. Where there is any doubt the A/EA should be consulted. Sleeves must be fire-stopped where passing through a fire barrier. Only galvanised fittings may be used on galvanised pipe work. Overflows will need a 1.5 degree slope to allow for flow and a fire rating when passing through fire barriers.

Particular attention should be paid to the bracketing of pipe work as required by the contract documents and any requirements for the guiding and anchoring of pipe work for the purpose of expansion should be noted.

7.15.31 Room air conditioners

These may be of the following types:

- single packaged, through wall or window
- ducted from main air conditioning plant

- split type with remote condenser unit
- split type for connection to remote central cooling plant.

They may also include, in certain circumstances, integral air heaters or humidifiers, with a flow and return to retain the altered environment.

7.15.32   Central plant cooling

Plant may be of the direct expansion (DX) type or chilled water coils connected to remote chiller plant. External units need to be positioned to prevent leaves and dirt clogging the exchanger and allow for easy access for maintenance.

7.15.33   Central plant cooling, heating and humidity

This plant would be either delivered complete or assembled on site. This would have a cooling refrigerated heat exchanger, a heating coil, humidifier and filters connected to a circulation fan. This type of unit can recirculate or allow fresh air into rooms at a controlled temperature. Overflows can become blocked and provision should be made to prevent damage to equipment.

7.15.34   Chilled water plant

It is likely that a specialist engineer may be engaged to comment upon the installation of the plant and to oversee and witness the commissioning of the plant. In this event, the Clerk of Works should liaise through the A/EA with the engineer as required.

7.15.35   Refrigerant pipe work

Refrigerant pipe work may be of copper or steel. Pipe work of both materials should be stored clear of the ground in clean and dry conditions with ends sealed until required for installation. Pipe work should be supported as stated in the contract documents and precautions taken to prevent cold bridging. Provisions should also be made to accommodate thermal expansion and contraction.

Copper pipe work: flared and brazed joints are the norm, although compression joints may be utilised for connections to pressure gauges and items of equipment. Brazing should be carried out in accordance with Heating and Ventilating Contractors' Association (HVCA) Codes of Practice and the relevant BS ENs. The Clerk of Works should check that a scheme of approval for welders is instigated and that welders achieve the necessary standard of competency.

Steel pipe work: welded or flanged joints are the norm, although screwed joints may be utilised on connections to equipment. Welding should be carried out by suitably qualified and certified operatives in accordance with HVCA Codes of Practice, BS 2971 and BS 2640.

7.15.36 Chilled water pipe work

Chilled water pipe work will generally be of black mild steel except for open condenser water systems, air washer, drain, vent and overflow pipe work, which will generally be of galvanised steel. Tube ends should be cleaned of scale, paint, oil, etc., and any rusting should be removed and treated with a suitable primer before installation. Galvanised fittings are only to be used on galvanised pipe work.

7.15.37 Thermal insulation

The requirements of the contract documents for the application of thermal insulation should be noted; many specifiers require that pipe work be painted prior to the application of insulation. Pressure testing should be undertaken before the application of insulation, and on pre-insulated pipe work joints should be left exposed for testing.

Chilled water and refrigerant pipe work insulation will normally incorporate a vapour barrier and it is of the utmost importance that this is not prejudiced by penetration with brackets or supports. Where the insulation is to be over-clad with hammer-clad metal, fixings must not be permitted to penetrate the vapour barrier. Adequate identification banding must be applied in accordance with the BS and contract documents.

7.15.38 Flushing and dosing

Method statements should be obtained from the contractor, with particular attention paid to the disposal of flushing and dosing water. The Clerk of Works should check with the A/EA, Environment Agency and the local water authority that the contractor's proposals are acceptable.

Flushing and dosing must be properly carried out and required water conditions must be obtained. Water samples should be taken and despatched as directed by the A/EA.

7.15.39 Catering

Refrigeration for catering purposes requires specific temperature ranges for different products. All equipment provided must be labelled for contents and correct to specification and current legislation. Walk-in freezers should have external ventilation and safety devices to prevent the door from accidentally closing.

Performance testing

Performance testing using simulated loads to the rating detailed in the specification must be monitored during setting up and testing. All test instruments must be calibrated by an accredited agency and have current certificates of calibration.

Method statements should generally be produced by the contractor for charging of any system and for all testing.

3 STATUTORY REQUIREMENTS AND TECHNICAL STANDARDS

(Note: under European legislation, the BS prefix will shortly change to EN.)

Publications to which site reference may be necessary include:

BS 779:1989 *Specification for cast iron boilers for central heating and indirect hot water supply (rated output 44 kW and above).* [Partially replaced by BS EN 303-1:1999 *Heating boilers. Heating boilers with forced draught burners. Terminology, general requirements, testing and marking,* and BS EN 303-4:1999 *Heating boilers. Heating boilers with forced draught burners. Heating boilers with forced draught burners. Special requirements for boilers with forced draught oil burners with outputs up to 70 kW and a maximum operating pressure of 3 bar. Terminology, special requirements, testing and marking.*]

BS 855:1990 *Specification for welded steel boilers for central heating and indirect hot water supply (rated output 44 kW to 3 MW).* [Partially replaced by BS EN 303-1:1999 *Heating boilers. Heating boilers with forced draught burners. Terminology, general requirements, testing and marking,* and BS EN 303-4:1999 *Heating boilers. Heating boilers with forced draught burners. Heating boilers with forced draught burners. Special requirements for boilers with forced draught oil burners with outputs up to 70 kW and a maximum operating pressure of 3 bar. Terminology, special requirements, testing and marking.*]

BS 1113:1999 *Specification for design and manufacture of water-tube steam generating plant (including superheaters, reheaters and steel tube economizers).* [Partially replaced by BS EN 12952 Parts 1–7 and 10 *Water-tube boilers and auxiliary installations.*]

BS 1894:1992 *Specification for design and manufacture of electric boilers of welded construction.* [Partially replaced by BS EN 12953-8:2001 *Shell boilers. Requirements for safeguards against excessive pressure.*]

BS 2640:1982 *Specification for Class II oxy-acetylene welding of carbon steel pipe work for carrying fluids.*

BS 2790: *Specification for design and manufacture of shell boilers of welded construction.* [Partially replaced by BS EN 12953 parts 1–6 and part 8 *Shell boilers.*]

BS 2971:1991: *Specification for Class II arc welding of carbon steel pipe work for carrying fluids.*

PD 5500:2006 *Specification for unfired fusion welded pressure vessels.*

BS EN 378 *Specification for refrigerating systems and heat pumps.*

BS EN 12797:2000 *Brazing. Destructive tests of brazed joints.*

BS EN 12799:2000 *Brazing. Non-destructive examination of brazed joints.*

BS EN 13133:2000 *Brazing. Brazer approval.*

BS EN 13134:2000 *Brazing. Procedure approval.*

BS EN 14324:2004 *Brazing. Guidance on the application of brazed joints.*

BS 8000-1:1989 *Workmanship on building sites. Code of practice for excavation and filling.*

Health and Safety at Work etc. Act 1974. Chapter 37.
Pressure Systems and Transportable Gas Containers Regulations 1989 SI 1989/2169
CIBSE Commissioning Code W, *Water distribution systems.*

HVCA publications
TR3 – *Jointing of copper and its alloys.*
TR5 – *Welding of carbon steel pipework.*
TR6 – *Guide to good practice for site pressure testing of pipework.*

7.16 MECHANICAL VENTILATION AND AIR CONDITIONING SYSTEMS

1 CONTRACT REQUIREMENTS

7.16.1 Duties

Conformity with specification and drawings should be checked. The many variable performance requirements specified for products to be installed require particular vigilance in checking the documentation and certification of deliveries and conformity with appropriate standards, bye-laws and other statutory requirements. Competent personnel are obligatory for some tasks and the Clerk of Works may be asked to confirm their qualifications.

The specification should be checked for product QA schemes applicable and the A/EA's instruction obtained on any duties arising.

This section should be read in conjunction with the Refrigeration section in 7.15.26 et seq.

2 QUALITY CONTROL

7.16.2 Design

These types of systems are always purpose-designed and manufactured with the specialist contractor carrying out detail design to suit the performance requirements stipulated in the particular specification and the building as constructed. Any drawings produced should be submitted to the Project Engineer for approval before manufacture commences and copies of approved drawings provided to the Site Inspector before installation commences.

7.16.3 Delivery, on-site storage and handling

Delivery of material to site should be monitored and checks made that it is stored safely and weather protected.

If the site is not ready to receive ductwork and plant, adequate facilities must be provided for storage. Ductwork should be stored clear of the ground and in such a manner that it is not subject to damage or deformation. Open ends of ductwork and plant should be protected against the ingress of debris during storage until required to be installed: during installation any open ends should be similarly protected. Dampers and terminal devices should be stored away from the working area until required to be installed.

Adequate measures should be in place for the handling of ductwork and plant items from the place of off-loading/storage to the work place, having due regard for bulky and heavy items.

7.16.4 Installation procedures

Ductwork should be checked to ensure that it is of the correct gauge as required by the contract documents. Where sheet metal ductwork is to be cut on site, the Clerk of Works should confirm that the correct tools are being employed, that all raw or rough edges, both externally and internally, are removed and areas where galvanising has been destroyed are cleaned, prepared and painted with zinc-rich paint. Checks should be carried out to ensure that no use is made of plant or ductwork as access platforms by following trades to undertake their own work. Flexible and bendable ducts should be inspected to ensure that they are not deformed and are not bent to a radius outside the manufacturer's tolerances. The installation should be checked against the contractor's working drawings as it proceeds, with any deviations noted.

7.16.5 Air handling plant

Plant items should be examined and checked for compliance with the contract documents and approved manufacturer's drawings. Any deviations are to be noted in the site diary and the contractor and A/EA notified. When installed, the Clerk of Works must check that plant has sufficient space around it for routine maintenance to be undertaken, that pipe work connected to the plant does not prohibit the opening of access doors or the removal of heating or cooling coils, etc., and that air handling unit sections are properly assembled, access doors are properly seated and there are no air leaks on the plant. Safety guards should be fitted to all fan drives.

All heating and cooling coils must be examined for damage and, if necessary, the contractor should comb the fins of the coils.

Where cooling coils are fitted, adequate allowance must be made for the collection and removal of condensate caused by the dehumidification process. Similarly, where humidifiers are installed, provision should be made for the removal of excess water. Room cooler units mounted in ceiling voids and at floor level may present particular problems in this respect.

Adequate bypasses must be fitted to heating/cooling coils for flushing.

7.16.6 Fans

Fans must be properly mounted in accordance with the manufacturer's instructions and adequate provision should be made for vibration isolation, by the use of anti-vibration mounts and flexible duct connections. The shaft and impeller assembly of all fans should be statically and dynamically balanced to BS 7058.

An equipotential bonding vibration loop should be provided across flexible duct connections.

7.16.7 Ductwork

The Clerk of Works should check that ductwork is effectively supported as installation proceeds and that insulation strips are incorporated in supports where required. After it has been levelled and straightened, checks for cleanliness should be witnessed before testing and commissioning commences.

Test procedures and results should be witnessed and calibration of test instruments and certificates of calibration checked. The specified test routine must be followed correctly and any results that are out of specification referred to the Project Engineer. If a high efficiency or a specific filter material has been called for, the Clerk of Works should check that the appropriate filter has been installed and that the airflow direction is correct.

The contract requirements for the leakage testing of ductwork should be checked and witnessed as necessary.

7.16.8 Filter replacement

The requirements of the contract documents for the provision and replacement of filter media before handover should be noted. Generally, all filters should be clean at the time of handover.

7.16.9 Noise attenuators

The ends of attenuators are to be kept covered until required to be installed. Before installation, they should be checked internally for any damage and any non-compliant units rejected.

7.16.10 Instruments

The requirements of the contract documents with regard to the installation of instrumentation, thermometers and pressure gauges, etc., should be noted. These must be installed in accordance with the manufacturer's requirements in areas where they will provide a representative reading.

7.16.11 Thermal insulation

Where thermal insulation is to be applied to ventilation ductwork, the Clerk of Works should pay due regard to vapour barriers and ensure that duct access doors and test points are not obstructed or covered over. Adequate provision must be made at points of support to prevent the piercing of vapour barriers and the compression of the insulation material. Support-piercing fasteners should be examined to ensure they are adequately fixed to the ductwork surface with suitable adhesive. Problems are often encountered with 'self-adhesive stick pin' fasteners because oil residues on ductwork surfaces are not properly cleaned off prior to fixing. Identification triangles and lettering should be applied in accordance with the contract documents.

7.16.12 Dampers

Fire and regulating dampers should be installed with sufficient access for their maintenance and sufficient and adequate access doors must be fitted in the duct-work. Fire dampers should be installed in proper mounting frames within the thickness of firebreak walls or floors. All dampers should be checked for operation in accordance with the CIBSE Commissioning Codes before the plant is put into operation.

The operation of any mechanical interlocks or connections with fire alarm interfaces should be examined during the checking of automatic controls.

7.16.13 Chillers

Where water treatment is required on chilled water systems or humidifiers, the Clerk of Works should check that dosing is to correct levels, that any safety labelling required under the Control of Substances Hazardous to Health Regulations 2002 (COSHH) is in place and that the Health and Safety Plan and File reflect safety procedures. Additionally, for evaporation cooling towers all required water tests and treatment, including Legionella or associated bacteriological tests, must be certified as having been complied with fully.

Some refrigerants are banned under the Montreal Protocol. Others which are permitted may still have a significant environmental impact if they are released into the environment and stringent precautions should be in place. The specification should be checked for any specific requirements but, additionally, the Clerk of Works should be familiar with the refrigerants being proposed/used and relevant statutory requirements or environmental good practice.

7.16.14 Fume and industrial extraction

Generally, the procedures to be followed are those for all ductwork, but there is a need for closer inspection regarding quality standards. Environmental health, chemical safety and biological containment needs mean that any extraction system dealing with the removal from a work station of airborne pollutants must be constructed and installed to a high standard and detailed records kept of the efficiency and performance achieved as these are used as the benchmark for later maintenance inspections of the installation. Therefore, the system must be installed to the design and meet or exceed the specified performance criteria: any short-comings must be reported to the A/EA and Project Engineer.

Diligence and care in the monitoring and recording of an extraction system that may handle a hazardous substance cannot be overstated as harm or injury to a person using the facility at a later date, that is caused by the substance that it is designed to handle may lead to legal action.

If the Clerk of Works is aware of the substance that the system is designed to handle, data on its level of hazard to health can be obtained from HSE Publication EH 40/2005 *Workplace exposure limits.*

3   STATUTORY REQUIREMENTS AND TECHNICAL STANDARDS

(Note: under European legislation, the BS prefix will shortly change to EN.)

Publications to which site reference may be necessary include:

BS 7508:1995 *Mechanical vibration. Methods and criteria for the mechanical balancing of flexible rotors.*
BS ISO 1940-1:2003 *Mechanical vibration. Balance quality requirements for rotors in a constant (rigid) state. Specification and verification of balance tolerances.*
DW/143 *Practical guide to ductwork leakage testing.*
DW/144 *Specification for sheet metal ductwork: low, medium and high pressure/velocity air systems.*
DW/154 *Specification for plastics ductwork.*
DW/172 *Standard for kitchen ventilation systems.*
DW/191 *Guide to good practice – glass fibre ductwork.*
(DW leaflets are available from HVCA Publications: see address in Chapter 15.)
HSE EH 40/2005 *Workplace exposure limits.*

7.17   ELECTRICITY SUPPLY, POWER AND LIGHTING SYSTEMS

1   CONTRACT REQUIREMENTS

The contents of the Quality Control section are divided into subsections as follows:

2A   high voltage – generation, supply and distribution
2B   low voltage – distribution, lighting and power

2C specialist supplies and distribution
2D specialist lighting
2E electric heating.

7.17.1 Duties

Conformity with the specification and drawings should be checked. The many variable performance requirements specified for products to be installed require particular vigilance in checking the documentation and certification of deliveries and conformity with appropriate standards, bye-laws and other statutory requirements. Competent personnel are obligatory for some tasks and the Clerk of Works may be asked to confirm their qualifications.

The specification should be checked for product QA schemes applicable and the A/EA's instruction obtained on any duties arising.

2A QUALITY CONTROL: HIGH VOLTAGE – GENERATION, SUPPLY AND DISTRIBUTION

7.17.2 Definitions

Under BS 7671 *low voltage* is defined as:

- not exceeding 1,000 V AC or 1,500 V DC between conductors
- 600 V AC or 900 V DC from any conductor to earth.

High voltage (HV) is therefore any voltage exceeding the above definition.

7.17.3 Authorised person

Any connection to or alteration of an HV system can only be carried out under the auspices of an 'authorised person' (AP) as defined under the Health and Safety at Work etc. Act 1974, Electricity at Work Regulations 1989 and Electricity Supply Regulations 1988 and by persons skilled and experienced in such work.

Reference should also be made to the preliminaries of the project specification and the Health and Safety Plan for the duties of APs. In association with the A/EA, the Clerk of Works should liaise between all parties to agree any demarcation and division of responsibilities.

No jointing or testing must proceed unless a method statement is available that has been checked and countersigned by a second AP.

7.17.4 Cable routes

In agreement with the Project Engineer, the Clerk of Works should confirm all cable routes and ensure that cable clearances have been gained. Particular attention should be paid to the safety of excavations and the trench bed before cables are laid.

Cables should be laid strictly in accordance with manufacturer's instructions and all jointing carried out as detailed by the jointing system manufacturer. The ambient temperature should not fall outside the manufacturer's specified limits and jointing must be carried out under clean and acceptable conditions, with staging to avoid contamination if the trench is wet or muddy and weather protection available. Cable radii must be in accordance with the manufacturer's recommentations.

7.17.5 Cable identification

For connection into, or alteration of, an existing system the role of the Clerk of Works is strictly limited to witnessing installation procedures and testing. It is the responsibility of the AP to identify cables, carry out all switching, earthing and proving dead. The AP should also be completely satisfied that connections have been made correctly and colour true before cancelling the Permit to Work.

If permanent identification labels are not available it is suggested that suitable temporary labels identifying each switchgear circuit are fitted before the Permit to Work is issued in order to avoid possible confusion and mismatching of cable to switch, as this could have serious operational consequences.

Notwithstanding the above advice, the Clerk of Works is strongly advised to refrain from identifying existing cables or circuits and to leave this to the AP. Full details including times of issue and cancellation of Permits to Work should be recorded. A copy of a Permit to Work, up to and including cancellation, should be obtained.

7.17.6 Transformers

After receipt on site, it should be confirmed that the voltage ratio, vector group and winding type are as specified. The transformer should be installed into a bunded area of sufficient capacity to contain the entire oil/liquid capacity of the unit plus 10 per cent. Cable connections should be monitored for phase correctness and, before energising, a check carried out that test certificates (including earthing) are complete and available; that any breather openings have been uncapped and any breather dryers (if fitted) are in good condition; and that ventilation is adequate.

Where work to old equipment is involved, the Clerk of Works should check that the transformers do not contain any hazardous materials. Legislation now forbids the use of polychlorinated biphenyls (PCBs), and this highly toxic and environmentally destructive chemical must be withdrawn from service. If such a hazard is discovered, all work in the vicinity should be prevented and the A/EA and Project Engineer informed.

7.17.7 Switchgear

Owing to the wide variety of HV switchgear available and the need to select carefully to suit requirements, any changes proposed from the specification must be referred to the Project Engineer; this applies as much to the protection equipment as to the switchgear itself. The manufacturer's detail schedule should be checked carefully; and if the switchgear is to operate in conjunction with any existing switchgear, e.g. cable inter-tripping, confirmation should be obtained on whether protection devices are compatible, although this element should be done by the Project Engineer.

All switchgear must be installed with sufficient room in front for removal and maintenance of component items (circuit breakers with trucks may require 2,000 mm); alternatively, positioning switchgear opposite a door opening of sufficient width may be acceptable.

There are a number of specifications pertinent to electrical switchgear depending on the operating voltages and locations. Advice should be sought from a specialist in this field if there is any doubt *whatsoever* regarding the suitability of switchgear for the intended job or location.

7.17.8 Standby generators

For installation, testing and commissioning purposes, HV generators generally follow the same procedure as low voltage sets with the exception that the increased voltages require additional safety requirements and a fully detailed method statement signed by an AP and countersigned by a second AP. All procedures, and particularly those regarding 'high voltage enclosures', must be strictly observed.

If the generating set is to be built up on site, the Clerk of Works should liaise with B&CE colleagues to check that any concrete foundations are in accordance with the specification before the erection team arrives on site. Additional rotational lineability checks will be needed before running the set to ensure that prime mover and generator are in line and will not put undue stresses on the coupling or create vibration.

The Clerk of Works must check for adequate ventilation and that attenuation is fitted in accordance with the project specification.

7.17.9 Substations

The Clerk of Works should check the builders' work requirements and check that adequate allowance has been made to accommodate the size and number of cables to be installed. In particular, the turning radius of cables should be given adequate consideration, especially at and between switchgear. Bases and plinths should be designed to accommodate cables, incorporating cutouts or ducts as required. Consideration must be given to the containment of oil that may escape from oil-filled transformers in the event of accidental spillage. Where substations are to be surrounded by walls or are in buildings, adequate provision must be made for the escape of personnel in the event of fire or other emergency.

The Clerk of Works must check that adequate allowance has been made in the planning of the substation for the removal and maintenance of equipment, access for cable jointing, withdrawal of circuit breakers and any future reasonable extension of switchgear. In case of any doubts, the A/EA and Health and Safety Co-ordinator should be consulted.

Particular attention should be paid to the requirements for earthing of the substation equipment and the contractor must be made aware of all obligations under the contract.

7.17.10 Testing

All tests required by the specification and the Project Engineer must be witnessed; all salient dates should be recorded in the site diary and a copy of all test results retained.

All HV pressure testing should be witnessed; all test equipment must be correctly calibrated and accompanied by current certificates of calibration. Test areas should be defined by temporary barriers and warning notices posted. Test voltages and duration should be in the job specification or as advised by the Project Engineer in writing. For jointing onto existing cables or equipment, test voltages and/or duration are reduced; further details are provided in the appropriate BS for the type of cable.

7.17.11 Identification labels

All identification labels for switches, circuits, cable boxes, etc., must be of a permanently engraved type with lettering at least 10 mm high and mechanically fixed, i.e. not using adhesives.

7.17.12 Safety and identification signage

Adequate and sufficient identification and danger notices must be fitted to equipment and substations and must be visible from the normal direction of access.

2B QUALITY CONTROL: LOW VOLTAGE – DISTRIBUTION, LIGHTING AND POWER

7.17.13 Definitions

Under BS 7671 *low voltage* is defined as:

- not exceeding 1,000 V AC or 1,500 V DC between conductors
- 600 V AC or 900 V DC from any conductor to earth.

7.17.14 IEE Regulations

All requirements for low and extra low voltage power design installation and control are contained in the IEE Regulations – currently (2001) 16th edition with 2004 amendments now issued as BS 7671 – and are enforceable in law in England and Wales through the Electricity at Work Regulations 1989 for commercial premises and through Building Regulations in Scotland.

The IEE publishes the regulations in book form and also publishes guidance notes for design, installation and testing. The Clerk of Works should request copies of all four publications from the A/EA or Project Engineer.

7.17.15 Design

Although the designer may have detailed the cable sizes and circuit protection devices, it is incumbent upon the electrical contractor to produce working drawings showing the cable routes, builders' work and all other items needed to install the circuits. This should include locations where fire stopping is required. The electrical contractor should also check the calculations in case the actual route or installation method chosen produces a value requiring a different size of conductor or protective device. These drawings should be submitted for approval prior to construction starting.

7.17.16 Revised voltage ratings in Europe

Because of the adoption of revised voltages across Europe, at 230 V single phase, 400 V three phase, it is now possible to install equipment, luminaires or lamps working at the reduced voltage on existing 240/415 V circuits. The Clerk of Works should be aware of the problems that can be created by long-term use of lower rated equipment and endeavour to ensure that 230 and 240 V goods are not inter-mixed. If 230/400 V goods are installed throughout the job the Clerk of Works should endeavour to ensure that the supply transformer is adjusted to produce the correct output by tap changing. Any problems should be referred to the Project Engineer. Although the voltage still falls within UK tolerances, it is advisable to check that distribution boards and operating/maintenance manuals are annotated that the system has been designed to operate at 230/400 V and any lamps and spares used or alterations to the system must be for the correct voltage. Any problems should be raised with the A/EA and the Project Engineer.

7.17.17 Buried services

Any buried services must be handled so as to avoid damage and in accordance with manufacturers' recommendations; also, the correct preparation and backfilling of trenches, together with specified warning tapes, tiles, etc., must be carried out. The cover and segregation of cables and other services must be adequate. In particular, compliance with the cable manufacturer's instructions as to the laying temperatures and minimum bending radii must be monitored. The exact positions of the cables and any joints should be recorded for later checking of the record drawings.

7.17.18 Buried conduits

The Clerk of Works should inspect conduits pre-installed for embedding in slabs or screeds before they are hidden, checking for site damage and corrosion, protection of cut threads and frequency of conduit boxes. Checks should also be made for electrical continuity where the conduit is to be used as a protective conductor (although this is not currently the usual method). The cover to buried conduits must be adequate and fixings must be secure to prevent movement during pouring and vibration of concrete. Particular care should be taken where conduits cross expansion and settlement joints, and the contractor should be consulted on this matter. Open ends of conduits should be temporarily plugged immediately to prevent the ingress of water and solid materials. Before cables are drawn in, conduits must be cleaned internally.

During first fix the Clerk of Works should check that chases are not cut too deep. Building Research Establishment (BRE) guidance notes recommend that they are not greater than one-third of the thickness of the block or brick, but are sufficient to allow the correct amount of plaster cover. Suitable fixings for the wall construction material must be used. The Ministry of Defence (MOD) Specification 034 *Electrical installations* has details for work on Crown Property. The Project Engineer or architect should be consulted for other types of contract.

7.17.19 Cable supports

All cable supports should be inspected for adherence to the specification, ensuring that fixing centres are adequate. In particular the cable manufacturer's recommendations with regard to the support of vertical cables should be noted. The IEE Regulations make no recommendations but Appendix 4 of the *On Site Guide* published by the IEE offers advice on methods of support which satisfy the requirements of Chapter 52 of the Regulations. Particular attention should be paid to ensuring that the contractor allows for the bending radii of cables when planning tray work or cable rack routes. Cut edges of cable trays and cable rack are to be deburred and given a coat of zinc-rich paint. Sharp edges should be fitted with protection for the cables. Coupling bolts should not come into contact with the cables and all cables should be fastened with proprietary ties. Attention should be drawn to the requirements for supplementary bonding. Cable ties for fire alarm cables must be non-flammable, e.g. stainless steel.

7.17.20 Cables

Cable drums must be unloaded carefully and properly stored in accordance with the manufacturer's recommendations. Cables must be handled with care and every effort made to avoid damage to them, to other services and to the building fabric. Particular attention should be paid to the manufacturer's recommendations with regard to bending radii, and the way in which cables are pulled into conduits, ducts, etc., should be monitored. Any damage to cables should be noted in the site diary and reported to the contractor and A/EA. The size of conductors and type of cable should be checked against the design drawings.

7.17.21 Conduits, trunking and ducting

Unless routes are indicated on drawings, their run should be determined with the contractor before work is started and the routes agreed with the Project Engineer on behalf of the A/EA. The Clerk of Works must check that the contractor pays due regard to the pulling in or laying of cables and subsequent access for future maintenance, paying particular attention to clearances between other services. Conduit, trunking and ducting runs should be run parallel with the lines of the building construction. Any sharp edges and burrs are to be removed as the works progress, a zinc-rich paint applied to all cut edges and adequate attention paid to allowing free passage for cables.

The Clerk of Works should check on trunking and ducting that earthing links are present. Reference should be made to the IEE Regulations for cable-carrying capacities of conduits, trunking and ducting. Before any wiring is carried out, all conduits, trunking and ducting runs must be inspected and tested in accordance with the specification. Adequate capacities with regard to category segregation should be confirmed by reference to the IEE Regulations.

7.17.22 Wiring accessories

The Clerk of Works should ascertain that wiring accessories have the required minimum degree of protection, conform with the specification and are mounted at the correct heights.

7.17.23 Connections to appliances and motors

The revision of the term 'stationary equipment' within the IEE Regulations should be noted; a domestic cooker is not regarded as a portable item and does not need a flexible connection. Furthermore, the Clerk of Works should pay attention to vibrating and rotating plant, machinery or motors and check that adequate allowance is made for movement and mechanical stresses.

7.17.24 Luminaires and lamps

The situation with regard to the lamping of luminaires should be clarified prior to handover. It should be established whether the specification or contract allows for the contractor's use of the luminaires as temporary lighting or if the A/EA is required to give permission. The Clerk of Works should check that the implications for relamping prior to handover have been agreed and understood.

Adequate supports must be available for suspended luminaires. In particular, the requirements where luminaires are to be incorporated into a suspended ceiling must be noted.

7.17.25 Emergency lighting

Reference should be made to BS 5266-1, the Project Specification and MOD Specification 034 (if applicable) and any Building Control Officer's requirements for escape lighting, battery cubicles and testing. The provision of mains failure simulation must be monitored.

7.17.26 Identification labels

All labels and distribution schedules must be fitted in accordance with IEE Regulations and the Clerk of Works must check that they reflect the 'as-installed' systems, including any construction stage alterations.

7.17.27 Generators

Low-voltage generators are normally delivered as skid-mounted package units that have been assembled and tested at the supplier's works. Site tests should be conducted as required in the specification and against the specified test load, i.e. a load bank.

If the generator is of a new type or from a new supplier, tests at the manufacturer's works or under controlled environmental conditions may be required. The Project Engineer should decide whether the Clerk of Works will be called upon to witness trials on his or her behalf. The A/EA should be consulted if the location for tests is any distance from site as there may be others better placed to visit the test site.

All fire and safety devices must be installed and working correctly before the set is run. Section 7.19 below (Petrol, Oil and Lubricants [POL]) has further information regarding fuel systems.

Adequate air requirements and noise attenuation must be installed to specification.

7.17.28 Testing

All testing and inspection is to be in accordance with BS 7671, sections 712, 713 *et seq*. All instruments must be in good condition and accompanied by certificates of calibration, even if newly purchased. Forms for results are as published by electrical contractors' associations and based on BS 7671 guidelines.

2C QUALITY CONTROL: SPECIALIST SUPPLIES AND DISTRIBUTION

7.17.29 Computers: 'off standard'

Some computer systems may be powered from sources that contain back-up sources or special electrical filters to eliminate surges, interferences, etc. Frequently, plug-in power points on such circuits are 'off standard' to prevent other appliances being plugged in. The socket outlets and plugs should comply with BS 1363 in all respects except that the shape and/or orientation of one or more pins of the plugs and corresponding socket tubes should be different from those on standard plugs and sockets.

Each socket should be labelled to indicate that it is a dedicated supply intended only for computers or similar equipment. See section 7.17.33 below for information on 'clean earths'.

7.17.30 Filters

Installations and equipment that require a 'clean' power supply free from electrical interference, etc., may be fed from an installation containing filters of various types. These remove interference, harmonics, spikes, etc., within defined ranges and tolerances. If required to be installed, the specified model should be strictly adhered to as variation could result in a failure to meet the requirements. The Project Engineer should be consulted in case of any doubt.

All earths from such filters should be run independently of any building or electrical earths to prevent cross-interference.

7.17.31 'No break' supplies

'No break' supplies and uninterruptible power supplies produce a similar result by various mechanical and electrical processes. Uninterruptible units are normally semi-sealed units converting the AC power to DC and then back to AC electronically with a battery source connected at the DC point in the system. These can range from a small under-table unit for a PC, up to modular units capable of supporting considerable loads (in excess of 1 MW). The battery back-up is normally of the sealed or low maintenance type and capable of supporting the uninterrupted power supply (UPS) at full load for fifteen minutes. A bypass circuit supplies 'mains' for use in case of breakdown.

Mechanical interface uninterruptible units are often specified where electrical separation is desired by the client between the client's equipment and its electrical power source. They can consist of a motor and generator on a common shaft with a heavy flywheel between to maintain momentum until a stand-by generator on the motor supply is able to take the load. Alternatively, a solid state rectifier supplying DC to a motor connected to a generator can be used. In this case, a battery source maintains the DC supply until the stand-by generator is on line.

Depending on the specific site requirement, either multiple units may be provided to allow for maintenance or a bypass switch provided.

All performance tests should be carried out at the specified load rating.

All test instruments should be accompanied by current statements of calibration. Dates should be recorded in the site diary and a copy of all test results retained for site records.

There are many variations on the very basic outlines described above. All installation testing and commissioning should be carried out in accordance with the equipment manufacturers' recommendations and method statements.

The Clerk of Works should be aware during testing that the DC voltages can be higher than usual voltages encountered; also, the large number of capacitors fitted in UPS units are an additional hazard. Sufficient time must be allowed for the charge to dissipate, or they may be discharged using an earthing stick. The Health and Safety Plan and File at handover must contain safety statements/ procedures.

7.17.32 Uninterrupted power supply (UPS)

Any special requirements of the project specification with regard to earthing, venti- lation and cooling of the UPS and battery rooms should be noted. Battery racks must be stable and properly secured. Generally, racks should be of acid-resistant material, which is likely to be plastic-coated steel. Particular attention must be paid to protection of the coating.

There may well be specific requirements with regard to off-site testing and, in the case of larger units, extended on-site testing. If off-site testing is witnessed by others, the Clerk of Works must check that test certificates accompany the equip- ment. The requirements for witnessing should be confirmed with the A/EA, and the Clerk of Works should confirm that test equipment, artificial electric loads and any other necessary facilities will be available at the required time.

7.17.33 Special earthing

For some installations the client may specify a 'clean earth'. This is run as a separate insulated earth (protective conductor) from the connection point of the equipment or earth pin of a dedicated 'off standard' socket outlet, to a point as near as possible to the source of electrical supply (e.g. the main earth bar). All other electrical earths are as standard.

Occasionally, for UPS and power filtration or conditioning equipment a separate insulated 'earth' stud will be fitted. This is a 'dump' point for the unwanted electricity components (e.g. spikes, harmonics and surges removed from the supply) to produce a clean sine wave. This should be treated in the same way as a 'clean earth'. Sometimes the voltage produced from this point can amount to several volts and may need to be routed to a separate earth rod located outside the main earth so that their zones of resistivity do not overlap.

If problems are encountered with sensitive electronic equipment malfunctioning, the earth system should be tested and monitored as the presence of voltages as low as 5 V can cause problems.

7.17.34 Extra low voltage (ELV) supply

The 16th edition of the IEE Regulations makes a subtle difference between safety extra low voltage (SELV) systems and functional extra low voltage (FELV) systems, which relate to the protective measures taken. The Clerk of Works should ascertain which applies to the systems in use. The change to the definition of nominal voltage should also be noted. ELV circuits must be segregated from other types of circuit in accordance with the requirements of the 16th edition of the IEE Regulations.

7.17.35 Builders' work

Builders' work holes, ducts, plinths, etc., for M&E items must be checked to ensure that these are adequate for their duty, correctly located and aligned.

2D QUALITY CONTROL: SPECIALIST LIGHTING

7.17.36 Application

This section covers all lighting other than general lighting and emergency lighting which is dealt with in subsection 2B above.

7.17.37 Design

Specialist lighting is normally designed, either by the equipment manufacturer or a person who specialises in such work, to the specific light output in terms of efficacy, colour rendering and light spread for a specific luminaire and lamp. Any alterations proposed by the contractor must be referred to the designers for their consideration. It should be borne in mind that even a change of lamp can create a change in appearance if the colour rendering is different: a change in manufacturer can sometimes cause unanticipated problems in this respect.

7.17.38 Low voltage display lighting

Low voltage display lighting requires close monitoring during installation as the higher currents required by the lower voltages may need wiring to be of a larger conductor size and/or higher temperature cables. Additionally, if the low voltage luminaries are installed on lighting trunking, the trunking power rating will need to be considerably increased.

For example, while the voltage of a 12 V lamp is 20 times less than normal, the current rating will need to be increased by 20 times for the same power, so a trunking feeding six 50 W 12 V lamps will need to be rated at 25 A!

There are special requirements for neon signs: where the operating voltage of the sign exceeds 'low voltage' an emergency switch must be provided. BS 7671 provides further details.

7.17.39 Luminaires generally

The Clerk of Works should check that luminaires are compliant with the specification and pay particular attention to the colour of lamps. The luminaires must be positioned in accordance with the contract and working drawings, they must co-ordinate and are not to be obscured by other services. The contractor should be encouraged to provide a co-ordinated ceiling plan indicating luminaires and diffusers, etc., to resolve any problems at the outset. If a clash with other services is noted, this should be brought promptly to the attention of the A/EA and M&E Project Engineer.

7.17.40 Aviation ground lighting (AGL)

Aviation ground lighting is a singularly different facility to most other lighting installations. Because of the need to maintain constant levels of brilliancy throughout a circuit, it is frequently arranged as a series circuit with each luminaire being connected to the primary circuit through an isolating transformer. This arrangement means that a relatively low current is used (e.g. 6.6 or 8.33 A) but the number of luminaires used can result in a voltage considerably higher than 1,000 V.

For this reason AGL control centres are restricted areas and should only be entered by persons authorised or accompanied by the 'authorised person'. All cabling used on the luminaire side of the control transformers must be 2,000 V and rated and colour coded for the length of its outer sheath using the colour specified in the design or maintenance manual. All earthing conductors should be bare stranded copper of 6 mm minimum size and buried directly into the ground. The Clerk of Works should check that cabling installed in trenches is not laid as a complete ring to control centres to avoid inducing currents via 'transformer effect' into other circuits.

As the circuits run from the control centre to the nearest luminaire and then interlace, no cable joints should be allowed between luminaires, and only if essential elsewhere. Sufficient slack should be allowed on circuits at each isolating transformer to allow its removal clear of ground level plus at least 300 mm.

Warning: for alterations to an existing system on circuit, the 'authorised person' should identify, cut and prove the circuit to be worked on, securely isolate the circuit and issue a Permit to Work. Colour identification must *not* be relied upon as the use of incorrectly coloured cables for repairs is all too common.

The Clerk of Works should *not* permit work on an existing airfield lighting circuit unless the electrical contractor's 'competent person' is in possession of a Permit to Work. Details of the issue and cancellation of any Permits issued should be recorded in the site diary. Any interruptions to work caused by activities beyond the contractor's control, e.g. flying, military activities, etc., should also be recorded, as should all testing and test results.

The design and spacing of AGL is controlled by the Civil Aviation Authority for civil airports and for military airfields is derived from Stannag 3316: both of these requirements comply with internationally agreed standards. The Clerk of Works must not agree any alterations proposed by the contractor unless authorised by the project AGL design engineer and client. The spacing of luminaires must be confirmed to be correct and, where appropriate, that the setting out dimension is derived correctly.

Some items of an AGL installation, e.g. PAPI (precision approach path installation) and IRFIS (inertial referenced flight inspection system), are positioned precisely and are used by aircraft in conjunction with other navigation aids. The setting out and positioning of such equipment is best done by experienced surveyors.

Generally, further installation information on AGL can be found in MOD Specification 034. If any difficulty arises or if advice on AGL installations is required, the A/EA should be requested to organise specialist help.

7.17.41 The industrial environment

For further reading, reference should be made to the CIBSE Lighting Guide LG1.

Luminaires in hazardous areas should be checked to ensure that the correct ingress protection (IP) rating and electrical classification have been applied (e.g. 'Buxton' rating for flameproof fittings). The Clerk of Works should ensure that any flameproof requirements for luminaires apply to associated wiring installations.

Where high bay luminaires are specified, due consideration must be given to relamping and maintenance. The Clerk of Works should check that the Health and Safety Plan and Health and Safety File at handover contain safe procedures.

7.17.42 Hospitals and health care buildings

For further reading, reference should be made to the CIBSE Lighting Guide LG2.

Luminaires in hazardous areas should be checked to ensure that the correct IP rating and electrical classification have been applied.

Many areas will have lighting controlled by dimmer switches, and the Clerk of Works should ensure that these are correctly selected and operate satisfactorily. Operating luminaires may incorporate pattern selection, and a check should be made that this function operates correctly and the luminaire focuses as required. Colour rendering may be particularly important in some areas. Special switching arrangements will apply in radiological areas, X-ray darkrooms, etc.

7.17.43 Areas for visual display terminals

For further reading, reference should be made to the CIBSE Lighting Guide LG3.

Lighting will have been designed to eliminate high luminance from the room or to ensure that any high luminances that are present are not reflected towards the operator. This may be achieved by downlighters, fixed or freestanding uplighters or a combination of these.

7.17.44 Sports lighting

For further reading, reference should be made to the CIBSE Lighting Guide LG4.

Luminaires may be difficult to reach, especially with mounting heights of up to 10 m. The Clerk of Works should check that adequate consideration has been given to the maintenance and relamping of luminaires with due regard to the Health and Safety at Work etc. Act 1974 and the CDM Regulations. The Health and Safety Plan and Health and Safety File at handover must contain safe procedures.

7.17.45 The visual environment in lecture, teaching and conference rooms

For further reading, reference should be made to the CIBSE Lighting Guide LG5.

Lighting schemes may incorporate luminaires for general display and presentation lighting, and may be under the control of sophisticated lighting consoles. Because there may be a greater than normal number of luminaires and other services (e.g. ventilation ductwork fitted in suspended ceilings), co-ordination of services is of the utmost importance.

Because of their location in large auditoria and over-raked seating, luminaires may be difficult to reach. The Clerk of Works must check that adequate consideration has been given to the maintenance and relamping of luminaires with due regard to the Health and Safety at Work etc. Act 1974 and the CDM Regulations. The Health and Safety Plan and Health and Safety File at handover must contain safe procedures.

7.17.46 The outdoor environment

For further reading, reference should be made to the CIBSE Lighting Guide LG6.

Lighting will not only be provided for the illuminance of walkways and roads but also for the display of architectural features or sculptures. Particular attention should be paid to the siting of luminaires, to the IP and electrical classification of fittings and electrical safety.

Because of mounting heights and locations, luminaires may be difficult to reach. The Clerk of Works should check that adequate consideration has been given to the maintenance and relamping of luminaires with due regard to the Health and Safety at Work etc. Act 1974 and the CDM Regulations. The Health and Safety Plan and Health and Safety File at handover must contain safe procedures.

2E QUALITY CONTROL: ELECTRIC HEATING

7.17.47 General

All appliances must be examined to check that they comply with the IEE Regulations. In particular, attention must be paid to appliances which may be installed in hazardous areas. The Clerk of Works should check that individual heaters can be isolated for safety and maintenance and that cables are suitably heat resistant where required.

7.17.48 Radial circuits

As no diversity is allowed under BS 7671 for heating installations permanently connected into an electrical circuit (Regulation 311-01 and 433), heating appliances that are heavily used should be wired as radial circuits to avoid overloading ring circuits (e.g. cookers, all types of water heater, hand dryers, storage heaters and all types of space heating not designed for occasional use only).

7.17.49 Under-floor heating

Under-floor heating installations use a higher resistance cable than standard cabling, usually with a double sheath single core unarmoured cable. Care should be taken during installation to ensure that the outer sheath is undamaged and is located correctly, and that later operations do not cause damage (see BS 7671, Regulations 522-06-04, 544-06 and 554-07).

Note: where normal electrical circuits pass through a heated floor they must have the appropriate ambient temperature correction factor applied.

For maximum conductor temperatures for floor warming cables see table 55C of BS 7671.

7.17.50 Water heaters: general

The requirements of Regulations 554-03, 554-04 and 554-05 of BS 7671 should be noted. The Clerk of Works should identify aggressive water conditions and check that heater elements are selected to provide adequate resistance, referring to Regulation

512-06 and Section 522 of BS 7671. Checks must also be carried out to confirm that appliances are suitably selected and installed in accordance with the manufacturer's instructions.

7.17.51 Instantaneous water heaters

Reference should be made to BS 7671, Regulation 554-05.

Instantaneous water heaters are unsuitable for use on installations where a water softener of the salt regenerative type is used because the increased conductivity of the water is likely to lead to excessive earth leakage currents from the usually uninsulated element. It is essential that all parts of this type of water heater are solidly connected to the metal water supply pipe, which in turn is solidly earthed independently of the circuit protective conductor. If the neutral supply to a heater with an uninsulated element is lost, current from the phase will return via the water and the earthed metal. Therefore, a careful check is necessary to ensure that there is no fuse, circuit breaker or non-linked switch in the neutral conductor.

7.17.52 Water heaters – non-vented

The use of unvented water heaters for multi-point purposes requires special connections to ensure that a safe working pressure is not exceeded. Reference should be made to BS EN 60335.

7.17.53 Electrode boilers and water heaters

Two or three electrodes are immersed in the water and a single-phase or three-phase supply is connected to them. There is no element and the water is heated directly by the current flowing between the electrodes. The electrical requirements are:

- for three-phase – a circuit breaker which opens all three phases and is equipped with overloads on all phases: bonding conductors equal to the size of the supply conductors (or larger) and connecting the heater shell to the armouring on sheath of the supply cable and the heater shell to the neutral conductor
- for single-phase – double pole linked circuit breakers with overload protection on phase and neutral. Bonding conductors to be at least the size of the conductors between the shell of the heater to the sheath, armour or earth of the supply cable, and the shell of the heater to the neutral. The supply must be one which has an earthed neutral
- for three-phase heaters fed from extra low voltages, special conditions apply. Reference should be made to BS 7671 for information.

7.17.54 Room heaters

The requirements of Chapter 42 of the IEE Regulations should be noted. The Clerk of Works should check that heaters comply with the relevant part and section of

BS EN 60335. Where the heater is to be installed in a bathroom, reference should be made to Regulation 543-07-01 and Section 601 of BS 7671. Installation of appliances should be in accordance with the manufacturer's instructions.

7.17.55 Cookers

The control switch or cooker unit should be placed within 2 m of the appliance. Where there are two stationary cooking appliances in one room in household premises, one switch may be used to control both appliances provided that neither appliance is more than 2 m from the switch.

7.17.56 Bathroom appliances

Means of isolation for heaters in bathrooms, e.g. instantaneous shower heaters, must be sited out of reach except by pull cord and of specific type (Regulation 544-05, 601-01 to 601-12). Shaver sockets must be fed from a double-wound transformer to BS EN 61558-2-5, protected to IP2X and protected by an RCD with an operating current no greater than 30 mA. Extract fans should have a three-pole isolator located outside the area.

7.17.57 Heater batteries

The requirements of the contract documents should be checked with regard to the switching, control and construction of heater batteries. All wiring must be compliant with Section 522 of the IEE Regulations and the Clerk of Works should check that any thermal cutouts required by the contract documents are provided.

3 STATUTORY REQUIREMENTS AND TECHNICAL STANDARDS

(Note: under European legislation, the BS prefix will shortly change to EN.)

Publications to which site reference may be necessary include:

Health and Safety at Work etc. Act 1974. Chapter 37.
Electricity at Work Regulations 1989. SI 1989/635.
Electricity Supply Regulations 1988. SI 1988/1057.
MOD Specification 034 *Electrical installations.*

HSE publications
GS 6 Avoidance of danger from overhead electrical lines.
GS 38 Electrical test equipment for use by electrician.
ESI (Electrical Supply Industry) Standards.
ESI 09-9 Waveconal cable.
IEC (International Electrical Commission) 502 – XLPE cables.

Institute of Electrical Engineers publications
Guidance Notes to the IEE Regulations.
On Site Guide to the 16th Edition Wiring Regulations
(The IEE Wiring Regulations 16th Edition: BS 7671).

British Standards Institute
BS 1363 *13 A plugs, socket-outlets and adaptors* (various parts and dates).
BS 5467:1997 *Electric cables. Thermosetting insulated, armoured cables for voltages of 600/1000 V and 1900/3300 V.*
BS 6346:1997 *Electric cables. PVC insulated, armoured cables for voltages of 600/1000 V and 1900/3300 V.*
BS 6480:1988 *Specification for impregnated paper-insulated lead or lead alloy sheathed electric cables of rated voltages up to and including 33000 V.*
BS EN 60076 *Power transformers* (Parts 1–10 various dates).
BS EN 61558-2-5 *Safety of power transformers, power supply units and similar. Particular requirements for shaver transformers and shaver supply units.*

Electrical switchgear
BS EN 60694:1997 *Common specifications for high-voltage switchgear and controlgear standards.* (AMD 10123) (AMD 13162) (AMD 13725) (Also known as IEC 60694:1996.)
BS EN 60947-2:2003 *Low-voltage switchgear and controlgear. Circuit-breakers.*
BS EN 60947-3:1999 *Specification for low-voltage switchgear and controlgear. Switches, disconnectors, switch-disconnectors and fuse-combination units.* (AMD Corrigendum 10766) (AMD 13240)
BS EN 60947-4:2001 *Specification for low-voltage switchgear and controlgear. Contactors and motor-starters.*
BS EN 60947-5:2004 *Specification for low-voltage switchgear and controlgear. Control/circuit devices and switching elements. Electromechanical control circuit devices.* (AMD 15484)
BS EN 60439-3:1991 *Low-voltage switchgear and controlgear assemblies. Particular requirements for low-voltage switchgear and controlgear assemblies intended to be installed in places where unskilled persons have access to their use – distribution boards.* (AMD 8302) (AMD 13466)
BS 7657:1993 *Specification for fuses (cut-outs), ancillary terminal blocks and interconnecting units up to 100 A rating, for power supplies to buildings.* (AMD 9504)
BS EN 60298:1996 *A.C. metal-enclosed switchgear and controlgear for rated voltages above 1 kV and up to and including 52 kV.* (AMD 10215) (AMD 13079) (Superseded but remains current – as at May 2006.)
BS EN 60439-1:1999 *Low-voltage switchgear and controlgear assemblies. Type-tested and partially tested assemblies.* (AMD 15026) (AMD Corrigendum 15498) (AMD Corrigendum 16033)

BS EN 62271-100:2001 *High-voltage switchgear and controlgear. High-voltage alternating-current circuit-breakers*. (AMD 14682)

Low voltage

BS 5266-1:2005 *Emergency lighting. Code of practice for the emergency lighting of premises*.

BS 5486:1989 *Low-voltage switchgear and controlgear assemblies*.

BS 7671:2001 *Requirements for electrical installations*. (The IEE Wiring Regulations 16th Edition.)

BS EN 60439 *Specification for low-voltage switchgear and controlgear assemblies*. (Various parts and dates.)

Lighting

As above, plus CIBSE Lighting Guides LG1 to LG12.

Electric heating

BS 3456 *Specification for safety of household and similar electrical appliances*. (Various parts and dates.)

BS EN 60335 *Specification for safety of household and similar electrical appliances*. (Various parts and dates.)

7.18 COMMUNICATIONS, SECURITY, FIRE AND CONTROL SYSTEMS

The Quality Control section is divided into the following subsections:

2A communications systems
2B security systems
2C protection systems: fire and lightning protection
2D control systems: general
2E building management systems (BMS).

1 CONTRACT REQUIREMENTS

7.18.1 Duties

Conformity with specification and drawings should be checked. The many variable performance requirements specified for products to be installed require particular vigilance in checking the documentation and certification of deliveries and conformity with appropriate standards, bye-laws and other statutory requirements. Competent personnel are obligatory for some tasks and the Clerk of Works may be asked to confirm their qualifications.

The specification should be checked for product QA schemes applicable and the A/EA's instruction obtained on any duties arising.

The following sections contain contractual requirements specific to this subject.

2A QUALITY CONTROL: COMMUNICATIONS SYSTEMS

7.18.2 Design and standards

Most communications systems are designed and installed by specialist companies to suit a performance specification and user requirements. Although individual components of equipment may be manufactured to various British Standards, the systems themselves are not covered in detail by any BS. BS 6701 is a code of practice for installation of apparatus intended for connection to certain telecommunication systems.

7.18.3 Government procurement

Some government departments (e.g. the Army and the RAF) have their own specifications for communications equipment and its enclosures. In fact, for many sites the contract is split between installation of a cable environment system and later installation of cables and devices by a specialist company; normally employed directly by the client after completion and handover of the construction project.

7.18.4 British Telecom, the Army and the RAF

British Telecom (BT), the Army and the RAF have their own specifications for the construction of external pit and duct systems and further specifications for internal distribution.

For BT systems they also supply free issue for installation by the contractor of duct materials, draw-pit frames and covers and building entry seals: the local BT external installation officer may be contacted via BT general enquiries freephone number (refer to local directory).

Similar specifications and information should be obtained from alternative communications contractors and the A/EA or Project Engineer.

7.18.5 Cable installation

The Clerk of Works should ensure that the company contracted is the one to whom the client has let the communications contract.

Within the building, communications cabling must be routed away from mains electrical cabling to avoid interference problems. Alternatively, cabling can be screened. Under BS 7671, communications cabling must not be run in the same conduit or trunking compartment as electrical cable (see IEE Regulations Part 2; 331-01, 512-05 and 528-01).

Where fibre optic cabling is to be used, particular attention must be paid to bending radii and handling. Many types of fibre optic cabling are fragile and *must not* be drawn through conduit, etc., a process that will lead to breaks in the cabling. Instead, most types of fibre optic cabling must be carefully laid in.

All cable routes should have either cables or an approved draw cord (not for fibre optics) left in them at handover.

7.18.6 Public address

The planning and installation of sound systems is detailed in BS 6259.

For installation on airfields and some other MOD establishments, there is a requirement for prioritised override operation of the system. The requirements should be detailed in the project specification. As prioritising is achieved by terminal links, it is essential during commissioning that the Clerk of Works checks that priorities are correct. There may also be sound tone generators for various warnings. The locations that can initiate the tones and areas to which they are broadcast will be in the specification or advised by the client.

If sound alarms are incorporated in other equipment, the Clerk of Works must establish that there is no conflict with site alarm tones: equipment alarms must be altered if necessary. The A/EA must be informed of any problems and instructions sought.

If used for voice alarm, requirements may need to be covered by specification for Category 3 circuits, as defined by the IEE Regulations.

7.18.7 Audio visual

Audio visual (AV) systems are advancing rapidly. New digital systems give a far higher picture quality and frequently use a mixture of fibre-optic and low-voltage cable connection systems. It is difficult to give definitive guidance due to the rapid evolution, but the best point of guidance is the quality of the final sound or picture; any poor or loose connections give rise to appreciable loss of quality. If the quality is not as good as expected from an incoming source, a portable signal generator should be connected as near as possible to the incoming point and used to check the internal system. See also subsection 2B below (Security systems).

7.18.8 Data

Data transmission within a building is normally done within a computer local area network (LAN) or similar system with one control station and modem or fixed line links between buildings and networks. The variations in style, type and quality of networks are considerable.

All such systems are designed and installed by specialists. Changes to the system once the original design has been agreed should be supported by confirmation that the design concept and method of operation is unaffected. Technology is evolving faster than specifications and designs.

Apart from the need to ensure that the electrical supply is adequate, reliable and backed up by UPS, the design specification is the only recommended guiding document to the standards required. See also subsection 2E below (Building management systems).

2B   SECURITY SYSTEMS

7.18.9   General

Building and property security can include a wide range of devices, including intruder detection systems (IDS), closed circuit television (CCTV) and access control/entry systems.

The appropriate trade association is the National Security Inspectorate which publishes codes of practice relevant to sections of the trade. The Department of Trade and Industry (DTI) also publishes standards related to some aspects of the industry, and some British Standards apply.

7.18.10   Specialist installers

For certain types of installation within some government buildings, a specialised security group must be employed. This is normally stipulated at design stage and only the specified company must be used for reasons of departmental or even national security.

Usually, the electrical subcontractor will be expected to install the system containment (e.g. conduits, boxes, etc.) and the specialist will install and commission the sensing and activating devices at a later stage. Sometimes the system wiring will be by the specialist, or it can be part of the general electrical installation but to the specialist's specification. In all cases, the Clerk of Works should check the contract specifications and ensure that the demarcation between responsibilities is clear and unambiguous.

Subject to the A/EA's agreement, it is suggested that a site visit by the specialist is arranged to take place at a suitable stage of the works to confirm positions of sensors, etc., before installation of conduits commences.

Segregation of electrical circuits should be undertaken in accordance with the IEE Regulations: see also subsection 2A above (Communications systems).

7.18.11   Intruder detection systems

Cabling will, in all likelihood, be run in secure conduits. Conduit runs should be co-ordinated with other services to avoid clashes. The Clerk of Works must agree the method of fitting detectors in doors and terminating cabling thereto and agree location of motion sensors as instructed by the A/EA.

The coverage of any infrared detectors must be checked to ensure that they cover the required areas and that any blind spots do not compromise the ability of the system to detect intruders.

7.18.12 Closed circuit television

Cameras must be carefully positioned to ensure that only the client's property is in vision: coverage of parts of the public highway is acceptable but not adjoining and adjacent private property.

The location and mounting positions of cameras should be agreed to give the best field of view, as instructed by the A/EA. Care should be taken with panning cameras to limit their travel to avoid both obstructions and views of other property. A mechanical restrictor may need to be fitted. For pole-mounted cameras, it is important to bear in mind that access for maintenance must be practical (e.g. that access to water-wash reservoirs is possible without recourse to specialist access equipment, that folding columns do not obstruct access for emergency or other vehicles when lowered, etc.). The Health and Safety Plan should be consulted and the Health and Safety File at handover must contain appropriate maintenance methods.

Special requirements apply to Home Office installations: the particular specification must be consulted.

7.18.13 Entry systems

Card and cipher access, electronic locking and motorised doors are among the systems that may be encountered. The Clerk of Works should attend, if required by the A/EA, any off-site inspection and witnessing at the manufacturer's works and agree the method of terminating cabling to electronic door locks, paying attention to the integrity of the security of the installation.

Access control systems that require the use of a keypad or insertion of a card should be positioned so that use by disabled persons is feasible without undue effort or stress. Alternatively, an assistance call point may be acceptable if the work is an adaptation of an existing building. However, the Disability Discrimination Act 1995, which has been applied progressively since 1999, will mean that no person with a disability should encounter inferior conditions, facilities or services.

7.18.14 Training

Training should ideally take place at the manufacturer's premises in advance of the testing and commissioning on site. The Clerk of Works should liaise between the client department and the contractor as requested by the A/EA.

7.18.15 Testing and commissioning

The Clerk of Works should liaise with the client department responsible for the operation of the security systems and invite their attendance during testing and commissioning.

2C PROTECTION SYSTEMS: FIRE AND LIGHTNING PROTECTION

7.18.16 General

This section covers the installation of lightning protection and fire alarm and detection systems.

7.18.17 Fire alarm cabling

Fire alarm cabling should be installed in accordance with the IEE Regulations, having due regard for segregation of circuits: reference should be made to Section 528 of the IEE Regulations. It is likely, for the majority of commercial and industrial applications, that mineral insulated copper clad (MICC) cabling will be used. Where the MICC cabling has an outer covering, the Clerk of Works should check that the copper sheath is protected by wrapping with plastic adhesive tape at terminations. Reference should also be made to BS 5839 Part 1.

7.18.18 Lightning protection

For general provisions, reference should be made to BS 6651, which covers all aspects of design, installation testing and maintenance.

During installation, the Clerk of Works should check that all tapes are routed in such a manner that 're-entrant loops' are avoided (see paragraph 15.8 and figure 22 of BS 6651). Checks should be made that all fixings are correctly spaced (see table 1 of BS 6651), and it should be noted that the spacing varies according to the length of the run and whether it is horizontal or vertical. If thermal fixing (e.g. 'cad welding', a form of thermit welding) is to be used to join tapes, then all 'hot working' procedures in force on the site must be obeyed.

MOD Specification 034 contains further details of materials and manufacture.

Where reinforcing bars are to be used as down conductors, or where other connection is specified to the building reinforcement, the Clerk of Works should liaise with the B&CE Site Inspector to ensure that this is incorporated during building construction. Tests of such connections are to be made before casting the structure and test certificates retained for inclusion in the Health and Safety File. Where dissimilar metals are used, adequate precautions should be taken to ensure that corrosion does not occur.

Exposed down conductors should be routed to avoid sharp right-angle bends and overhangs.

7.18.19 Electromagnetic pulse protection (EMPP)

EMPP is only installed in rooms requiring this very specialised form of screening. Installation and proving can only be carried out by one or two companies.

The room is completely encased in a metal sheath with all components lap covered, and door openings also contain metal components within the seal to ensure total shielding. All incoming services must be routed through filters (for electrical circuits) or special glands (for non-electrical communications). Ventilation grilles and ductwork also have special design considerations. Within the enclosed area, all equipment and fixings are secured so that the integrity of the outer sheath is not impaired.

Testing is normally carried out by the installation contractor but must be to the client's performance specification written for that particular project.

7.18.20 Testing and commissioning

Lightning protection systems should be tested in accordance with BS 6651.

Fire alarm testing and commissioning should be undertaken in accordance with the project specification. It is likely that the Building Control Officer will require to be in attendance for the final testing and commissioning, but it is advisable that the M&E Site Inspector witnesses testing before that stage.

2D CONTROL SYSTEMS: GENERAL

7.18.21 General

Control systems for heating, hot water, air conditioning and ventilation can range from the simple to the highly sophisticated. MOD Specification 036 contains outline information on the sensing points for various types of controller. The project specification will outline the type of control required, or a control philosophy and the manufacturer whose equipment was used as a basis for the design specification.

For gas-fired systems reference should be made to 7.16 above for technical requirements and standards.

Approved working drawings should be received on site in good time for them to be studied before installation commences.

7.18.22 Conduit trunking and trays

The Clerk of Works should ensure that routes are co-ordinated with other building services, paying particular attention to segregation.

7.18.23 Cable installation

Cable installation should be undertaken in accordance with MOD Specification 034 and the IEE Regulations. Particular attention should be paid to cable segregation and protection and handling if fibre optic cabling is used (see subsection 2A above). Flexible cables to detectors and motors, etc., should be kept as short as possible. Cable ends should be permanently identified.

7.18.24 Detectors

Particular attention should be paid to the location of detectors to check that they are located in representative positions and in accordance with the manufacturer's instructions.

7.18.25 Control cubicles and panels

The Clerk of Works should monitor that all cubicles and panels are constructed to the degree of protection required by the contract documents and BS EN 60947-1:2004 and check that all internal wiring is colour coded and bunched and run on trays or within trunking. Cable ends should be permanently identified. Where the contract drawings are only indicative, the location of panels should be agreed with the Project Engineer and contractor. Off-site inspection may be required: the Clerk of Works should check with the A/EA for attendance required.

7.18.26 Commissioning and performance testing

Before testing of the control system is commenced the Clerk of Works must ensure that all plant under its control is fully commissioned. With the A/EA's agreement, the persons responsible for the maintenance of the facility after handover should be invited to attend.

During inspection and commissioning, it is essential that the proving of all operational and safety devices is witnessed. It should be noted that for some items, such as fusible links, actual operation is not practicable but shorting out of electrical devices or operation of mechanical release buttons will prove the operational capability of the system.

High temperature cut-outs must always be checked on domestic hot water services.

Before commissioning, the Clerk of Works should check the operating temperature required as indicated for domestic hot water and endeavour to obtain a temperature outside the zone in which Legionella is considered to be a higher risk (i.e. outside the zone 20–46 °C). If it is higher than 60 °C, then the provision of warning notices (risk of scalding) should be considered at all outlets. Any doubts as to appropriate temperature should be referred to the Project Engineer.

Requirements for interfaces with other elements, e.g. lighting, fire/smoke alarms, security systems, etc., should be checked.

7.18.27 Training

The requirements of the contract documents for the training of client staff should be checked. Through the A/EA, the Clerk of Works should liaise as necessary with the client and contractor. It may be preferable for training to be undertaken at the manufacturer's works prior to commissioning and performance testing being carried out.

2E BUILDING MANAGEMENT SYSTEMS (BMS)

7.18.28 General

Building or energy management systems may be stand-alone for each individual building or may be networked to a central location or via modem to a remote location. They may incorporate a computer at the 'head end' where interrogation and adjustment of the system can be undertaken and a local keypad control at each outstation or require an interrogative computer to be plugged in at the outstation.

7.18.29 Technological change

Building management systems are designed, installed and commissioned by specialist companies. Developments and progress in computers and microchip technology mean that changes in equipment offered by manufacturers often render the job specification outdated before the project has reached the installation stage.

Conversely, new technology is often marketed before it has been fully tested and proved in practice and to be offered the 'first installation of the new range' can bring with it totally unforeseen problems.

7.18.30 Cable installation

Cable installation should be undertaken in accordance with MOD Specification 034 or contract specification and the IEE Regulations. Particular attention should be paid to cable segregation and protection and handling if fibre optic cabling is used (see subsection 2A above).

The Clerk of Works should liaise with the main contractor/mechanical subcontractors for supply connection to motorised valves, dampers and equipment.

7.18.31 Commissioning and performance testing

Before commencing testing of the BMS, the Clerk of Works must check that all plant under its control is fully commissioned and monitor that sufficient personnel are in attendance to witness both the reactions at the head end and also at the plant being controlled. With the A/EA's agreement, the persons responsible for the maintenance of the facility after handover should be invited to attend.

Often, the sheer size of a BMS installation and the number of sensor or control points will make it very difficult to carry out a 100 per cent check of the accuracy and effectiveness of them all. A 10 per cent sampling check spread across the project will normally be sufficient to provide a reasonable statistical check on the quality and accuracy. However, the actual sampling rate and acceptable pass/fail rate must be agreed with the Project Engineer and A/EA. Should the check produce unacceptable results, the A/EA and Project Engineer must be informed immediately and further instructions sought. It is suggested that, either:

- the contractor is asked to recheck the system and provide evidence and then the 10 per cent check is repeated, or
- the percentage-sampling rate is increased.

The final check of working capability is for the system to run for a predetermined period (say 14 days) without a software or system failure. The system needs to be fully operational and all the equipment it is managing must be working normally for the reliability trial to be successful.

7.18.32 Training

The requirements of the contract documents for the training of client staff should be noted. Through the A/EA the Clerk of Works should liaise as necessary with the client and contractor. It may be preferable for training to be undertaken at the manufacturer's works prior to commissioning and performance testing being carried out.

3 STATUTORY REQUIREMENTS AND TECHNICAL STANDARDS

(Note: under European legislation, the BS prefix will shortly change to EN.)

Publications to which site reference may be necessary include:

General
IEE Regulations (16th edition) (BS 7671).
BS 6259:1997 *Code of practice for the design, planning, installation, testing and maintenance of sound systems.*
BS 6701:2004 *Telecommunications equipment and telecommunications cabling. Specification for installation, operation and maintenance.*
MOD Specification 034 *Electrical installations.*

Security systems
National Security Inspectorate:
NACP20 *Code of practice for planning, installation and maintenance of closed circuit television systems.*
NCP 30 *Code of practice – access control code of practice for planning, installation and maintenance.*

BS 4737 *Intruder alarm systems*. (Parts 1–5, various dates.)
BS EN 50131-1:1997 *Alarm systems. Intrusion systems. General requirements.*

Fire and lightning protection
As above, plus:
BS 4422:2005 *Fire. Vocabulary.*
BS 5839 *Fire detection and alarm systems for buildings*. (Parts 1–9 various dates).
BS 6651:1999 *Code of practice for protection of structures against lightning.*

Controls, etc.
BS 6346:1997 *Electric cables. PVC insulated, armoured cables for voltages of 600/1000 V and 1900/3300 V.*
BS EN 60730 *Specification for automatic electrical controls for household and similar use*. (Various parts and dates.)
BS EN 60947-1:2004 *Specification for low-voltage switchgear and controlgear. General rules.*
BS EN 61558-1:1998 *Safety of power transformers, power supply units and similar. General requirements and tests.*
BS EN 61558-2.23:2001 *Safety of power transformers, power supply units and similar. Particular requirements for transformers for construction sites.*
MOD Specification 036 *Heating, hot and cold water, steam and gas installations for buildings.*

Building management systems controls
There are British Standards that deal with the many elements used within any one BMS. Reference should be made to the relevant standards dependent upon the range of elements used within any specific system, e.g. heating, electrical, air conditioning, refrigeration, etc.

7.19 TRANSPORT SYSTEMS: LIFTS, HOISTS, CRANES AND PETROLEUM, OIL AND LUBRICANT (POL) INSTALLATIONS

1 CONTRACT REQUIREMENTS

7.19.1 Duties

Conformity with the specification and drawings should be checked. The many variable performance requirements specified for products to be installed require particular vigilance in checking the documentation and certification of deliveries and conformity with appropriate standards, bye-laws and other statutory requirements. Competent personnel are obligatory for some tasks and the Clerk of Works may be asked to confirm their qualifications.

The specification should be checked for product QA schemes applicable and the A/EA's instruction obtained on any duties arising.

Sections below contain contractual requirements specific to this subject.

Installation of such equipment is normally carried out by specialists or manufacturers. The requirements of the contract documentation should be noted, in particular with reference to the attendance of specialists, 'competent persons' and insurers. The Clerk of Works should liaise with the A/EA in good time when the presence of these specialists will be required.

2A QUALITY CONTROL: LIFTING EQUIPMENT

7.19.2 Lifts

For lifts and other enclosed shaft machines, it is essential that the main structure is within tolerance before installation commences. Accuracy should be checked by the main contractor against the dimensions given in the specialist contractor's working drawings. If the shaft is outside specification, the A/EA should be informed immediately.

With the assistance of the B&CE Site Inspector, the preparation for the builders' work associated with the lift installation should be checked, with particular attention paid to verticality and alignment, landings, bases, plinths, channels and any cast-in items. A check should be made that no services installation or access route, other than those provided for the lift equipment and personnel, share or pass through the machine room or lift well.

Provision must be made from the lift well for the ventilation, directly or by ducts, of smoke to the open air in the event of a fire. The lift motor room must be adequately ventilated. Provision must be made for the installation of a tubular heater to prevent frost attack of grease and oils.

Where the lift is to serve as a fireman's lift, the Clerk of Works should liaise, through the A/EA, with the Building Control Officer, whose duty it is to inspect the operation of the installation. Requirements in contract documents for automatic control for fire operation, e.g. all cars returning to the ground floor, should be checked, as should any intercom/alarm provision for occupants.

Maintenance tools must be provided and mounted by the contractor as required by the contract documents (in the motor room if possible).

7.19.3 Safety in lift shafts or other openings

During construction work and installation of the equipment, the Clerk of Works should check that all openings have adequate physical barriers to prevent personnel or equipment falling into the shaft. During installation, this may mean a rigid fence or screen around openings to exclude all trades other than those directly involved in the installation. The Health and Safety Plan should be consulted for safe working procedures and the A/EA and the Health and Safety Co-ordinator informed immediately of any concerns.

Adequate ladder access must be provided to the lift well. In the case of hydraulic lifts, the Clerk of Works should check that a purpose-made prop has been provided to stop creep during maintenance and inspection and that a suitably placed STOP device has been provided in the well (see BS 5655 Parts 1 and 2).

Attendance by a specialist insurance engineer will be required to witness load testing and testing of the safety devices. Via the A/EA, the Clerk of Works should liaise between the insurer's engineer and the contractor to arrange this attendance.

A check should be made that all fire-stopping requirements for services have been adhered to.

7.19.4 Safety in machine and pulley rooms

The Clerk of Works must ensure that contractors are aware of their responsibilities with regard to making provision for safe working in machine and pulley rooms in accordance with BS 7255:2001, particularly Section 9.

7.19.5 Lifting beams

Where lifting beams are installed over lift shafts, or as part of a crane installation, these must be marked with safe working loads and any client register numbering required by the contract documents. Beams must be insurance inspected before handover and this may require load testing. The Clerk of Works must ensure that the contractor is aware of his or her responsibilities and is in attendance when the specialist inspections take place.

7.19.6 Hoists

Document hoists will require the same attention as lifts for builders' work requirements, and attendance by the insurance engineer requires the same level of liaison.

7.19.7 Cranes

The Clerk of Works should check builders' work drawings for any cast-in items, bases and plinths and ensure that these are adequate and correct and ensure that the contractor co-ordinates the installation of the other M&E services with the crane installation to avoid any clash of services. Testing and commissioning, in accordance with BS 466, of the installation should be witnessed in association with the insurance engineer and safety officer as necessary.

7.19.8 Test weights

The Clerk of Works must beware during commissioning and testing that floor loadings are not exceeded when test weights are brought in and out and should check that the contractor is aware of any potential problems. Particular attention should be paid to potential damage to suspended access floors or other sensitive areas.

7.19.9 Statutory inspection by 'competent person'

All lifts and usually all lifting equipment are subject to statutory inspection by a 'competent person' before being put into service and must be inspected at regular intervals thereafter. Copies of all test certificates should be obtained and should be included in the Health and Safety File at handover.

2B QUALITY CONTROL: PETROLEUM, OIL AND LUBRICANT (POL) INSTALLATIONS

7.19.10 Types of installation

Petroleum, oil and lubricant installations fall into several different categories: motor transport refuelling, aviation fuel storage and handling systems, vehicle lubrication and servicing, heating fuel storage and fuel for stand-by generator sets.

Motor transport refuelling: generally for MOD and civil sites the main source of advice on design, construction and installation can be found in the Association for Petroleum and Explosives Administration (APEA) *Guidance for design, construction, modification, maintenance and decommissioning of petrol filling stations*. There may be additional requirements to satisfy the local licensing authority regulations – these should have been taken into consideration at planning stage and should be contained in the particular specification.

Aviation fuel storage and handling: apart from a completely new installation, all work *must* be carried out following 'authorised person' (AP) and 'person in charge' (PIC) procedures, with the operating authority providing the AP and the contractor the PIC. Any equipment and pipe work, etc., to be worked on should normally be certified 'gas free' before work commences. The Site Inspector's role is limited to checking that the installation is as designed and to witnessing tests.

Due to the training, medical and material needs of such duties it is not envisaged that any Site Inspector will undertake AP or PIC roles. The Clerk of Works must make certain not to extend his or her duties or accept duties in such a way as to impinge on or interfere with AP or PIC duties.

Vehicle servicing bays and heating fuel installations: all necessary requirements are to comply with fire precautions. Control of pollution regulations and local authority requirements must be fulfilled, e.g. all bunds must be in place, pipe work identified and protected, tank alarms tested and operational, fill points labelled with grade of fuel and capacity of tank.

7.19.11 General

When working in the proximity of existing installations the Clerk of Works should ensure that the contractor complies with the Health and Safety Plan and any 'Permit to Work' system, and should be acquainted with the Permit system and able to monitor the contractor's performance.

7.19.12 MOD 'authorised person'

On MOD establishments an 'authorised person' (AP) will have been appointed. At an early stage the Clerk of Works should make contact with the AP and continue to liaise with him or her throughout the works. When testing and commissioning pipelines, storage tanks, pumps and dispensing equipment, the attendance of the AP and of the client department which will take ultimate responsibility for the installation and equipment should be invited.

7.19.13 Storage tanks

Any off-site inspection and testing should be attended as required by the contract documents and the A/EA. If the off-site inspection is to be undertaken by others, then the test certificate should be checked on receipt of the tank on site. The tank must be examined on delivery for damage to the shell, connections and any protective coating, in the latter case ensuring that remedial works are immediately undertaken to prevent any corrosion. Where the tank is to be buried, adequate holding down straps must be fitted and the tank filled prior to burying to prevent it 'floating'. The tank should not be emptied until the surrounding mass concrete has cured.

Where the tank is to be erected from sections or plates on site, then, in liaison with the B&CE Site Inspector, the Clerk of Works should check that the builders' work base is correctly constructed and incorporates any holding down bolts and cutouts.

7.19.14 Pipe work

The contract documents should be checked for the type and grade of material to be used in construction of the pipeline. Any special requirements for welding or specific construction methods should be noted. Where welding is to be undertaken, the Clerk of Works should ensure that the operatives are competent (and hold current certification) in the particular welding procedures to be adopted. The levels and routes of pipe work must be checked to avoid co-ordination problems with following trades, and correct installation of any check valves, if required, must be ensured.

7.19.15 Fuel dispense columns

These may be client or contract supplied. Where the client is to provide the equipment then the Clerk of Works must confirm that it will be available when required by the contractor to avoid any delay. When commissioning the dispensing equipment, the client's representative and Weights and Measures representative should be in attendance and the Clerk of Works should liaise as necessary through the A/EA.

3 STATUTORY REQUIREMENTS AND TECHNICAL STANDARDS

(Note: under European legislation, the BS prefix will shortly change to EN.)

Publications to which site reference may be required include:

Lifting installations
BS 466:1984 *Specification for power driven overhead travelling cranes, semi-goliath and goliath cranes for general use.*
BS 2853:1957 *Specification for design and testing of steel overhead runway beams.*
BS 4617:1983 *Methods for determining the performance of pumps and motors for hydraulic fluid power transmission.*
BS 5588-5:2004 *Fire precautions in the design, construction and the use of buildings. Code of practice for firefighting stairs and lifts.*
BS 5655 *Lifts and service lifts.* (Parts 1–14, various dates.)
BS 5656-1:1997 *Safety rules for the construction and installation of escalators and passenger conveyors. Specification and proformas for test and examination of new installations.*
BS 5656-2:2004 *Escalator and moving walks. Safety rules for the construction and installation of escalators and moving walks. Code of practice for the selection, installation and location of new escalators and moving walks.*
BS 7255:2001 *Code of practice for safe working on lifts.*
CP 3010:1972 *Code of practice for safe use of cranes (mobile cranes, tower cranes and derrick cranes).* (Partially replaced by BS 7121. Parts 1–3, various dates.)
HSE Guidance Note PM 55 *Safe working with overhead travelling cranes.*

POL installations
BS 799 *Oil burning equipment.* (Parts 1–8, various dates.)
BS 7117-2:1991 *Metering pumps and dispensers to be installed at filling stations and used to dispense liquid fuel. Guide to installation.*
BS 7117-3:1991 *Metering pumps and dispensers to be installed at filling stations and used to dispense liquid fuel. Guide to maintenance after installation.*
BS EN 13012:2001 *Petrol filling stations. Construction and performance of automatic nozzles for use on fuel dispensers.*
BS EN 13617-1:2004 *Petrol filling stations. Safety requirements for construction and performance of metering pumps, dispensers and remote pumping units.*
BS EN 13617-2:2004 *Petrol filling stations. Safety requirements for construction and performance of safe breaks for use on metering pumps and dispensers.*

BS EN 14015:2004 *Specification for the design and manufacture of site built, vertical, cylindrical, flat-bottomed, above ground, welded, steel tanks for the storage of liquids at ambient temperature and above.*

Association for Petroleum and Explosives Administration (APEA) *Design, construction, modification, maintenance and decommissioning of filling stations*, 2nd edition, 2005.

Preparing for handover

8.1 STRATEGY DEFINITION

Project handover involves the transfer of overall responsibility for the works from the construction team to the client's user organisation(s).

The handover strategy should be developed by the architect/employer's agent (A/EA) in conjunction with the client to suit the client's financial, operational and other requirements. This could include:

- phased handover, partial possession or sectional completion releasing key areas before overall completion
- partial possession enabling early access for specific activities, for example specialist fitting out, while the remainder of the construction work is completed
- Operation and Maintenance/Building Manuals and a statement of the person authorised to keep them and their place of storage. A draft copy could be prepared so that those who need to use them may review the contents.

It is good practice to establish the handover strategy early in the project as part of the detail design stage and to incorporate it into the master programme. However, there is enormous variation between projects.

Certain elements may be addressed in the specification, such as training provision by the contractor's installers for the client's maintenance team on safe operation and maintenance aspects.

As detailed design develops, the handover strategy should develop into a more detailed handover plan. This could cover:

- project completion
- timetable for handover and lead-in activities
- responsibilities during the process
- training requirements
- handover procedures (including to non-client organisations)
- involvement of maintenance staff/organisations
- demonstrations and witnessing requirements
- any 'familiarisation' programmes required
- commissioning plans with appropriate method statements
- lift tests
- fitting out
- documentation, including the Health and Safety File
- environmental impact information
- advice to client (e.g. on transfer of insurance liability)
- handing over of keys from main contractor
- Operation and Maintenance/Building Manuals and a statement of the person authorised to keep them and their place of storage. A draft copy should be prepared so that those who are required to access the information are able to.

After the plan has been developed with the design team and the client, the client should formally approve it.

8.2 CLERK OF WORKS' AND SITE INSPECTOR'S ROLES

The Clerk of Works will be expected to monitor the procedures and actions identified in the commissioning and handover plans. The A/EA or services engineer may require the inspector to witness appropriate tests. Some inspections may need to be carried out or witnessed by external parties, such as insurance inspectors and the fire or safety officers. The client's maintenance organisation may also wish to be present. During commissioning all appropriate health and safety measures should be in accordance with the method statement attached to the commissioning plan. These measures may include 'Permit to Work' areas or isolation of certain equipment during testing.

Where self-certification is legitimately carried out by subcontractors, the A/EA will need to check that all requirements for certification have been clearly allocated to contracts, so that the Health and Safety File and the Operation and Maintenance/Building Manual will be complete. The A/EA may be required to assist and monitor delivery of the Testing and Signing Certificate.

Where appropriate, the Clerk of Works should liaise with the Health and Safety Co-ordinator (as required in the Construction (Design and Management) Regulations 2007) to establish that test certificates for service installations are being obtained and incorporated in the Health and Safety File.

8.3 DEFECTS AND DEFICIENCY (SNAG) LISTS

It is generally accepted good practice to keep the 'snag' list to a minimum by encouraging the contractor to take action to remedy faults well in advance of the final handover or occupation date, whichever is earlier.

The Clerk of Works should carry out a thorough preliminary inspection with the contractor, record all defects and omissions, and, after agreeing them with the A/EA, issue instructions that they are to be put right before the date of handover where possible or by a given date. A long initial snag list should indicate that the work is not ready for inspection. In a phased handover, such as a housing project, after the initial snagging, items picked up subsequently should not be expected to keep reappearing.

It is increasingly common to use a defects tracking computer-aided system on sites. The system can be utilised to log defects and clearance dates, sorting into trades and locations if required. The re-sort facility is particularly useful, as the lists can be prepared on a room-by-room basis and then sorted into separate lists for subcontractors.

The keys to successful snag lists are *method* and *consistency*. All inspectors have their own ways of achieving this; for example, in a building of two or more storeys, starting from the top and working down – on entering a room, checking for defects on the ceiling first, then the walls in a clockwise direction starting from the entrance door, including windows and any stores off the room, any fixed furniture and finally the floor, before checking the door and exiting.

It is the responsibility of the Clerk of Works to check that the snag list is being cleared (agreeing division of building, civil engineering, M&E and landscape responsibilities), and to carry out the final snagging inspection, ensuring that all special tools, specified spares, fire appliances and notices are in place. Building Control may have separate requirements (i.e. Part L, public licensing issues), and the Clerk of Works may well be involved in monitoring these to completion.

8.4   WITNESSING AND TESTING – PROCEDURES GENERALLY

Clerks of Works should try to ensure that adequate prior notice is given to allow them to arrange workloads to suit, and that a method statement is available. It is not uncommon for the commissioning programme to be telescoped because the contract is delayed, leaving an impossible witnessing programme. It is wise to alert the architect as soon as an indication of this kind of problem becomes apparent.

It is the duty of the Clerk of Works to check that all test instruments have been calibrated and are accompanied by a current certificate.

Buildings or facilities must be in a fit state for the test and represent acceptable conditions, e.g. it is *not* acceptable to carry out heating or ventilation tests if doors are propped open for other trades to work.

Where tests are to be carried out by a 'competent person', the Clerk of Works must ensure that the contractor is aware of the requirement. It is also suggested that if the 'competent person' is not a representative of a company known to the Clerk of Works as practitioners in this specialised field, a company brochure and list of clients for whom they have carried out similar work should be requested before testing and inspection proceeds. The architect should be alerted if any uncertainty remains about the competency of the 'competent person'.

8.4.1   Witnessing generally

It is good practice to confirm early in the project with the client and/or the architect the extent of witnessing required and confirm the amount of time available to be spent on this activity. Work will have to be prioritised; for example, there is little need for a Clerk of Works to be present all the time for inspections carried out by a 'competent person' or independent specialist if both the A/EA and the Clerk of Works are happy with the method statement and their initial activities on site. However, if any dissatisfaction remains with the procedures or quality of any testing and commissioning it must be reported to the A/EA or services engineer and the problem discussed.

Full site diary records of all timing and commissioning activities must be kept, including when 'competent persons' and other specialists are on site.

8.5 HANDOVER DOCUMENTATION

The Construction (Design and Management) (CDM) Regulations 1994 (or as amended by CDM Regulations 2007) set out the requirements of handover documents (refer to the CDM Regulations Approved Code of Practice). In practice, the needs will be defined in collaboration with the Health and Safety Co-ordinator.

8.6 AS-INSTALLED OR AS-BUILT DRAWINGS

The Clerk of Works should monitor progress on (and accuracy of) contractors' as-installed drawings and the compilation of data for the Operation and Maintenance/ Building Manual as directed by the A/EA and the Health and Safety File as directed by the Health and Safety Co-ordinator.

8.7 COMMISSIONING

Commissioning involves a great deal more than just the services – lifts, the wet risers, air conditioning, etc. On the construction side, windows, roofs and 'man-safe' systems all need commissioning as well, often for insurance purposes, but the following sections all deal with the services element.

8.7.1 Witnessing

The Clerk of Works' role here may include:

- witnessing final high voltage (HV) and other electrical tests and obtaining and countersigning the test certificates
- checking that all pre-testing and pre-commissioning cleaning of pipe work and ductwork is carried out
- witnessing all pressure tests on pipe work and ductwork leakage tests where applicable
- witnessing and assisting the insurance and fire officers for certificate testing, if applicable, on behalf of the client.

If applicable, the Clerk of Works may have a responsibility to check that arrangements are made for the initial delivery of solid and liquid fuels in time for plant start up.

8.7.2 Plant commissioning

- Before use, calibration of any instruments to be used for commissioning tasks must be checked.
- As agreed with the M&E project engineer and A/EA, the Clerk of Works must witness that air and water distribution systems are correctly balanced, checking this at measuring stations confirmed with the M&E project engineer.

The commissioning of all plant, e.g. boilers, pumps, fans, compressors, coolers, chillers, air handling units, water treatment and control and indication systems, must be witnessed. The operation of *all* safety devices must be checked by simulating emergency conditions.

- The Chartered Institute of Building Services Engineers (CIBSE) Commissioning Codes contains further useful information (see chapter 15).
- The Clerk of Works should liaise with specialists appointed for the testing of air conditioning for hospital operating theatres, computer suites and process systems, intruder detection systems, noise, vibration and contamination control in nuclear, biological or chemical protected buildings and any other highly specialised systems.
- Any remaining site M&E proving and performance tests must be witnessed to ensure that certification is correctly completed. The project M&E engineer and others concerned should be notified immediately if anything arises that is likely to jeopardise the handover arrangements.

8.8 PLANNED MAINTENANCE

If requested by the A/EA, the Clerk of Works should check that the planned maintenance detail sheets have been completed in time for their inclusion in the Operation and Maintenance (O&M) Manuals before handover.

8.8.1 Operation and Maintenance/Building Manuals

It is part of the duties of the Clerk of Works to collect, as agreed with the building Project Manager and M&E project engineer, documentation for the A/EA to collate into the Manual and to ensure that all M&E manufacturers'/contractors' operating and maintenance instructions and test certificates are provided, including:

- the actual performance data obtained from commissioning
- the schedule of M&E equipment
- the planned maintenance log book
- any risk assessments and Health and Safety Plans
- the fire alarm and emergency lighting inspection and test certificates required under BS 5839-1:2002 and BS 5266.

The Clerk of Works will assist the M&E project engineer to ensure that the Maintenance and Operating Instruction Manuals are adequate.

8.9 SUMMARY OF TEST CERTIFICATES

The following table gives a summary of the main categories of tests that may need to be witnessed and the certificates to be included in the O&M Manuals/Health and Safety File.

	Item	Source
1.	Electrical Installations Test Certificates	Tests carried out by the electrical contractor and witnessed by Clerk of Works Results recorded on agreed forms
2.	Earthing, Lightning Protection, Anti-Static Precautions, etc., Test Certificates	Tests carried out by the electrical contractor and witnessed by Clerk of Works Results recorded on agreed forms
3.	Lifting Equipment Test Certificates	Architect to raise order on 'competent person' (CP) Test carried out and certificates issued by CP
4.	Lifts and Hoists (and Lifting Beam) Test Certificates	Tests carried out and certificates issued by CP
5.	Steel Wire Ropes Test Certificates	Certificates issued by the rope manufacturer
6.	External Heating Mains Test and Commissioning Certificates	The contractor, or the commissioning specialist approved by the architect, is responsible for showing that the installation meets with the design criteria
7.	Heating and Domestic Hot Water Installations Test and Commissioning Certificates	Off-site tests for some items of equipment are required. These are carried out at the manufacturers' works, where the test certificates are issued, e.g. for boilers, calorifiers, pumps, fans, motors, starters and control gear The contractor, or the commissioning specialist approved by the architect, is responsible for fully commissioning each installation as specified and for issuing the Commissioning Certificate
8.	Gas, Air, Water, etc., Part System Pressure Test, Test Certificate	Test carried out by the contractor according to specification and witnessed and test certificate countersigned by the Clerk of Works
9.	External Gas Mains and Internal Gas Installations Test Certificates	Distribution mains external to site and service pipes within the site up to and including the primary meter are the responsibility of British Gas/Transco Certificates for the installation beyond that point are the responsibility of the contractor

	Item	Source
10.	Mechanical Ventilation and Air Conditioning Test and Commissioning Certificates	Off-site tests for some items of equipment are required at the manufacturer's works. The manufacturer will be responsible for the issue of the test certificates, e.g. fans, pumps, electric motors, starters and control gear, air heaters, refrigeration plant The contractor is responsible for fully commissioning each installation, issuing the Commissioning Certificate for Ventilation and Air Conditioning
11.	Pressure Vessels Test Certificates and Reports	The certificates are issued by the 'competent person' The architect is to arrange for the 'competent person' (for boilers and pressure vessels) to undertake: ● approval of design, examination under construction and test at the manufacturer's works, and issue of a Certificate of Test unless these services have been arranged by the manufacturer ● examination and test of second-hand plant under purchase ● initial examination and test after installation on site and issue of report forms prescribed under the Factories Act ● examinations of test welds where required
12.	Safety Officer's Report	Where advised necessary by the A/EA, the report is completed by the client's Safety Officer

Handover, practical completion and defects rectification stage

9.1 HANDOVER: GENERAL PROCEDURES

The takeover of completed works from the contractor, and the acceptance of the works from him by the client with any agreement for subsequent maintenance, is a contractual event. Handovers need not involve the whole site; they may be of only one part of it, and this is often known as phased, partial or sectional completion. The A/EA will normally give directions as to when the handover will occur and any specific procedures to be followed, but the Clerk of Works will often be asked to provide advice and reports on the state of the works. The A/EA will need to liaise with the client and any maintenance organisation beforehand to ensure readiness and to make certain that any difficulties or problems are resolved before formal handover to the client.

Detailed procedures for takeover and handover are to be agreed with the A/EA. These will depend on the particular requirements of the client, and the A/EA is responsible for making the necessary arrangements.

Generally, not less than four weeks before the probable date of handover to the client of any part of the works, and eight weeks or more in advance in the case of a complete installation, the A/EA should notify the client with a request to make preliminary arrangements to take over the building or other works services. When occupation or partial occupation of a building is to be taken before actual completion of the contract, the A/EA will also give notice so that arrangements for client's maintenance and changeover of building insurances can be made.

As soon as possible after notice is given, a site meeting should be held, attended by the A/EA, client and maintenance organisation or their representatives, to discuss any outstanding items and to agree the takeover date.

The Health and Safety File will require a schedule of principal materials used in construction. The Health and Safety Co-ordinator (as required by the CDM Regulations 2007) and the A/EA will determine how this is to be produced and may require the site Clerk of Works to assist in the preparation. The Clerk of Works should check that the A/EA has been provided with all test reports and certificates, prior to the practical completion date. The contractor is ordinarily responsible for provision of as-built drawings, although the consultants may prepare part of them. In either case, these should be checked against the Clerk of Works' own record of variations and from site knowledge.

9.1.1 Defects and deficiencies (snag lists)

Depending on the form of contract, a list of outstanding defects will be compiled as the project approaches handover. The A/EA and the Clerk of Works, supported by the design consultants, should inspect the works and compile a list suitable to be attached to any Practical Completion Certificate. It is advisable to check whether the contractor should also be in attendance.

9.1.2 Training of client's maintenance team

Where required, the training of the client/users' maintenance organisation should be arranged to achieve the requirements of the handover plan, including any installation or manufacturers' instructions.

9.1.3 Health and Safety File and as-installed drawings

All information necessary for the end user to maintain and operate the final works is to be incorporated into the Health and Safety File. This is reviewed by the Health and Safety Co-ordinator before issue to the client.

It is good practice to monitor progress on (and accuracy of) contractor's as-installed drawings or the last issue of contract drawings 'for construction'. This will include the compilation of data for the Maintenance Manual and Health and Safety File as required by the Health and Safety Co-ordinator.

9.1.4 Pre-completion planning meeting

A pre-completion project meeting should be held at a suitable time before antici-pated project completion (generally this will be approximately two weeks before-hand). The meeting is normally attended by the client and consultants and may include deliberation on the following:

- a review of quality being delivered and level of defects
- performance to date and expectation of completion date
- state of appearance and cleanliness
- extent of incomplete works
- progress on services commissioning and testing
- Health and Safety File documentation
- damage
- readiness of client's organisation to take on the building and consequent respon-sibilities (e.g. day-to-day maintenance, running costs and insurance)
- certification from the Building Control Officer.

The purpose of the meeting is to review the standards of construction achieved and all outstanding or incomplete works, including documentation for the Health and Safety File. From this review, the likely date of project completion is established and any further actions agreed.

9.1.5 Keys

The Clerk of Works may be asked to check availability of keys immediately before hand-over with the contractor and to ensure that the keys are clearly labelled. This does not just apply to door keys, but window, manhole and any services keys also figure. If, for any reason, the Clerk of Works is obliged to receive important keys significantly in advance of handover (e.g. because of staged completion), the A/EA should provide a security key case and carry out appropriate security measures, perhaps with the client's security advisor. The contractor may also have a key release form.

The contractor is likely to require a receipt for any keys handed over; this is normally the A/EA's responsibility unless delegated to the Clerk of Works.

Where special security locks and keys are specified (security lock keys and master keys should not normally be consigned to the contractor), there may be specific requirements for installation and protection of high security locks before, during and after installation; the Clerk of Works should check the project specification and consult with the A/EA.

In any event, any key handed over to a client or client's representative *must* be signed for.

9.1.6 Operation and maintenance of the finished building and maintenance documents

It is likely that maintenance documents specified in the contract, including those provided by suppliers and subcontractors, will go straight into the Building Manual. It is also good practice to see that these are completed in the prescribed format and are ready for handing over to the client on the due date. The client's cleaning contractors may require access to the cleaning requirements early, e.g. regarding any special flooring.

The Clerk of Works may be asked by the Health and Safety Co-ordinator to check that all information required for the Health and Safety File has been prepared and issued by the designers, contractors and any other parties.

9.1.7 The handover meeting

It is normal practice that the client and consultants attend the project handover meeting. If everybody is satisfied that construction work is practically complete and documentation is in an acceptable state, then the Practical/Partial Completion Certificate can be signed by the A/EA. Generally appended to the certificate is a complete list of outstanding works and defects. This is to be agreed by all the parties involved. However, it should be made clear that this does not alter the contractor's responsibility for remedying any defects identified after project practical completion, within the specified defect rectification period.

The A/EA is normally responsible for creating the Practical Completion Certificate. Forms produced by the respective professional institute (e.g. RIBA) are often used. The Clerk of Works' role is normally confined to the production of an up-to-date schedule of outstanding works and defects and deficiencies (snag list), which is attached to the certificate.

Once project completion has been certified, no additional works can be instructed by the client, the A/EA or the Clerk of Works under the original contract.

The Project Completion Certificate is issued to the contractor, with copies to the client and all the project consultants. A copy should be retained on the inspector's site files and the end of the rectification period (defects liability period) recorded in the site diary.

If, however, at the meeting it is agreed that the works are *not* in a fit state to hand over, for whatever reason, the A/EA has the authority to issue a Non-Completion Certificate. The Clerk of Works may be asked to assist the A/EA to record the reasons for its issue.

Handover of the project should not proceed until project/practical completion has been achieved. Significant risk attaches to any other strategy. Once this has taken place the client controls the project and becomes responsible for security, building insurances, day-to-day maintenance and operation. Access for defects rectification must be co-ordinated through the client's nominated representative.

Arrangements are made for clearance of defects as they occur throughout the defects rectification period. The original project team generally makes these arrangements. The Clerk of Works may be asked to check and agree any areas of damage made by client's removal operators or from 'white goods' deliveries.

9.2 CONDITION AT COMPLETION

The contractor is normally required to remove all temporary markings, coverings or protection unless otherwise instructed, and to clean and clear the works of debris and rubbish, leaving the premises on completion in a fit condition for occupation and use. If any special degree of cleanliness is required, e.g. in technical or prestige areas, this should be detailed in the specification or otherwise ordered. The contractor's attention should be drawn to these matters in the course of the defects and deficiencies inspections.

9.3 PARTIAL POSSESSION AND SECTIONAL COMPLETION

If it becomes evident that dates specified in the contract for obtaining partial possession of sections of the site or for completing and commissioning engineering services in advance of the main contract are unlikely to be met, the A/EA must be informed as soon as possible.

9.4 POST-HANDOVER AND RECTIFICATION (DEFECTS LIABILITY) PERIOD

This period may have other titles, such as the rather misleading 'maintenance period' stated for government contracts.

The period runs from practical completion (i.e. the date on the Practical Completion Certificate) for the period specified in the contract. This is usually six or twelve months. Twelve months is a desirable period for M&E installations so that a complete annual heating/cooling cycle is experienced.

During this period, any residual works and defects should be completed by the contractor. There is also the possibility that other defects may come to light during the first year of occupancy, for which the contractor is also responsible.

The Clerk of Works may be involved in:

- monitoring the completion of items known about at handover and recorded on the snag list
- inspecting and advising on defects that come to light during this period (there may be a dispute over whether the defect was caused by the occupier or is the responsibility of the contractor) and adding these to the snag list when instructed by the A/EA
- advising on events which have led up to contractual disputes, such as claims for loss, expense, disruption and extensions of time
- completing and filing records.

9.5 RECORD DOCUMENTATION

On completion of the contract the Clerk of Works should seek instructions from the client regarding the return of all drawings, specifications, bills of quantities and other contract documents, the Clerk of Works' own copies of instructions, a copy of the contractor's programme showing actual progress made and other formal records. Especially valuable records include relevant photographs, site diaries, daily labour returns and the Clerk of Works' dimension book giving measurements of works covered up, e.g. on additional foundation excavations. Where the A/EA is an outside appointment, all records should be passed to the client.

The Clerk of Works' site records may often be the most authoritative contemporary evidence of disputes between the contractor, the design team, the A/EA and the client. Included in these records is the Clerk of Works' marked-up drainage drawing, often a most useful record of the revisions that actually occurred during construction.

9.6 SURPLUS MATERIALS AND EQUIPMENT

The A/EA may identify surpluses which are client property and not part of the 'spares' list, and issue directions for disposal.

9.7 PREPARATION OF DEFECTS LIST DURING RECTIFICATION (DEFECTS LIABILITY) PERIOD

When repairs are required during the defects rectification period, the A/EA should determine whether they are the contractor's responsibility and, if so, advise the contractor so they can be rectified as soon as possible within an agreed time frame. If the Clerk of Works has reason to believe that the contractor is not keeping up or making sufficient progress, the A/EA should be informed immediately. The reporting of defects should *not* be left until the end of the defects rectification period(s), which, it should be noted, may vary for building and M&E works.

Any additional defects, reported from any source including the client/client's agent should, if appropriate, be reported to the A/EA before being added to the snagging database/list.

9.8 CONTRACTUAL CLAIMS AND DISPUTE RESOLUTION

For claims and counterclaims, the A/EA must consider all the possible implications and consequences of the potential and issued instructions. At the earliest possible time, steps should have been taken to detect any circumstances which might develop and give rise to additional expense or claims, and consideration given to ensuring that adequate contemporaneous records have been kept and maintained in order that expenses and damages may be properly ascertained. The A/EA should liaise closely with the quantity surveyor on all these matters.

Claims for prolongation and disruption expenses arising in the circumstances provided for in the contract or stemming from unreasonable delay by the project team in issuing or approving drawings which the contractor is required to submit, and extra-contractual claims, will ordinarily be negotiated by the quantity surveyor.

The A/EA must advise the client of any claims received together with the A/EA's comments and recommendations, and the Clerk of Works may be asked to give an account of events and demonstrate site records. The site diary is often the most complete documentary evidence of the events leading up to the claim situation. The quantity surveyor may require the assistance of the Clerk of Works in order to facilitate settlement of any extra-contractual claims.

The client should be kept informed of developments if the client has instructed the Clerk of Works to report directly rather than through the A/EA.

It should be noted that resolution of claims would normally attract an additional fee or time charge. The Clerk of Works should seek agreement from the client before committing resources.

9.9 INSPECTION AT EXPIRY OF RECTIFICATION (DEFECTS LIABILITY) PERIOD

On expiry of the rectification period (or before, if possible), the Clerk of Works should check that the contractor has completed all outstanding work, and has made good all defects listed on the Practical Completion Certificate and all defects subsequently reported during the rectification period.

Once satisfied that all outstanding work is completed and all defects made good, the A/EA will issue to the contractor the 'Certificate of Making Good', sending copies to the client, quantity surveyor and Clerk of Works.

9.10 PERFORMANCE REPORTS AND PROJECT FEEDBACK

It is good practice for the Clerk of Works to assist the A/EA to complete performance reports on the contractor and subcontractors as required by the client.

The Clerk of Works should provide feedback on the project generally, including on any design-related issues, to the client and request feedback accordingly. Any matters that could prevent problems recurring on future projects should be identified. Feedback should be given at any time during the contract, not only at completion.

Typical performance feedback may include information on:

- suppliers
- contractor
- subcontractors (domestic or otherwise)
- materials used
- the Clerk of Work's own performance
- consultants
- client staff
- design details
- training needs
- key performance indicators (KPIs).

Published and model forms for Clerks of Works

10.1 SPECIMEN CLERK OF WORKS PROJECT REPORT

10.1.1 Notes on use and completion

For the purpose of these notes, it is assumed that JCT SBC05 is the building contract being used. However, the Project Report Form shown on pages 174–5 can be used under other forms of contract.

(1) The name of the project, which will be its contractual title, and its address, i.e. the address of the works or site, should be entered. These descriptions should be maintained consistently throughout all forms and records relating to the project. The project reference number is given to the project for administrative purposes.

The serial report number and the week ending date should be entered. This will be the Sunday at the end of that week. If project reports are to be less frequent than one a week, the most convenient approach will be to complete the form as appropriate and attach separate weekly sheets as required for trades on site, weather, etc.

The name of either the architect or the employer's agent and the name of the contractor, all as shown in the building contract, should be entered. The Clerk of Works' own name, together with telephone and fax numbers on site, should be entered.

The contract start date should be the date stated in the building contract for possession or commencement as appropriate. The contract completion date should be the date stated in the building contract or as last revised following any extension of time.

The progress against programme entry should indicate where, in the Clerk of Works' view, slippage has occurred or the main contractor is ahead of programme. The entry may be expressed in days or weeks, or as a percentage deviation from the current programme issued by the main contractor.

(2) The number of person days per trade for each day of the week should be entered. For example, four operatives working all day will be entered as four person days (assuming a working day is seven hours on site). Two operatives both working all morning only will be one person day. Two operatives working one in the morning and one in the afternoon will also be one person day. Enter the total number of person days for each day of the week.

If agreed with the A/EA, this panel may be left blank and the main contractor's labour return form substituted or attached in addition. An important purpose of these entries is to enable the A/EA to verify that the main contractor has been proceeding regularly and diligently. Care is therefore needed to make sure that entries for the appropriate categories are consistent, week on week, and that operatives are not accidentally included twice (e.g. as machine operators and as ground workers).

It will also be helpful to identify which trades operatives are working for a nominated subcontractor (or named subcontractor in the case of the Building Contract Intermediate/Building Contract Intermediate with Contractor Design (IC/ICD) contract). This information will be invaluable for an A/EA reviewing extensions of time or direct loss and expense applications relating to nominated subcontractors.

(3) The weather report entries should include a temperature reading. Ideally, this will be taken at the same time each morning and afternoon, otherwise a rise and fall reading of minimum and maximum temperatures can be given. In normal conditions, entries under a.m. and p.m. can be expressed as standard weather report headings (e.g. rain, bright, cloudy, thunder, sunny, dull). However, to alert the A/EA to weather conditions which might affect the main contractor's performance it might be expedient to agree to make the record under limited headings (i.e. snow, frost, rain, high winds, hot, dry), rating them on, say, a 1–5 scale which might assist computer analysis. Whatever approach is adopted, consistency of expression is important.

In the case of high-rise construction, weather conditions at ground level can be markedly different from those at high-level elevations. This should be borne in mind and noted as appropriate.

Person hours lost due to adverse weather conditions should be given for each day, with the weekly total and total to date recorded.

(4) All visitors to site should be noted, with names, functions and dates.

(5) Under General Comments the Clerk of Works might draw the A/EA's attention to some matter that requires immediate action; for example, a boundary dispute with the owners of neighbouring property.

(6) The entry for site directions should include Clerk of Works directions.

(7) Delays or events with potential to cause delay should be listed. The latter are often expressions of opinion by a vigilant Clerk of Works, but they will be invaluable when the A/EA is considering claims for extensions of time.

(8) Defective work observed, including instances of non-compliance with the building contract in respect of workmanship, materials, working methods, etc., should be recorded, together with a note of any action taken by the main contractor to remedy such deficiencies.

(9) Drawings/information received on site should include any A/EA's instructions and information issued by the main contractor (e.g. method statements)

which might have been requested. Also included might be relevant notices or explanatory leaflets received from the Health and Safety Executive.

(10) Drawings/information required on site by the Clerk of Works should include items already requested but not so far received.

(11) The entry under plant/materials should include items delivered to site during the week and measures for their protection as required by the building contract. The removal from site of any unfixed materials and goods should be noted, and whether this was done with the consent of the A/EA as required by the building contract.

(12) The progress to date panels include items or operations described in a way that is generally accepted within the building industry. The percentage entries indicate the percentage of work actually achieved as measured against the percentage of work which should have been achieved according to the main contractor's current programme. For example, by the end of that week 70 per cent of the roof covering should have been completed, but in fact only 60 per cent has been carried out. There is therefore a 10 per cent shortfall against programme for that operation.

(13) The general report will summarise the contents of the Clerk of Works' diary for that week, and this information might be invaluable to the A/EA when dealing with extensions of time and loss and expense applications. Both the reports and the site diary entries might subsequently be used as evidence in arbitration or litigation proceedings, and Clerks of Works should bear this in mind when compiling and setting out facts and observations.

(14) The health and safety entry might draw the A/EA's attention to instances of non-compliance with the regulations (e.g. in respect of safety clothing or scaffolding) or work not in accordance with the method statement or safety plan, etc. Any action taken by the Clerk of Works or intervention by the health and safety inspectorate should be noted.

(15) The entry under site housekeeping will describe conditions on site during that week. For example, the site might have become a quagmire because of continuous heavy rain, making working conditions extremely arduous. Observations of this kind will help the A/EA when dealing with notices of delay.

(16) Enclosures might include main contractor's labour returns (see (2) above), site directions issued by the Clerk of Works and reports. The latter might concern the weather, air quality, cube tests, commissioning, performance of components, etc.

(17) The distribution of the Project Report should be agreed with the A/EA, to whom the top copy should be sent.

(18) The Clerk of Works whose name is given on the face of the form should sign and date the Project Report.

CLERKS OF WORKS PROJECT REPORT

PROJECT: _____ REF: _____

ADDRESS: _____

NO: _____

Architect/Contract Administrator:	Week/Month ending:
	Contract Start Date:
Main Contractor:	Contract Completion Date:
Clerk of Works Phone/Fax No:	Progress +/− to Programme:

TRADES	MON	TUES	WED	THU	FRI	SAT	SUN
Site Staff							
Groundworkers							
Steelfixers							
Steel Erectors							
Concretors							
Drainlayers							
Machine Operators							
Carpenters							
Scaffolders							
Bricklayers							
Roof Finishers							
Wall Cladding							
Window Fixers							
Glaziers							
Floor Screeders							
Plasterers							
Tilers – Wall/Floor							
Dryliners/Partitions							
Ceiling Fixers							
Decorators							
Floor Finishers							
Heating/Ventilation							
Plumbing							
Electricians							
Hard/Soft Landscape							
Roadworks							
Public Services							
TOTAL							

WEATHER REPORT

	AM	°C	PM	°C	Time Lost
Mon					
Tue					
Wed					
Thur					
Fri					
Sat					
Sun					

Stoppages (Hours)

Total to Date

Visitors (include Statutory Inspectors)	Date

SITE DIRECTIONS ISSUED

No	Item	Date

DELAYS INCLUDING DEFECTIVE WORK (ACTION TAKEN)

DRAWINGS/INFORMATION RECEIVED ON SITE

DRAWINGS/INFORMATION REQUIRED ON SITE

PLANT/MATERIALS DELIVERED TO SITE OR REMOVED

WORKS – MATERIALS: TESTED OR COMMISSIONED

SPECIMEN

Progress to date	Programme		Progress to date	Programme		Progress to date	Programme
	%	%		%	%		%	%

Preliminaries			Blockwork Internal			Electrical 2nd Fix		
Excavation			Cladding/Curtain Wall			H & V 2nd Fix		
Shutter/Reinf			Windows-glazing			Ceiling Grid/Tiles		
Concrete Structure			Joinery 1st Fix			Decoration		
Steel Erection			Plastering			External Works		
Main Drainage m/h			Drylining/Partitions			Hard/Soft Landscape		
Floor Construction			Floor Screeds			Roadworks		
Floors Suspended			Plumbing 1st Fix			Mains: Gas-Electrical		
Roof Structure			Electrical 1st Fix			Mains: Water-Telecoms		
Roof Coverings			H & V 1st Fix			Lifts		
Drainage fw.sw.			Wall/Floor Tiles			Alarm/Computer Systems		
Brickwork External			Plumbing 2nd Fix			Defects/Handover		

GENERAL REPORT: SUMMARY OF WORKS IN PROGRESS

HEALTH AND SAFTETY: ACTION TAKEN

SITE HOUSEKEEPING: CONDITIONS/CLEANLINESS: ACCESS AND EGRESS

Enclosures: G.C. Labour Return [ ] Site Directions [ ] Reports (State) [ ]	OFFICE ACTION:
Distribution as Agreed	
Client [ ] Architect [ ] Project Manager [ ] Quantity Surveyor [ ] Office [ ] Others [ ]	
Clerk of Works Date	

10.2 SPECIMEN MAIN CONTRACTOR'S LABOUR RETURN

10.2.1 Notes on use and completion

To be completed by the main contractor and submitted weekly to the Clerk of Works.

(1) The name of the project and its address should be entered and should be consistent with the Clerks of Works' report. The week number, as shown on the programme for the works, should be entered together with the date of the Sunday at the end of that week. The project reference number will be the unique number given to the project for administrative purposes.

(2) The number of person days per trade for each day of the week should be entered. For example, four operatives working all day will be entered as four person days. Two operatives, one working in the morning and one in the afternoon will be one person day.

(3) A list should be entered of the main contractor's resources on site during that week. All heavy plant and specialist equipment should be included, but not standard minor items such as hand tools. Any equipment on site that has been hired by the main contractor should be separately identified.

(4) Entries should clarify which materials and goods have been ordered and delivered in the course of the week and which are still awaiting delivery.

Main Contractor's **Labour Return**

Project: _____ Ref. No: _____
Address: _____ Week No: _____
_____ Week ending: _____

Institute of
Clerks of Works

TRADES (Man days)		Mon	Tue	Wed	Thu	Fri	Sat	Sun
	Person in charge							
	Scaffolders							
	Groundworkers							
	Drivers and plant operators							
	Steel fixers and concreters							
	Bricklayers and masons							
	Roofers: Finishes							
	Carpenters and joiners							
	Steel erectors							
	Window fixers							
	Plumbers							
	H & V engineers							
	Electricians							
	Lift engineers							
	Plasterers and screeders							
	Tilers: Wall and floor							
	Ceiling fixers							
	Floor finishers							
	Glaziers							
	Painters							
	Drainlayers							
	Statutory undertakers							
	Road pavers, Tarmac workers							
	Total man days							

PLANT ON SITE

MATERIALS AND GOODS Ordered and awaiting delivery

Delivered to site

Signed _____ (for Main Contractor) Date

This Return is to be completed by the main Contractor where this is required under the contract conditions,
and submitted weekly to the Clerk of Works.

10.3 SPECIMEN CLERK OF WORKS DIRECTION FORM

10.3.1 Notes on use and completion

Directions may be given to the contractor by the Clerk of Works in respect of matters which are empowered under the building contract and which may be the subject of an A/EA's instruction. A direction will be of no contractual effect unless confirmed by an A/EA's instruction within two working days. Any action before such confirmation will be premature and taken at risk.

The intention of a Clerk of Works Direction is to alert the A/EA about information or action which, in the opinion of the Clerk of Works, is relevant at this time.

(1)   The name and address of the A/EA, employer and contractor should be completed as named in the building contract.

(2)   The works should be identified (i.e. site address) and date of contract, as entered in the building contract.

(3)   The job reference, sequential number of the direction and date of issue should be given.

(4)   The content of the direction should be expressed clearly and concisely, itemising matters as appropriate. Care should be taken that numbers and dimensions are accurate and legible.

(5)   The declaration should be signed by the Clerk of Works.

(6)   The original should be issued to the contractor and, at the same time, a copy sent to the A/EA.

**Clerk of Works
Direction**

Architect/CA:
address:

Employer:
address:

Contractor:
address:

Works:
situated at:

Contract dated:

Job reference:

Direction no:

Issue date:

Under the terms of the above-mentioned Contract, I issue the following direction.

This direction shall be of no effect unless confirmed in writing by the Architect/Contract Administrator within 2 working days, and does not authorise any extra payment.

Direction	Architect/CA use
	Covered by Instruction no:

Signed _____ Clerk of Works

| *Distribution* | ☐ Contractor | ☐ Architect/CA | ☐ | ☐ Site records file |

F510 for SBC

RIBA ⌗ Reproduced by agreement with the RIBA

The Clerk of Works with special reference to duties under the JCT Standard Building Contract (SBC05)

11.1 ARCHITECT'S DUTIES

The architect under the terms of the RIBA Architect's Appointment is required to 'administer the building contract, including reviewing the progress of construction works against the contractor's programme'. The architect is not, therefore, required to make frequent or constant inspections and, where these are required, a Clerk of Works should be employed by the employer, who has such an entitlement under the Joint Contracts Tribunal (JCT) standard form of contract, and/or a resident architect appointed under the Architect's Appointment.

11.2 CLERK OF WORKS' REMIT

Under Clause 3.4 of SBC05, the Clerk of Works' duty is 'to act solely as inspector on behalf of the Employer under the directions of the Architect/Contract Administrator'. This Clause also states that any Clerk of Works direction 'shall be of no effect' unless it falls within the powers given to the architect under the conditions and is 'confirmed in writing by the Architect within two working days of such a working direction being given'. The dangers of a contractor acting immediately on a Clerk of Works direction and something going wrong, then the architect refusing to issue an appropriate instruction, are obvious. There are, however, emergency situations where such immediate action must be taken and the Clerk of Works' experience and skills will be required to avoid any contractual difficulties.

11.3 SUMMARY OF CLERK OF WORKS' DUTIES

In practice, the duties of the Clerk of Works are somewhat broader than laid down in the building contract and can be summarised as including inspections, reporting in detail, advising and generally being the eyes and ears of the architect on site. The satisfactory discharge of those duties requires a wealth of practical experience, sound technical knowledge and interpersonal skills.

11.4 DUTIES OF THE CLERK OF WORKS

11.4.1 Register of drawings

A register of drawings must be maintained and all contract documentation carefully filed. In order to carry out his or her duties efficiently, the Clerk of Works must have an intimate knowledge of the contract drawings, the preamble, the bills of quantities and any other contract documents. The Clerk of Works should therefore ensure that there is ready access to that information, requesting this from the architect if it is not offered.

11.4.2 Errors and discrepancies

The architect should be notified of any errors in or discrepancies between the drawings, preambles, bills of quantities or other documents.

11.4.3 Decisions and variations

The architect should be notified immediately of any significant problems that arise on site, or if any decisions or variations are required. Queries should not be stored until site meetings but raised as they occur.

11.4.4 Work in accordance with the contract

The JCT Standard Building Contract (SBC05) states in Clause 2.1 that the contractor shall carry out and complete the works in a proper and workmanlike manner and the powers given to the architect to issue instructions in the case of non-compliance will rely on the Clerk of Works' vigilance on site.

Work should be inspected for execution in accordance with the contract documents and with any instructions which may be issued from time to time by the architect. When necessary, work in the contractor's, subcontractors' or suppliers' yards should be inspected as should any unfixed materials and goods stored off site when requested. Any tests which may be detailed in the contract should be witnessed and recorded. Directions to the contractor regarding defects which are noted should be issued in writing and a remedy sought promptly.

11.4.5 Materials meeting standards

Materials and goods are to be inspected for compliance with the stated standards and to ensure that they are properly stored and protected. The Clerk of Works should inspect delivery notes, examine materials for Kitemarks and CE marks, etc., and obtain necessary certificates as routine procedures.

11.4.6 Clause 3.18

The Clerk of Works should confirm with the architect whether or not Clause 3.18 is to operate regarding the acceptance of work or materials not in accordance with the contract. In certain circumstances the architect, with the employer's agreement and after consulting the contractor, may allow such work.

11.4.7 Directions

Directions must only be given to the main contractor through the site manager/agent. Directions should never be given directly to workmen or subcontractors' representatives. Clause 3.4 of SBC05 states that directions given to the contractor by the Clerk of Works shall have no effect unless confirmed in writing by the architect within two working days of such direction being given, which is extremely difficult to achieve in practice. The Clerk of Works should issue written directions, dated and numbered with copies being passed to the main contractor, the architect, the quantity surveyor and one copy kept on site by the Clerk of Works.

11.4.8 Negligence or non-compliance

The architect should be informed immediately if there is continuing negligence or non-compliance after the contractor's attention has been drawn, both orally and in writing, to any lack of observance and there is any reason to believe that any work is being sub-let without the architect's written consent as required under Clauses 3.7.1 and 3.7.2.

11.4.9 Unfixed goods

Vigilance must be maintained to ensure that unfixed materials and goods are not removed from the site by the contractor, unless with the architect's written approval. Clause 2.24 refers.

11.4.10 Site progress meetings

The Clerk of Works should attend site progress meetings as required and confirm the accuracy or otherwise of the contractor's progress report.

11.4.11 Daily diary

It is the duty of the Clerk of Works to maintain a daily diary recording such items as:

- temperatures, rain, snow and high winds, with particular reference to 'exceptionally adverse weather'
- records of tests carried out
- any delays that are evident and the reasons for them
- concrete pouring and striking of formwork, etc.
- site labour and any labour problems on site
- visits by the Building Control Officer, statutory authorities, professional team or client
- details of any condemned work or work to be covered up
- verbal instructions or information given by the architect, civil or structural engineer or mechanical services engineer
- details of attendance at day works
- progress against programme.

Since the site diary may have to be produced when dealing with contractor's claims, it is essential that all entries are factual and can be substantiated.

11.4.12 Weekly reports

Clerk of Works and weather reports are to be submitted weekly in the form required by the architect or employer and progress should be verified by recording the actual programme on the master programme.

11.4.13 Levels and setting-out on new work

The Clerk of Works should verify with the contractor's representative the levels and setting out of the building. It should be noted that under Clause 2.10 of SBC05 it is the contractor's responsibility alone to set out works and establish all levels in accordance with the contract drawings and that inspection by the Clerk of Works does not relieve the contractor of his or her obligation.

11.4.14 Record drawings and certification

The Clerk of Works must verify that the contractor maintains such record drawings and certifications as are required by the contract. These normally consist of internal and external drainage, electrical installation, heating and ventilating installations.

11.4.15 Health and safety

Clause 3.25 sets out the requirements that each party must undertake to comply with the Construction (Design and Management) (CDM) Regulations. The employer is required to ensure that the Planning Supervisor and the Principal Contractor carry out their duties under the CDM Regulations. The employer may not be completely familiar with the requirements of the CDM Regulations and the Clerk of Works can be of great assistance in advising on whether the Planning Supervisor and Principal Contractor are carrying out their duties appropriately. Any breaches of the Health and Safety Plan should be drawn to the attention of the Principal Contractor. (Note: The role of Planning Supervisor is due to be replaced by the Health and Safety Co-ordinator after the introduction of the CDM Regulations 2007 – see chapter 6.)

Any accidents to persons, structures, equipment or plant should be recorded.

11.4.16 Materials and workmanship

Since Clause 2.3 requires the contractor to carry out and complete the works using materials and workmanship of the quality and standard specified in the contract documents, it follows that the contractor alone is responsible for making certain that the works are satisfactorily completed before asking the architect to certify practical completion. It is also important where works are specified to be to 'the reasonable satisfaction of the Architect' that the Clerk of Works checks that the standard approved by the architect is maintained throughout that element of the works.

The Clerk of Works should maintain the systematic preliminary inspections and keep the architect informed of progress to completion and any difficulties likely to arise, and only when notified by the contractor that the works, or part of the works, are complete should the Clerk of Works then undertake a final inspection with the architect.

It is customary for the Clerk of Works at various stages of the works to draw the contractor's attention to items requiring corrective actions. Approaching practical completion there are often lists of defective and incomplete works being produced by the Clerk of Works, usually referred to as defects and deficiencies (snag) lists.

Such lists have no contractual significance under SBC05 and it should be noted that it is the contractor's responsibility to provide workplace supervision and ensure that proper contract information is available to enable the operatives to achieve the specified or approved standards. Where BS EN ISO 9001:2000 is adopted by the contractor, the quality control and audit procedures may be relevant.

Architects and Clerks of Works are recommended to avoid the use of the term 'snagging lists', instead referring to 'incomplete or defective work'. Clerks of Works should be discouraged from producing repetitive and extensive written lists of such incomplete and/or defective work as that is the responsibility of the contractor.

The architect must finally make the decision as to whether the completeness of the works is sufficient to merit a Practical Completion Certificate.

In some instances, the Clerk of Works may be involved in assisting the architect to prepare Schedules of Defects at the end of the rectification period for rectification by the contractor prior to the issue of the Certificate of Making Good.

11.4.17 Quality assurance

The Clerk of Works can play an important role in respect of QA procedures in contracts where BS EN ISO 9001:2000 is being applied.

11.4.18 Building control compliance

The contractor has a contractual obligation to comply with the statutory requirements and the Clerk of Works should be aware of Building Regulations requirements and should inspect for compliance.

11.5 MATTERS BEYOND THE SCOPE OF THE CLERK OF WORKS

The Clerk of Works shall not:

- modify the design without the prior approval of the architect
- accept instructions other than from the architect

- approve the contractor's method of carrying out any remedial measures without the approval of the architect
- direct the contractor on methods of working unless agreed by the architect
- agree to commitments with subcontractors or suppliers.

11.6 SPECIFIC DUTIES

11.6.1 Day works

When the contractor contends that work, in the contractor's opinion can only be valued on a day work basis, as opposed to measurement in accordance with the Clause 13.5 valuation rules, reasonable notice of such work must be given to enable the Clerk of Works to be present and to keep records and/or sign day work sheets as the authorised representative of the architect. The sheets should be signed 'for record purposes only' since it is the architect who will decide, together with the quantity surveyor, whether or not the work is to be paid as day works. The Clerk of Works should never sign vouchers unless completely satisfied that they present a correct record of labour, plant and material; not when the Clerk of Works has not been present as a result of inadequate notification; nor when they are submitted outside the specified period in Clause 5.7, i.e. not later than the end of the week following that in which the work has been executed.

11.6.2 Time and material sheets

It is the practice of some contractors to submit for the Clerk of Works' signature 'time and material' sheets for items regarded as quantifying for extra or varied work. These vouchers shall not be signed by the Clerk of Works under any circumstances.

11.6.3 Liability

The Clerk of Works may be specifically appointed by the employer or the architect or be a permanent member of the staff of the employer or of the architect.

The Clerk of Works will be liable for his or her own acts of proven negligence, subject to the considerations of contractual liability and the vicarious liability of an employer for the actions lawfully carried out by an employee in the course of his or her duties influencing the outcome of any dispute involving such matters.

11.7 APPOINTMENT

The ICW publishes a Clerk of Works Appointment Document (Independent Practices) for use where clients wish to employ the services of self-employed Clerks of Works and a Memorandum of Agreement for use in conjunction with it.

The services which may be required are listed, along with the conditions of appointment and the remuneration. The fees may be on a time charge, lump sum basis or percentage of the total construction cost. The Memorandum requires all of those facts to be recorded.

Clerks of Works are engaged under various types of contract other than JCT SBC05, the most commonly used form, and should acquaint themselves with the conditions of contract which will determine the extent of their powers under the contract.

Some thoughts on self-employment

12.1 EMBARKING ON THE SELF-EMPLOYED ROUTE

Modern working practices within the site inspection and Clerk of Works disciplines are making the prospects and, indeed, attractions of self-employment more and more appealing to many. The days of large Clerks of Works' departments in local authorities are well and truly over for the majority, as even they outsource their requirements to agencies or specialist consultancies on an 'as and when required' basis. However, while there is little doubt that most of those who opt for the self-employed route are successful, and develop a more enjoyable and rewarding career as a result, none of them would pretend that it is an 'easy' option, or that success will come without hard work.

This chapter relates purely to the thoughts of some ICW members who have followed the route of self-employment; some have set off on this journey of discovery fairly recently, others have been established for many years. It is not a definitive guide to actually taking the plunge, but is simply a few of their thoughts that should be of interest and guidance to those that are considering joining their ranks.

12.1.1 A starting point

- The first consideration will usually have to be the establishment of a base – the point from which business will be conducted, enquiries received, paperwork dealt with and the other administrative functions of being one's own boss carried out.
- It is always wise to seek the advice of an accountant in order to be able to consider the advantages and/or disadvantages of working from home or operating from an alternative venue.
- Crucially, it is important to establish – probably even before the first commission is accepted – exactly what can or cannot be claimed as legitimate business expenditure, and the many and various ways in which expenditure can be offset against liability for tax.
- Working from home has many advantages, although it requires discipline in ensuring that the work/domestic harmony line is maintained.
- 'Taking an office' on a leasehold basis can be costly and it must always be borne in mind that the commitment will continue – rent, rates, utilities, etc. – even when work is slow or during an annual holiday period.
- Consideration should be given to how paperwork will be managed – especially as most work days will be spent out on site. An ever-increasing amount of correspondence is via e-mail these days, which is fast but demands constant checking and downloading. This will be an important factor in the choice of base of operations.

12.1.2 Getting around

- One of the key elements of developing the costs of providing a freelance service is the inclusion of overheads in the figures. Apart from the costs of 'operating' from the business base, wherever it happens to be, there is also the consideration of the costs involved in getting to and from site.

- The normal method of travel is by motor vehicle, and again the advice of an accountant will need to be sought at the outset in order to minimise any tax or other liabilities that can result from the usage of a private vehicle for business purposes.
- In considering transport, the following points should be borne in mind:
  - ○ engine size and CO_2 emissions have a very distinct bearing on tax liability
  - ○ the total costs of the vehicle – taxation, servicing, routine replacement of tyres, exhausts, etc., fuel costs and depreciation – all need to be considered, factored into the overall costs and reflected in the rates charged for services.

12.1.3   Sourcing work – things to remember

- It is essential to advertise in the ICW directory – it is relatively inexpensive and is distributed widely.
- Advertising in local papers, trade magazines and the Yellow Pages for the areas in which operations will be based should provide substantial feedback.
- It is advisable to make full use of local papers and trade magazines to establish which projects have planning approval – it is usually possible to contact the client or the project managers.
- Agencies can be a handy source of work between schemes and while looking for short-term contracts.
- When taking on agency work, an up-to-date CV is essential. PAYE or Limited Company status is a legal requirement to be employed by them.
- Networking with other Clerks of Works, via ICW Chapter Meetings, can provide a good source of contacts. Likewise, maintaining a network of industry/professional contacts may provide information on projects or other potential work sources as they arise.
- The professional approach to all projects is one of the simplest methods of sourcing further work. 'Word of mouth' is a very powerful marketing tool for those that provide the highest quality of service, but can be totally ruinous if the highest levels of professionalism are not apparent to co-workers or employers on the project.
- It is essential always to be wary of the less than scrupulous individuals who will, from time to time, seek tenders with no intention of following through, or of considering the levels of service that would seem to be required on the project. These are often difficult to identify, but an instinct for the genuine requests and the spurious will develop over time.

12.1.4   Does marketing work?

- Marketing most definitely does work and is an essential and necessary part of any working budget, particularly whilst trying to establish a reputation and source work.

- It must be remembered that marketing rarely produces immediate effects – its main aim is to market an awareness of services on offer and to put those services in the 'line of sight' of potential future employers.
- A website with as much information about the services offered as possible and, if approved by previous clients, details of previous projects and, crucially, comprehensive contact details including an e-mail address is an effective marketing tool.
- Once a website is developed, it is essential to register with as many search engines as possible in order that general searches will bring the requisite details forward.
- Professional credentials (particularly membership of ICW) should be displayed with pride, as many clients will consider employing only those that possess these qualifications.
- It is important to make full use of stationery, business cards and other 'giveaway' material to market services and credentials. They are inexpensive and can be very effective.

12.1.5   Cash flow – the crucial factor for the self-employed

- The need for regular payment should be established at the start of any contract or project and built into the terms of engagement.
- With slow payers, it may be advisable to send weekly reminders rather than waiting for a month. A month can easily become two then three or more months overdue.
- If dealing with a large organisation, personal contact with the finance department can establish a satisfactory working relationship and, by careful liaison, the possibility of speeding up the payments process.
- Invoices should state a deadline for payment of 14 or 28 days, but it is important to be aware that most organisations will wait until the last day prior to the deadline before making the payment. A period of 7 or 14 days should only be considered if a swift settlement is essential, but it must be borne in mind that many organisations will not accept contracts on this basis – cash flow is a similar consideration for them as well.
- Payment by BACS (which is made directly to a bank account) is usually the quickest way to receive monies. Accepting cheques will entail a delay of 5 to 7 days while they clear, which should be factored into onward bill payment procedures.
- If a contract ends at the beginning or middle of a month, the invoice for services should be sent out immediately, rather than waiting until the end of the month.
- Allowances for public holidays, and for the private holidays of anyone involved in the approval of accounts, should be made and billing arrangements adjusted accordingly.
- It is vital not to feel guilty about chasing for payment if it has passed the date by which normal payments should have been received – self-employment does not have to equate to financing someone else's organisation.
- It is not always a good idea to work for a percentage of the contract cost, as this can ultimately vary significantly from the envisaged income. An hourly figure, plus

phone, postage, travelling costs and associated expenses gives a far more workable and reliable means of forecasting income, which would not be diminished should the contract extend.

12.1.6 Taxation issues

- It will pay dividends to employ a good accountant and to make full use of his or her expertise in accessing advice and assistance.
- An accountant's bill is tax deductible.
- It is the person who signs the tax form, rather than the accountant or adviser, who will be prosecuted if it is incorrect, so it is always essential to ensure that all documents are fully understood.
- It is possible to take out insurance which covers tax investigation costs of up to £50,000, should something go awry. This is relatively inexpensive and is a wise investment.
- A disciplined attitude towards finance is essential – as is the provision of a separate building society or bank account to retain any tax monies as this has to be paid in advance. An accountant will advise on the amounts to be paid for the year ahead and establish monthly payments, so it is vital to ensure that these funds are deposited into an appropriate account monthly and are readily available when the Inland Revenue tax demand arrives.
- Payments should be made well in advance and at least 14 days allowed for the funds to arrive with the Inland Revenue, as interest will be charged on late payments by the Revenue Office and other financial penalties may be incurred.
- Tax returns, and any other information required by the Inland Revenue, should be submitted promptly.
- National Insurance must also be paid alongside tax, so allowances must be made accordingly.
- Numerous guides to taxation are readily available on the high street – but are certainly no substitute for an experienced accountant!
- Any large capital expenditures should be made at the end of a tax year, so that the benefit can be claimed as soon as possible, rather than waiting a full twelve months to claim.
- No credence should be given to people who say they pay no tax – HM Revenue and Customs catches up with everyone eventually, and it is safest work on that basis.
- It is simply a bad idea to try to claim for purchases that are not genuine business expenses. A meeting with the tax inspector is stressful enough without having to answer questions on items for which tax relief was claimed five years previously that may, to the inspector, appear to be of dubious origin.
- A good quality accountancy package, such as SAGE Instant, is a wise investment. Most accountants use it so account preparation should take less time at the end of the year, with correspondingly lower costs.

- Obtaining and safely retaining receipts for any business purchases is an essential factor in a self-employment enterprise.
- Books must be kept properly, and the advice of an accountant is invaluable in setting up the necessary books, and dealing with such issues as VAT once turnover has reached a sufficient level. An accountant can provide guidance through the relevant processes, checking records regularly until the newly self-employed practitioner has acquired an appropriate degree of competence.

12.1.7   Essential insurance

- A specialist construction insurance broker is the safest means of ensuring adequate cover, as they will have the knowledge, experience and expertise to make provision for all likely eventualities. ICW recommends Holbrook Insurance Brokers, who also provide specific cover for Clerks of Works.
- Third party insurance is a must, with the minimum being usually £1 million. However, certain specialist activities or sites may not be covered by some policies such as piling, fuels, specialist MOD sites and airports, railways, etc., so it is always essential to check the small print.
- Brokers will provide advice on indemnity. It is best to be circumspect in advising persons of indemnity value – many simply do not need to know, and often their motives may be suspect.
- Private personal insurance to cover individual requirements, such as illness, injury or unavoidable absence from work, is a vital consideration as commitments still have to be met, whether money is coming in or not.
- In the event of a self-employed Clerk of Works employing others, in addition to professional indemnity and public liability insurance, employers liability insurance will have to be considered (see section 13.3 below).

12.1.8   Good practices

- The duty to protect clients' interests at all times must be kept firmly in mind. Meticulous, accurate records must be kept, through written, photographic and video evidence, as appropriate. It is a good idea to keep a diary of all conversations and events.
- Any other evidence, such as examples of materials, maker's information notes and technical literature, as appropriate, may be vital at a later date in proving a case.
- It should be made clear from the start of any project that the role of the Clerk of Works is not to design but to check the quality of the works.
- Flexibility is necessary to ensure that clients achieve the result they want. Every job is different, and the service provided should be tailored to suit the client so that, if the opportunity arises, they will consider a further engagement at a future date.
- Formal contracts can be rather stuffy and are time consuming if they are totally bespoke for every contract. An experienced Clerk of Works should be able to convert a standard engagement letter to suit every situation.

- It is essential to keep up to date with new regulations and British Standards; one of the best ways is to attend an ICW Chapter to advance Continuing Professional Development (CPD), but reading the construction related media and/or visiting appropriate websites is helpful in keeping abreast of changes.
- In a perfect world, a self-employed Clerk of Works should aim to have three jobs on the go – one just starting, one in the middle and one just finishing, to provide a constant supply of work.
- It is important to cultivate a forward-thinking attitude. Particularly towards the end of long projects, new contracts will have to be sourced and plans made accordingly.
- It will sometimes be necessary to work full time on one project while looking for options before the end of the project. Most clients will be sympathetic to this situation. A reminder of availability for return site visits, if the client should require them, is never a waste of time.
- Things can become very fraught with contractors at times, but it is essential to maintain professional relationships at all times, not to take adverse comments personally and to try to gain the respect of co-workers and employers.
- Computer literacy is a prerequisite, enabling reports and photographs to be sent to clients via e-mail. A laptop for site visits may initially seem expensive but the investment will soon provide a good return in time saved.
- A digital camera is an essential piece of equipment on site to record activities and defective works or, in an emergency, a mobile phone may also be capable of capturing the necessary images.
- A get-out clause in the letter of engagement, with termination possible by either party at one month's notice, is a sensible precaution should the working relationship prove untenable.

12.1.9 Bad practices

- Arguments must never be allowed to develop with workers. A problem must always be reported to the site agent and, if it cannot be satisfactorily resolved, the Clerks of Works Direction form should be completed.
- It is unacceptable to give scribbled notes or verbal directions to site workers.
- The filling in of the site diary should never be left for another day. It must be completed each day before leaving the site.

12.2 ANECDOTES

The following comments from Clerks of Works may serve to illustrate some of the points detailed above.

- 'I was recently asked to do a list of defects for a family who had just moved into a new house. The building firm was refusing to do any work. I found four A4 sheets of defects; the worst was a hole in the eaves that you could pass a child through. There were newel posts under one metre high that were 38 mm out of plumb; the kitchen floor had 12–15 mm dips throughout and the entire staircase was not square with the hall wall by 50 mm. The family was eventually moved out for two weeks and the contractor did what he thought was rectification; but instead of squaring up the staircase, he moved the landing! I just could not believe the stupidity.'

- 'Try to treat everyone fairly – for example, I have one client who was a foreman for a contractor when we first met, and he is now the director of a development company, I like to think that he uses me now because I was fair with him in the past.'

- 'I was asked to do the project management, quantity surveying, etc., two years ago for works in a large building, including restoring a grade 2 listed hallway, converting barns into business units and building a new warehouse. A quote had come in at £2.5 million. On completion of the job it cost £1.25 million and is giving a return of over 15 per cent. It has also won five awards including Building of the Year from RICS and a Clerk of Works award. Every time I pass the site I feel proud, and that is what makes it all worthwhile.'

- 'About seven years ago while working for a local council while their Clerks of Works were off ill, I was checking work done on council house refurbishments. I use a mirror with torch attached to look over top cupboards and behind pipes (ex-army bomb squad, I think). One morning I arrived at site and standing outside was a labourer with a 6′ piece of 2″ × 2″ which had on the top a 2′ × 1′ mirror. I asked what he was doing and he said he had been sent to help me.'

Insurance aspects

13.1 PROFESSIONAL INDEMNITY INSURANCE

Clerks of Works and Site Inspectors, in common with all professionals, are required to exercise reasonable skill and care in the provision of professional services and advice which are relied on by others. Failing in this duty may be viewed as negligent and result in the need to compensate the party who suffers the loss. Professional indemnity (PI) insurance provides protection against just such negligent acts, errors or omissions.

Unless the Clerk of Words is a full-time or part-time employee, it is likely that personal professional indemnity insurance will be required. Whilst this is clearly the case with limited companies and partnerships, many sole practitioners working as sub-consultants seem to rely on vague assurances from those engaging them, such as 'Our PI insurance covers your work'. What is often not appreciated is that the firm engaging them as subconsultants and (perhaps more importantly) the firm's insurers retain rights of recovery (called subrogation rights) against the sole practitioner subconsultant in the event of his or her negligence. In other words, even though the lead consultant's PI cover may apply, the claim can then be passed on to the subconsultant, who therefore still requires personal PI cover. Unless a written confirmation is obtained from the lead consultant that

(a) the firm's PI insurance applies in respect of the subconsultant's work and
(b) that the firm and its insurers waive and will continue to waive all subrogation rights/rights of recovery against the subconsultant then

personal PI insurance should be arranged by the subconsultant to ensure adequate cover.

13.1.1 'Claims made' basis of cover

It is important to understand that PI insurance works on a 'claims made' basis of cover. The cover that applies is the cover in force at the time the individual insured first became aware of a possible claim, irrespective of when the work was undertaken.

13.1.2 'Run-off' cover

The nature of the construction industry means that claims (particularly PI claims) can arise many years after a building project has been completed. The 'claims made' basis of PI cover, detailed in section 13.1.1 above, means that to be protected against such claims cover must be in place at the time the insured party becomes aware of the claims, which may be years later. If the business continues to trade, a current PI policy will undoubtedly be in force at the appropriate time. If, however, trading has ceased and the self-employed party has gone back into employment or retired, the solution is to purchase run-off cover which provides insurance in respect of any continuing liabilities which may arise out of past work. This may only be available on an annual basis.

13.1.3 Retroactive cover

Unless qualified by a retroactive date, a 'claims made' PI policy wording will normally provide full retroactive cover for continuing liabilities arising out of work performed by the firm or individual in the past. At the time of writing this is generally the case in Holbrook Insurance's scheme for ICW members with policies containing no retroactive date, so providing full retroactive cover. This is often possible even where a firm or individual has been trading without the benefit of PI cover for a number of years.

In the open market, however, it is common practice to impose a retroactive date, which is usually the date that PI cover is first taken out. Subsequent renewals, even with a different insurer, will normally follow the retroactive date on the previous policy. This puts a backstop on the 'claims made' policy wording and means that cover is only provided for claims arising out of work performed after the retroactive date. See the case studies in section 13.4 below.

13.2 PUBLIC LIABILITY INSURANCE

Public liability insurance provides cover for a Clerk of Works or Site Inspector in respect of sudden and accidental damage to other people's (third parties') property or injury to such third parties. An example would be a Clerk of Works accidentally knocking a brick off some scaffolding and it falling on a third party's car or head causing damage or injury respectively.

For similar reasons to those detailed in the professional indemnity insurance section above, Clerks of Works and Site Inspectors are best advised to have public liability insurance unless they are full-time or part-time employees and this cover is maintained by their employer. Employers should obviously have public liability cover for principals, partners or directors and all employees as well as any self-employed persons who do not or may not maintain their own cover. See section 13.4.1 below.

13.3 EMPLOYERS LIABILITY INSURANCE

Employers liability insurance provides cover in respect of the employer's liability for injury or illness sustained by an employee in the course of their employment. It is compulsory under the Employers Liability (Compulsory Insurance) Act 1969. Although the legislation is complex and detailed guidance may need to be sought, it is worth mentioning that, as well as being compulsory for employees, it is also compulsory for firms to have employers liability insurance for self-employed people who are 'employees in all but name'.

13.4 CASE STUDIES

13.4.1 Case study 1

A self-employed Clerk of Works relies on a verbal assurance from a representative of the firm engaging him (Firm X) that his work for them is covered by 'their insurance', meaning both professional indemnity and public liability insurance. The Clerk of Works does not arrange his own professional indemnity or public liability insurance.

A few months later the Clerk of Works fails to notice a significant departure from the architect's design and specification, which he could reasonably have been expected to notice in performing his regular inspections and supervisory duties as set out in his contract. The client subsequently incurs significant costs in rectification of the defective works as well as delay and resulting financial losses.

Whilst it appears, at first, that the PI insurers of Firm X are dealing with the matter, as soon as they discover that the error/omission was made by a self-employed Clerk of Works, Firm X's insurers exercise rights of recovery against him (on Firm X's behalf). As the Clerk of Works has no insurance and is personally liable, the settlement is funded out of his personal assets, including savings, house, etc.

The same principles could also apply in respect of a public liability claim.

13.4.2 Case study 2

A Clerk of Works retired after a number of years trading on a freelance self-employed basis. Despite being made aware of the 'claims made' basis of cover and the need for 'run-off' cover (see section 13.1 above for details) he did not take this out.

A claim was made against him a number of years after he had retired in relation to work performed prior to his retirement. Despite the fact that he had professional indemnity cover in force at the time he performed the work, because with PI cover it is the time that the insured party *first becomes aware of the claim* (not when the work was performed) that counts, the Clerk of Works had no cover and was personally liable, with the potentially devastating consequences outlined in case study 1.

13.4.3 Case study 3

A Clerk of Works, who had been working on a freelance self-employed basis for almost a year without insurance, arranged PI cover in the open market. Although he was not aware of any possible claims when he arranged the PI cover, six months later he became aware of a possible claim. He notified the insurers who pointed out that his policy contained a retroactive date, which was the same date that he arranged the PI cover. This meant that the policy only provided cover in respect of work performed after that date, so the Clerk of Works remained personally liable.

A professional institute

14.1 CODE OF CONDUCT

1. Election to, and acceptance of, membership of the Institute binds those so elected to this Code of Conduct, and also to the Institute's Memorandum and Articles of Association. This Code of Conduct applies to all members, regardless of grade held, type or status of employment, whether they continue to practise or not and whether they are in membership in the United Kingdom or elsewhere.
2. All in membership undertake to further the aims and objectives of the Institute to the best of their abilities throughout their period of membership, and to promote and advance the ethos of membership to their colleagues and fellows, and through this encourage them into membership.
3. All members shall conduct themselves in such a way that the respect, reputation, honour and dignity of the Institute is upheld, maintained and enhanced at all times.
4. All members shall carry out their professional duties to the highest standards commensurate with the Institute's motto, contained on its Coat of Arms, 'Potestate, Probitate et Vigilantia' 'Ability, Integrity and Vigilance'.
5. All members shall endeavour to maintain, through Continuing Professional Development (CPD) or other means, the highest levels of knowledge, both in spirit and deed, to ensure that they are able to comply with the requirements of law as they apply to the construction industry, including, but not restricted to, matters of Health, Safety and Welfare as well as those that relate to the equal and fair treatment of all, regardless of creed, colour, gender, religious belief, sexual orientation or physical impediment.
6. Members shall never knowingly damage or otherwise harm the name, standing or reputation of others.

This Code of Conduct does not form a part of the Institute's Memorandum and/or Articles of Association.

14.2 THE PROFESSIONAL BODY FOR THE CONSTRUCTION INSPECTORATE

Established in 1882 by a small group of Clerks of Works, the Institute of Clerks of Works has undergone many changes in the ensuing years. However, its name and its original principles of formation – to safeguard the requirement for ensuring quality in construction and the provision of value for money to the client – remain sacrosanct.

Whilst it continues to be the wish of the membership that the title of the Institute remain unchanged, they have nevertheless recognised that the role and duties traditionally associated with Clerks of Works are now undertaken by a far more diverse range of construction professionals, under a wide variety of job titles and, often, as an intrinsic but substantial element of another role.

In recognising this, the Institute also recognises the far wider range of construction-related disciplines that have a key role to play in the delivery of value for money to the client. The Institute firmly believes that each of these disciplines has its own specific area of expertise and knowledge that – as a progressive and learned body representing the wider construction inspectorate – is an essential component in the Institute's own ability to be truly representative of the discipline that it exists to promote.

14.3 BENEFITS OF MEMBERSHIP

One of the major issues that has traditionally surrounded the role of the Clerk of Works is that, on site, they are to be seen to be a benefit to the project through a fair and firm appraisal of the ongoing works. They are seen very much as policemen and, in truth, that is exactly what they are. It is little wonder then that the majority will find that, although the role is probably one of the most professionally essential and satisfying in the industry, it is one of isolation. The basic understanding of this particular problem was identified during the earliest stages of the formation of the Institute, and remains true even in the modern construction arena.

14.3.1 Chapters

The cornerstone of Institute membership revolves around its network of Meeting Centres – The Chapters – originally developed to provide a focal point for members, working in isolation, to meet and discuss professional issues with their contemporaries. Over the years, the network has developed to provide a presence throughout the United Kingdom, Ireland and Hong Kong. Centres are strategically located to cover the following areas:

- Scotland:
  - Central
  - Highlands and Grampian
  - Northern Ireland
- Ireland:
  - Dublin (from mid-2006)
- Wales:
  - South Wales
- England:
  - North West
  - North East
  - North
  - Cumbria and North Lancashire
  - Deeside
  - North Cheshire
  - Merseyside

  - Staffordshire and District
  - East Midlands
  - Home Counties (North)
  - East Anglia
  - London
  - South East
  - South
  - Western Counties
  - South West
- Hong Kong.

Chapters usually meet monthly and undertake formal CPD, visits, lectures and a wide variety of professional and social programmes as circumstances dictate.

14.3.2 Other benefits

Members enjoy a variety of other benefits which include:

- the monthly journal *Site Recorder*, which gives details of related industry news, regulatory issues, health and safety developments, legal issues and a host of other topics relevant to the construction inspectorate, along with a dedicated recruitment and new products section
- access to technical advice and assistance through the Institute's Professional Standards Committee
- access to a specialist insurance brokerage service, dealing specifically with the requirements of the construction inspectorate
- priority access to a specialist recruitment consultancy dealing specifically with the construction disciplines
- access to a range of annual seminars and the Institute's Annual Conference weekend
- discounted ICW publications.

14.3.3 The biggest benefit

Membership of the Institute is recognised throughout the construction industry as the optimum level of qualification for Clerks of Works and, indeed, for those of differing title but allied or similar functions. Not only does it demonstrate to fellow professionals that an individual has been deemed to possess the requisite expertise and knowledge to have been accepted into membership – no mean feat in itself – but also demonstrates the same unimpeachable level of professionalism to potential employers.

14.4 PRINCIPLES OF MEMBERSHIP

Membership of the Institute of Clerks of Works is available to suitably qualified individuals who meet the following criteria:

'They are engaged in any aspect of the inspection, superintendence of construction and/or maintenance of buildings or any other works to ensure the proper/specified use of labour and/or materials, regardless of any title given to or held by the incumbent, nor whether the role is of a practical, educational or advisory nature.'

(Article of Association 2(c))

The range and application of this definition (of a Clerk of Works) is at the complete discretion of the Council, whose determination will be absolute.

14.5 REQUIREMENTS AND PROCEDURES

The latest requirements for gaining entry to the Institute are available either directly from the Institute's Headquarters, by request through e-mail (info@icwgb.co.uk) or by consulting the Institute's website and downloading the relevant paperwork (www.icwgb.org).

14.6 ACCEPTANCE INTO MEMBERSHIP

With the exception of students (who have a separate method of entry to membership) all candidates for membership go through a structured interview procedure conducted by senior members of the Institute, occasionally assisted by relevant professionals from chartered or other bodies, depending on the discipline of the interviewee, prior to acceptance into membership.

The interview procedure will be conducted at either a local meeting centre or at the Institute's Headquarters in Peterborough, whichever is more convenient. However, the format of the interview is identical:

- *professional practice interview*: based on the applicant's career to date, general construction-related information, health and safety, and information based on their specific discipline
- *identification of materials and their usage*: based on a selection of photographic records, candidates will be required to identify a number of construction-related materials and discuss their usage.

The interview is likely to last between 1.5 and 2 hours.

14.6.1 Grade of membership on entry

The grade of membership offered is dependent on a recommendation being made by the Interviewing Panel, which itself is based on all of the information presented to the Panel with each application and the results of the interview itself.

The Panel will recommend one of the three following courses of action:

- that the candidate be offered Licentiate membership (LICW) with a recommendation that a further interview be conducted after a period of consolidation for upgrade to full Member
- that the candidate be offered full Member grade (MICW)
- in the event that the members of the Interviewing Panel do not feel it appropriate to offer either of the above grades following interview, they will provide a synopsis of areas that need to be developed prior to a further interview taking place and will recommend a minimum time period before that interview occurs.

Candidates will, on completion of the interview, be given the opportunity to provide feedback to the Institute in relation to the conduct of the interview itself.

14.6.2 Election to membership

Following the deliberations of the Interviewing Panel, those recommended for election to Licentiate would have their names put forward to the Institute's Council for ratification, by no later than the end of the month following the interview.

In the case of those recommended for the immediate grade of Member, their names will be included in the next issue of the Institute's journal (*Site Recorder*) for ratification by the wider membership, again by no later than the end of the month following the interview.

14.6.3 Notification of election

Candidates are informed, by letter, immediately following election to membership, at which time they will be required to pay the balance of the subscriptions due for the remainder of the year, and are notified that their direct debit mandate will be activated to effect this.

Successful applicants will also be entitled to receive a Certificate of Membership at that time, which is normally presented to them at their most convenient local meeting centre. If this is not possible, then alternative arrangements will be made at their entire convenience. At this time, they will also receive a copy of the Institute's Memorandum and Articles of Association – its internal rules – and a copy of ICW's Code of Conduct, to which all members are bound by acceptance of membership.

14.7 SUBSEQUENT UPGRADES TO MEMBERSHIP

14.7.1 Licentiate to Member

At the time that Licentiate grade is offered, the Interviewing Panel will also make a recommendation with regard to the minimum time that the candidate will require to develop and consolidate their knowledge prior to making an application to upgrade to Member. This will vary from one to four years and will normally be communicated to applicants at the time that the results of their interviews are made known to them. The average period of consolidation is two years. At the time of upgrade to Member, however, all applicants must be 'practising' as Clerks of Works or similar and must undergo a further interview.

14.7.2 Member to Fellow

There is no interview required for upgrade to Fellow, since this level of membership recognises, subject to certain criteria, the commitment of the individual to the Institute and the discipline. Fellowship is normally available on completion of ten years in the Member grade and, at the time of application, confirmation than an individual is still practising the role.

14.8 IN CONCLUSION

The Institute has a long and very well regarded history and status within the construction industry and the designations LICW, MICW and FICW are accepted as the benchmark of professional recognition and standing by fellow professionals and employers alike.

For further information on the Institute see www.icwgb.org

Institution of Engineering Designers (IED)
Courtleigh, Westbury Leigh,
Westbury,
Wiltshire BA13 3TA
Tel: 01373 822801
www.ied.org.uk

Institution of Gas Engineers and Managers
Charnwood Wing, Holywell Park,
Ashby Road,
Loughborough,
Leceistershire LE11 3GH
Tel: 01509 282728
www.igem.org.uk

Institution of Lighting Engineers (ILE)
Regent House, Regent Place, Rugby,
Warwickshire CV21 2PN
Tel: 01788 576492
www.ile.org.uk

Institution of Structural Engineers (IStructE)
11 Upper Belgrave Street,
London SW1X 8BH
Tel: 0207 2354535
www.istructe.org.uk

Insulated Render and Cladding Association (INCA)
PO Box 12, Haslemere,
Surrey GU27 3AH
Tel: 01428 654011
www.inca-ltd.org.uk

Local Government Association (LGA)
Local Government House,
Smith Square,
London SW1P 3HZ
Tel: 020 7664 3131
www.lga.gov.uk

Mastic Asphalt Council (MAC)
PO Box 77,
Hastings TN35 4WL
Tel: 01424 814400
Fax: 01424 814446
www.masticasphaltcouncil.co.uk

National Assembly for Wales
Cardiff Bay, Cardiff CF99 1NA
Tel: 029 20 825111
www.cymru.gov.uk

National Energy Foundation (NEF)
Davey Avenue, Knowlhill, Milton Keynes,
Buckinghamshire MK5 8NG
Tel: 01908 665555
www.nef.org.uk

National Federation of Roofing Contractors (NFRC)
24 Weymouth St,
London W1G 7LX
Tel: 020 7436 0387
www.nfrc.co.uk

National House Building Council (NHBC)
Buildmark House, Chiltern Avenue,
Amersham,
Buckinghamshire HP6 5AP
Tel: 01494 735363
www.nhbc.co.uk

National Housing Federation (NHF)
Lion Court, 25 Procter Street,
London WC1V 6NY
Tel: 0207 0671010
www.housing.org.uk

National Inspection Council for Electrical Installation Contracting (NICEIC)
Vintage House, 37 Albert Embankment,
London SE1 7UJ
Tel: 0207 5642323
www.niceic.org.uk

National Insulation Association (NIA)
3 Vimy Court, Vimy Road,
Leighton Buzzard LU7 1FG
Tel: 01525 383313
www.insulationassociation.org.uk

National Specialist Contractors' Council (NSCC)
Carthusian Court, 12 Carthusian Street,
London EC1M 6EZ
Tel: 0870 4296351
www.nscc.org.uk

Chapter 15

The National Trust
Heelis, Kemble Drive, Swindon,
Wiltshire SN2 2NA
Tel: 0870 6095383
www.nationaltrust.org.uk

NBS
The Old Post Office, St Nicholas Street,
Newcastle upon Tyne NE1 1RH
Tel: 0845 4569594
www.thenbs.com

Neighbourhood Energy Action (NEA)
St Andrew's House, 90–92 Pilgrim Street,
Newcastle upon Tyne N1 6SG
Tel: 0191 261 5677
www.nea.org.uk

**Office of the Deputy Prime Minister
(ODPM)**
Eland House, Bressenden Place,
London SW1E 5DU
Tel: 0207 9444400
www.odpm.gov.uk

**Royal Incorporation of Architects in
Scotland (RIAS)**
15 Rutland Square,
Edinburgh EH1 2BE
Tel: 0131 2297545
www.rias.org.uk

**Royal Institute of British Architects
(RIBA)**
66 Portland Place,
London W1B 1AD
Tel: 0207 5805533
www.riba.org

**Royal Institute of Chartered Surveyors
(RICS)**
12 Great George Street,
London SW1P 3AD
Tel: 08703331660
www.rics.org.uk

Royal Town Planning Institute (RTPI)
41 Boltoph Lane,
London EC3R 8DL
Tel: 0207 9299494
www.rtpi.org.uk

Scottish Executive
St Andrew's House,
Regent Road,
Edinburgh EH1 3DG
Planning Helpline: 08457 741741
www.scotland.gov.uk

**Society for the Protection of Ancient
Buildings (SPAB)**
37 Spital Square,
London E1 6DY
Tel: 0207 3771644
www.spab.org.uk

Timber Trade Federation (TTF)
Clareville House,
26/27 Oxendon Street,
London SW1Y 4EL
Tel: 020 7839 1891
www.ttf.co.uk

**Town and Country Planning Association
(TCPA)**
17 Carlton House Terrace,
London SW1Y 5AS
Tel: 0207 9308903
www.tcpa.org.uk

TRADA
Stocking Lane,
Hughenden Valley,
High Wycombe,
Buckinghamshire HP14 4ND
Tel: 01494 569600
www.trada.com

**Water Regulations Advisory Service
(WRAS)**
Fern Close, Pen-Y-Fan Industrial Estate,
Oakdale,
Gwent NP11 3EH
Tel: 01495 248454
www.wras.co.uk

**Wood Panel Industries Federation
(WPIF)**
28 Market Place, Grantham,
Lincolnshire NG31 6LR
Tel: 01476 563707
www.wpif.org.uk

Index

Index

Index

Index